On Shifting Ground

GENDER AND JUSTICE

Edited by Claire M. Renzetti

This University of California Press series explores how the experiences of offending, victimization, and justice are profoundly influenced by the intersections of gender with other markers of social location. Cross-cultural and comparative, series volumes publish the best new scholarship that seeks to challenge assumptions, highlight inequalities, and transform practice and policy.

On Shifting Ground

CONSTRUCTING MANHOOD
ON THE MARGINS

Jamie J. Fader

UNIVERSITY OF CALIFORNIA PRESS

University of California Press
Oakland, California

© 2024 by Jamie J. Fader

Library of Congress Cataloging-in-Publication Data

Names: Fader, Jamie J., author.
Title: On shifting ground : constructing manhood on the margins / Jamie J. Fader.
Other titles: Gender and justice (University of California Press) ; 11.
Description: Oakland, California : University of California Press, [2024] | Series: Gender and justice ; 11 | Includes bibliographical references and index.
Identifiers: LCCN 2023023381 (print) | LCCN 2023023382 (ebook) | ISBN 9780520380769 (cloth) | ISBN 9780520380776 (paperback) | ISBN 9780520380783 (epub)
Subjects: LCSH: Men—Pennsylvania—Philadelphia—Identity—21st century. | Men—Pennsylvania—Philadelphia—Social conditions—21st century. | Generation Y—Pennsylvania—Philadelphia—Social conditions—21st century. | Men—Pennsylvania—Philadelphia—Interviews—21st century. | Generation Y—Pennsylvania—Philadelphia—Interviews—21st century.
Classification: LCC HQ1090.5.P4 F334 2024 (print) | LCC HQ1090.5.P4 (ebook) | DDC 305.3109748/110905—dc23/eng/20230620
LC record available at https://lccn.loc.gov/2023023381
LC ebook record available at https://lccn.loc.gov/2023023382

33 32 31 30 29 28 27 26 25 24
10 9 8 7 6 5 4 3 2 1

To the women and the elders of Frankford,
who are supporting the men in this book
and are holding the community together
with little recognition

Contents

Preface

The seeds of this book were planted by my first book, *Falling Back*, which examined the transitions to adulthood among young men of color who were incarcerated in a juvenile corrections facility and returned to their communities in Philadelphia with the goal of becoming "productive citizens."[1] My ethnographic research with these young men led me to conclude that subjective perceptions of adulthood and masculinity had a complicated relationship with criminal offending and legal system involvement during their postincarceration transitions. The vast majority of young men I studied embraced the idea that adulthood signified a movement away from their prior childish engagement in drug sales and agreed that a loss of freedom was not worth past profits. Yet they struggled to establish alternative means of constructing adult masculinity as working men or involved fathers. With profoundly limited success in legal employment, these young men were unable to enact the breadwinner role and thus to contribute meaningfully to their family of origin's household or to the financial well-being of their children. A common refrain during this period of negotiation was "slow money is good money." Yet slow money, whether earned legally in low-wage employment or illegally through drug sales, was rarely sufficient and stable enough to buy them the markers of adult

masculine identity. Their positions within their families' homes, in relation to their girlfriends and babies' mothers, and in their children's lives
were tenuous and unstable. Moments of actualized masculinity were temporary and fleeting. With this description in mind, the reader might not
be surprised that many of them "fell back," not in the way they intended—
to embrace conventional roles and activities—but rather into old routines
and habits of solving problems that put them at risk of involvement in the
adult Criminal Legal System (CLS).

Falling Back followed these young men for three years after their return from a juvenile facility and ended when they were 21 to 23 years old.
Having maintained close relationships with some of them and tracked all
of them using official and readily available criminal records and contacts
with family members, I reported on them again as they entered their thir-
ties. At that time, eight had been incarcerated in the adult system within
the five years prior to the follow-up, eight of the fifteen young men had
been re-arrested during the prior two years (with two others incarcerated), and three were serving long-term probation. Only three of the thirteen men still living in Pennsylvania had avoided CLS contact as adults.
To be sure, these men had well-known risk factors for adult incarceration,
including system involvement and incarceration as adolescents and impoverished schools, families, and communities. But I was surprised by the
sheer ubiquity of adult contact with the system.

The instability of their lives was equally striking. They wrestled with
housing and food insecurity, lasting discouragement about their prospects
in the labor market, untreated mental health problems, frequent losses of
friends and family members to violence or chronic illness, and continued
"drama" (as they called it) in their relationships with their babies' mothers
and families of origin. Tragically, Warren (age 30) became the victim of a
home invasion and fatal shooting.[2]

I knew from reading about the changing nature of transitions to adulthood that as millennials, these men were likely to adopt adult roles later in
life than had members of previous generations, but the degree of precarity and chaos in their daily lives was still astonishing. I began to wonder
what I would find if I studied a larger, more diverse set of men who were
in in the next stage of adulthood (roughly ages 25 to 34). This age cohort
had received comparatively little attention in the life course research in

sociology, which focuses on transitions to adulthood in work and family, and criminology, which focuses on persistence in or desistance from criminal careers. The research that followed men for decades found that it is the norm to age out of crime, but because these were such long-term studies, they captured the experiences of baby boomers who came cf age in a time of unprecedented postwar prosperity. I wondered if these patterns would hold up using a contemporary sample of millennials, who, according to the most common definition, were born between 1981 and 1996.

My first book drew on my close and enduring relationships with these young men, which allowed me to document their lives in rich detail, but it had some drawbacks that I wanted to address in my next study. First, with only fifteen men, I was not able to make any comparisons between subgroups, such as those whose families were disrupted by the consequences of criminal activity and those whose families remained intact during their childhood. Second, the men in *Falling Back* came from a juvenile facility and returned to neighborhoods in very different sections of Philadelphia, I was unable to analyze the significance of their community context. After returning to Philadelphia as a faculty member in the Department of Criminal Justice at Temple University in the fall of 2014, I was quickly convinced by my geographer colleagues that neighborhoods were a major factor in structuring conventional and criminal activities, as well as the operations of the justice system. The Frankford Men's Study was designed to address these limitations, although it presented new ones, which I discuss in chapter 1. My research team and I conducted in-depth interviews with forty-five men who varied in their racial/ethnic identification and (with one exception) did not have a four-year college degree.

This inquiry benefits from research I did on drug sellers in Philadelphia during and just after the Great Recession (from 2009 to 2012). With the help of Warren and Leo from *Falling Back*, I recruited and interviewed twenty active and former drug sellers to learn about their perceptions of the risk of arrest or incarceration and of working in drug sales versus in a legal job. I found that half of the sample were both working in low-wage legal jobs *and* selling drugs but were still living in poverty.[3] Neither form of work alone was sufficient to make ends meet. These men articulated the benefits of keeping a foot in each of these worlds, such as having a pay stub when stopped by the police and questioned about carrying cash. A major takeaway from the Philadelphia Drug Sellers Study was just how unprofitable and undesirable it was to sell drugs as an adult. These street-level distributors were at the bottom of the supply chain and took on all the risk of visible hand-to-hand exchanges, which they attempted to reduce in a variety of ways, while earning very little per shift.[4] They talked at length about their plans to get out of the drug game altogether, telling me about how they were "stacking" (saving their money) to go back to school or capitalize on the city's building boom by buying and flipping houses. Nevertheless, the fact that they continued in the trade despite articulating its high risk and low returns illuminates that drug selling operates as a strategy for making ends meet for those who are relegated to the low-wage sector of the labor market or excluded from legal employment altogether because of their criminal records.[5]

As I completed the drug-sellers study, I was developing a working theory that diminished labor force participation for men and less informal regulation of the drug economy (i.e., the death or weakening of the street code) could be extending criminal careers for marginalized men out beyond the long-established predictions of the age-crime curve.[6] In short, I suspected that these men were still relying on the drug economy for income but "selling smarter" by integrating legal and illegal work and avoiding risky techniques like open-air, hand-to-hand exchanges. I was (mostly) wrong. The men in this book taught me that involvement in criminal activities is inconsistent with how they view themselves; with their preferences for stability and a lack of drama; and with the expectations of their romantic partners, family members and children to "show up" for them by staying in the community and out of jail. In short, I began to appreciate the powerful effects of maturation as individual and relational processes. This book begins with a chapter on desistance from criminal offending and then unravels the strands of human development that supported it. It is my aim in *On Shifting Ground* to integrate sociological concepts explaining the contemporary production of social inequalities with a life course perspective on the effects of the CLS on a generation of marginalized men that has grown up in its wake.

Acknowledgments

This book could never have been written without the support of residents and leaders in the Frankford community of Philadelphia. I owe a great debt to a number of individuals who helped me to find men to interview and, later, to sort through my findings. Thanks especially to Bob Smiley, editor of the *Frankford Gazette*, who gave me free advertising space in his paper and engaged in an ongoing dialogue about crime in the neighborhood, and to Father Jon Clodfelter, who allowed us to use St. Mark's Church to conduct interviews and gave me my first insider's tour of Frankford. State Representative Jason Dawkins and his chief of staff, Darrion Shuford, were always supportive of my research and allowed me to leave flyers in their office. Blair Jordan at Joy of Living was very helpful in providing access to men in the recovery community. Pete Specos, president of the Frankford Civic Association, allowed me to observe countless community meetings and gave good hugs.

Numerous colleagues have provided crucial support during this research. Kathryn Edin gave me useful advice on the study design and sampling strategy. Abbie Henson was my right hand during data collection and was a gifted interviewer and meticulous project manager. Jesse Brey, who also conducted interviews and criminal record checks, provided many helpful insights during the analysis. Eva Juarez and Scott VanZant conducted interviews and observations. My father-in-law, Dennis Kelly, enthusiastically did field research at Frankford bars. Ronni Nelson provided editorial assistance. Maura Roessner and Claire Renzetti, my editors at UC Press, championed this book from the outset, and I appreciate the guidance provided by the anonymous reviewers they chose.

The ideas presented here have been shaped by my intellectual family, most notably Elijah Anderson and Kathryn Edin. Eli's groundbreaking ethnographic work in Philadelphia was the source of my ongoing interest in the social situation of Black men in urban communities. Kathy's expertise in urban poverty, survival strategies, fatherhood, and welfare policy complemented her skill in constructing research designs. I have also drawn on the research of my graduate school colleagues in sociology at the University of Pennsylvania, who have investigated sustainable social ties among the poor and desistance and redemption among young Black men and have shown that communities typically thought to be "socially disorganized" are actually highly organized.[1]

Kate Auerhahn, Sarah Boonstoppel, Pat Carr, Jason Gravel, Laurie Krivo, John Laub, Andrea Leverentz, Ajima Olaghere, Caterina Roman, Michael Sierra-Arévalo, Peter Simonsson, LaTosha Traylor, Jen Wood, and Amarat Zaatut offered support and feedback as I developed drafts. My teachers, including Eli Anderson, Randall Collins, Kathy Edin, David Grazian, Michael Katz, Robin Leidner, Eric Schneider, Lawrence Sherman, and Tukufu Zuberi, provided the best academic training I can imagine. Shadd Maruna has been inspiring always and indispensable at several key moments. Grey Osterud is the secret to any good writing I've managed to do for more than a decade.

My chosen family sustains me daily. My best friend and partner, Christopher "Kit" Kelly, feeds me intellectually, spiritually, and most days, literally. Phil and Ellen Harris have been there at my worst moments and loved me like parents for more than half my life. Mary, Dennis, Amanda, and the rest of the Kelly clan have been a source of acceptance, laughter, and bottomless glasses of wine over the years. I appreciate my connection with the Allen side of the family more than they know. Faye Allard is the person I call when it seems like things are falling apart. Allison Redlich, Janet Stamatel, and I forged lasting friendships under fire in our first academic positions. Jill McCorkel, whose sharp intellect and tenacity I admire beyond compare, has been a sounding board for more decades than seems possible. I deeply value the street wisdom shared by Mike Adams, Lonnie Greene, and Dante Long and the critical ideas shared by Kenneth Sebastian León, Colie "Shaka" Long, Reuben Miller, Ranita Ray, Rebecca Stone, Caitlyn Taylor, Jason M. Williams, and Sean K. Wilson. My righteous and clear-eyed undergraduate and graduate students at Temple University, especially Jesse Brey, Ronni Nelson, Megan Shaud, Gabbi Spence, Autumn Talley, and Dijoneè Talley, inspire hope about the future of the academy. I would never have made it through the long and uncertain process of writing through a global pandemic without my husband, my dogs, my wanderlust, a steady stream of fiction, Stevie Nicks, cannabis, my therapist, and my Philadelphia neighbors and community.

Finally, the forty-five men who shared their lives during the course of lengthy and personal interviews are the heart of this book. I hope I have done your stories justice.

1 Introduction

As American millennials—adults born between 1981 and 1996—faced the second economic recession of their working lives in 2020, the *Washington Post* dubbed them "the unluckiest generation."[1] Members of this cohort were ages 11 to 28 during the Great Recession of 2007–9 and 24 to 39 when the pandemic-induced recession began. As a result of this one-two punch, millennials have higher unemployment rates, less accumulated wealth, and unprecedented levels of student debt, so they are more vulnerable to economic instability than members of prior generations at the same age. The Stanford Center on Poverty and Inequality describes them as "canaries in the coalmine," important in their own right but also because their experiences signal the changing configuration of the labor market.[2]

For Black men growing up in poverty, the future that others had predicted was even bleaker. In the mid-1990s these millennial boys were characterized as future "superpredators," a vicious breed of criminals. In a screed published in the archconservative *Weekly Standard*, political scientist John Dilulio contended that within a decade young Black men would trigger a massive spike in violent crime in the United States.[3] Even though crime was declining by the time this narrative took hold, the threatening specter of superpredators spurred a host of "get tough" legal reforms that contributed to a massive rise in incarceration, the militarization of the police, and the introduction of police into schools, all of which targeted communities of color.[4] When I reference the term *superpredator* throughout this text, I am using it as shorthand to refer to twenty-five years of regressive policies that were justified on the basis of a racist moral panic.

On Shifting Ground examines the process of becoming a man in a place and time that is defined by an expanding criminal legal apparatus and contracting economic opportunities. Drawing on forty-five in-depth interviews with a diverse sample of millennial men without a college education, I analyze the key tensions that organize their lives: hypervisibility to the police and feared invisibility to others; isolation and individualism versus connectedness and generativity; stability versus "drama"; stagnation versus progress; hope versus fear; and stigma and shame versus positive, masculine affirmation. Risk permeates every aspect of their lives, flowing from their precarious position in relation to the labor market and criminal legal system (CLS) and spilling over into their strategies for making ends meet, forming supportive social ties and avoiding dangerous ones, constructing a positive sense of self, engaging in civic activity, and navigating public space. In an unfamiliar and shifting cultural landscape of adult masculinity, these men strive to define themselves in terms of what they can accomplish in the face of negative labels, seeking to avoid "being a statistic." The title reflects the fact that these two structural shifts have created unstable and unpredictable terrain for men to navigate as they work to see themselves and be seen by others as men. With well-worn pathways to adulthood no longer passable, they must improvise paths for themselves despite their particular and multiple disadvantages.

The men whose stories are told in this book reside in a Philadelphia community organized around the supervision of persons returning from jails and prisons and from inpatient drug and alcohol treatment facilities. In Frankford, a racially diverse neighborhood in northeast Philadelphia, long-shuttered factories have been replaced by halfway houses, recovery and sober houses, and outpatient drug treatment clinics. This "high-reentry" community is distinguished by a constant churn of men in and out of confinement and whose homes are increasingly difficult to distinguish from carceral spaces. Many grew up with parents who were in the first wave of mass incarceration; some became caught up in it themselves, while others remained in the community and struggled to avoid it. The CLS, starting with the police as gatekeepers, has crept into and altered nearly every other social institution. The carceral system and the postindustrial economy within which it has emerged shape pathways to adult manhood and the life chances of marginalized men. Moreover, they do not navigate these pathways alone. Their family members, romantic partners, friends, and members of their community offer them critical resources and at the same time set limits and expectations for them. The conclusions drawn in this book are relevant not only to men but also to the women who support them and who bear the brunt of their disconnection from mainstream institutions.

WHY MILLENNIALS?

Millennials, especially those who are economically and/or racially marginalized, occupy a uniquely vulnerable space in a changing landscape of contracting economic opportunities and an expanding criminal legal apparatus. These millennials, now aged 27 to 42, are far from "entitled," as their predominantly White, upper-middle-class counterparts were caricatured before the pandemic.[5] They occupy the bottom rung of a labor market bifurcated into high- and low-wage sectors. They are particularly susceptible to retractions of public assistance and other benefits previously provided by the government. Although college degrees are more common among millennials than in older generations, those without a college education are falling further behind than their counterparts in prior cohorts in terms of employment and income.[6]

Millennials constitute the largest and fastest growing segment of those who are either employed or actively looking for a job.[7] Even before the pandemic layoffs, 42 percent of them were freelancers in the growing "gig economy."[8] Those who drive for Uber or deliver food for GrubHub appreciate flexible scheduling but shoulder the risks of their jobs without liability protection or health or retirement benefits provided through their employers, who classify them as independent contractors rather than employees. Those who attend college face steep increases in the cost of tuition and graduate with an average of almost $39,000 in student loan debt.[9] The default rates among the 19.8 million millennials who carry educational debt spiked in 2011, as many sought refuge from the recession in for-profit colleges.[10]

This generation was the first to grow up during the steepest increase in rates of incarceration in the history of the United States. Many had parents and other family members who were imprisoned as a result of harsh drug policies aimed at inner-city communities of color.[11] They live in neighborhoods that are simultaneously overpoliced and underpoliced, where calls for assistance are ignored or require long waits and where at least half of murders are never solved.[12] Many of these inner-city communities are destabilized by losing and reabsorbing a disproportionate number of men, and to a lesser extent women, who are removed to and returned from jails and prisons.[13]

The millennials who are the subject of this book navigated the crucial transitions of adolescence and young adulthood during a time of unprecedented expansion of the CLS. The "surveillant assemblage" includes new forms of formal legal supervision (e.g., GPS monitoring), but more importantly, it fuses the legal system with other social institutions such as education, public welfare, and the labor market.[14] Millennials were the first generation to experience zero-tolerance disciplinary policies in their schools, leading to what is now known as the "school-to-prison pipeline." With rapidly expanding information-sharing capacity via the internet, their contacts with the CLS left behind a readily accessible and durable digital footprint.[15] Criminal records are now regularly made public and used by employers, rental agents, and public welfare professionals for decision-making purposes. Mug shots or photos of turnstile jumping are posted on social media by police departments. Homeowners and business owners can now link their camera feeds to the police department, widening the space that is surveilled. Restaurant chains' data on the location of a pizza delivery is shared with law enforcement agencies ready to serve a warrant.[16]

In short, the CLS has become a defining social and economic institution for millennials, particularly those without college degrees, which reflects and reinforces their economic marginalization. As adults, the men in this book are attempting to disentangle themselves from this sticky web of social control; they strive to become "productive citizens" despite encountering substantial barriers erected by the CLS. They must also challenge the stigmatic labels applied by the system and internalized by others (and sometimes themselves), working to redeem themselves in the eyes of family members and potential romantic partners. These men—particularly

Black men—must navigate the conflicting needs to be invisible to avoid the police yet visible and recognizable as individuals to their loved ones.[17]

Interviews with the Frankford men demonstrate that the CLS affects every aspect of their lives, from their limited ability to use public space and create social ties with neighbors, peers, and family members to their very definitions of self. The system is a central part of their life histories: their stories of trauma, of which family members stood by them when they were incarcerated, of missing their children's early milestones, of being disconnected from their schools. It teaches young people about their marginalized position in society, which puts them on the wrong side of the law. It circumscribes their definitions of adulthood: you are adult when you are treated as one by the system; of masculinity, as being able to control your own life and care for others; and of success: I'm not locked up. Their connection to the CLS is a master status and source of stigma they must overcome to develop a positive masculine identity.[18] It restricts their plans for getting ahead educationally or economically by creating debt and imposing economic burdens on family members. It is always ready to drag them backward, requiring consistent efforts to simply remain in place.

So far, I have argued that the millennial generation is a worthwhile subject of study because of their vulnerable positions in relation to an increasingly insecure labor market and the growing power of the CLS. Some may question the utility of generational labels and point out that their cutoffs are arbitrary. To be sure, fifteen years covers much territory. My intention is not to reify these categories or insist that someone born in 1980 has a demonstrably different life trajectory than someone born in 1981. Nevertheless, cohorts are a useful heuristic device for understanding the effects of structural and cultural shifts on individuals' lived experiences. Although this generation contains wide variations in circumstances, we know little about millennials without a college degree, who are more exposed to risk. This book focuses specifically on these men, both those who are White and those who are Black, Latino, or biracial.

WHY MEN?

As with millennials, the declining economic prospects of men have received a fair amount of popular attention. Indeed, a decade ago journalist

Hanna Rosin provocatively forecast "the end of men"—or, more precisely, of patriarchal power—as women surpassed men in their levels of education and stable employment and in their growing access to formerly male-dominated fields.[19] Unsettled perceptions of men are reflected in condemnations of "toxic masculinity" on the one hand and of concern about "incels," groups of involuntarily celibate men who are violently angry at being rejected by women. The #MeToo movement has created new accountability for men's treatment of women in the workplace, with numerous high-profile celebrities and politicians forced out of their positions because of sexual harassment and assault. Predictable backlashes have also occurred, with groups defending men's rights and a largely White male presence among active hate groups, such as those who marched in the Unite the Right rally in Charlottesville, Virginia, in 2017 and those involved in the January 2021 insurrection at the Capitol.

Beneath the cultural dialogue around men and masculinity is a set of stark facts about men's declining labor force participation. Even before the pandemic recession, men were significantly less likely to be employed or looking for work than in prior decades.[20] The number of less educated men of prime working age (25 to 54) has decreased by 10.7 percentage points since 1960, with a total loss of ten million men from the workforce.[21] The Great Recession of 2007–9 had a disproportionate impact on traditionally male blue-collar industries. Many of these men never rejoined the workforce after what some called the "mancession," leading to a surge in "deaths of despair," or early death attributable to suicide, drug overdose, or alcoholic liver disease.[22] Some men may never become or expect to become part of the formal labor force altogether.

Men are also falling behind in higher education, as anyone who attends or works at a university knows. The *Atlantic* noted in 2021 that "colleges have a guy problem," pointing to the gender disparity in college enrollment (with a 6:4 ratio of women to men) and the steep decline in college enrollment in the last five years, 70 percent of which occurred among men.[23] Men are also significantly less likely than women to complete their education at every level. In the 2018–19 academic year, seventy-four men for every one hundred women graduated with a bachelor's degree.[24] Women now make up the majority of graduates with associate's, bachelor's, master's, and doctoral degrees. This disparity bodes ill for the future, since economists and sociologists see a widening gap in opportunities for those with and without a college diploma.

The gendered, raced, and classed reconfiguration of higher education and the labor market has had spillover effects for marriage and living arrangements. Men are now more likely to be single (not married or co-habitating with a romantic partner) than women, and their declines in marriage and partnership are driven by their eroding economic positions. In a 2017 survey, 71 percent of Americans said that being able to support a family financially was very important for prospective male spouses or partners, while only 32 percent said that was true for prospective female spouses or partners. In short, unemployed men are perceived as less marriageable than their working counterparts and may face serious challenges when looking for a romantic partner.[25] Most Black women (62%) and Black men (55%) are single, a figure that reflects both the poor employment prospects and the disproportionate incarceration of Black men. Single men with few economic prospects rely on family members to survive; one-third of unpartnered adult men live at home with their parents.[26]

Men also garner the lion's share of attention from agents of the CLS. Men's vulnerability to arrest has increased since the advent of "proactive policing," in which officers attempt to prevent crimes rather than respond to them after the fact.[27] Even as crime has declined steadily since the mid-1990s, arrest has become a common feature of young adulthood. By the time they reach age 23, 38 percent of White men and 49 percent of Black men have been arrested.[28] Astonishingly, arrest has become increasingly prevalent among young adults who self-report *no criminal activity*, a phenomenon known as the "great decoupling" of behavior and sanctions.[29]

Men are also subject to greater risk of incarceration, especially men of color and men with low educational attainment. Among those born in 1965–69, 29 percent of Black men had experienced a spell of incarceration by age 30; the rates were even higher among Black men without a college diploma (30%) and those without a high school degree (60%). These staggering figures led sociologists Becky Pettit and Bruce Western to conclude that incarceration is a "new stage in the life course of young low-skill black men."[30] The effects of legal system contact are a primary driver of social inequality and precarity.[31]

MEETING MEN IN FRANKFORD

Frankford, located in the inner northeast section of Philadelphia, was selected because it has a high rate of violent crime, is among the few racially diverse neighborhoods in this hypersegregated city, and absorbs a disproportionate number of people released from jail and prison into the community. Those characteristics make Frankford the ideal place to explore the convergence of disappearing economic prospects and heightened exposure to the CLS. Table 1 contains neighborhood descriptors and is found in the appendix.

This study, carried out from 2014 to 2019, compares Black, Latino, and White men at two levels of education: high school dropouts who may have a general equivalency diploma (GED) and those with at least a high school diploma.[32] The men who were interviewed included twenty-three who identified as Black, five who identified as Latino, and seventeen who identified as White.[33] We had great difficulty in enlisting Latino men, which is not surprising given the well-publicized immigration raids that occurred throughout this period. Of the forty-five men, twenty-six had at least a high school diploma. When comparing White men to men of color, there were no differences in their likelihood of having dropped out of high school, but White men were significantly more likely to have GEDs, while men of color were more likely to have earned high school diplomas. All but one of six men with some college, including those with associate of arts (AA; one) or bachelor of arts (BA; one) degrees, were men of color. This reflects a nonrandom sample of White men who disproportionately had criminal histories and were in the community for substance use recovery. All participants had resided in Frankford for at least a year, and many had lived there their whole lives. Table 2, which describes each participant, is found in the appendix.

We recruited men by advertising in the local newsletter and making announcements at community meetings, posting flyers at corner stores and barber shops, and approaching men in public. The staff of churches and community agencies, landlords, and local residents connected us with men we might interview. But we found that very few of the men who had already been interviewed could connect us with other men in the community. In fact, this was the first clue that withdrawal from social networks was prevalent among men in Frankford.

When the in-depth interviews were conducted, these men were between the ages of 23 and 39. We met in a private room in a church with a central location. Most recorded interviews lasted between two and four hours. We wrote down additional details, such as the men's demeanor and mannerisms. Interview questions ranged widely: we asked about their daily routines, perceptions of the neighborhood, contact with the police and other agents of the legal system, family and social ties, and strategies for making ends meet (including drug sales) and included questions centering on identity, stigma, masculinity, and adulthood. Turning to their life histories, we asked about their families, romantic relationships, work, schooling, and criminal activity. To understand Frankford, we regularly attended community meetings, events, and venues from 2014 to 2019.[34]

My research team and I employed empathic interviewing, which helped many men feel more comfortable sharing intimate details of their often-traumatic lives. Some cried during their interviews, and many said that having someone listen to their stories made them feel better. We spoke with men who were vulnerable in multiple ways, subject to homelessness, food insecurity, addiction, victims of violence, formerly incarcerated, locked out of the labor market, and failing to meet their own definition of "a real man." It was heavy work to hear their stories, attempt to represent them in ways that capture the complexity of their situations, and imagine policies and practices that could meaningfully improve their lives.

To protect the privacy of everyone we spoke with, I use pseudonyms for the men and women who are represented here and refer to community leaders by their titles. Before introducing the interpretive perspectives underlying this book's analysis and the chapter outline, I examine the financial situations of the men we interviewed.

ECONOMIC PRECARITY

The Frankford men faced multiple barriers to steady employment at a living wage, including a lack of educational credentials, felony records, and spotty work histories. Some had visible signs of stigma, such as tattoos on the face or neck; had tics that revealed mental illness, brain injury, or disabilities; or lacked clean clothing because they were homeless. All these men were vulnerable; most of them lived precariously from day to day. Trauma, physical and intellectual disabilities, addiction, spells of incarceration, chronic health problems, histories of violent victimization, homelessness, and food insecurity were common.

Analysis of the Frankford men's employment reveals that the traditional distinctions made by the federal government—employed, unemployed but actively looking for work, or not in the labor force—fail to describe the full range of work activities in which they were engaged and do not fit subjective perceptions of who was "employed." For example, Wesley, a 26-year-old Black veteran, considered himself unemployed and engaged in online job searches nearly every day, even though he regularly contributed $600 per month to the household budget by doing odd jobs such as janitorial work and cleaning out houses. Most of the men used a variety of strategies to make ends meet, including support from family members and friends, legal and quasi-legal hustles, and receipt of various public assistance streams.[35]

Over half of these men (twenty-five of forty-five) were generating regular income through legal employment (broadly defined) at the time of our interview. Common forms of on-the-books work included jobs in construction and home repair, food service, health care, technology, and nonprofit sectors. Off-the-books (OTB) work, which is not reported to the government and thus is neither taxed nor eligible for benefits such as the earned income tax credit (EITC), unemployment insurance, and workers' compensation, is irregular, and those men who rely on it often do different kinds of informal work simultaneously. Among the Frankford men, day labor in the construction industry was most important, but they also repaired cars; did janitorial work or cleaned out houses; provided personal services such as help with computer problems, fitness training, haircuts, and tattoos; and engaged in creative endeavors such as silk screening or picture framing. Few men relied on drug sales or other illegal activities for income when we interviewed them, although many had done so during their teens and twenties.

Almost three-quarters of the men we interviewed (thirty-three) had unstable work histories, which can be attributed to a wide range of factors, including disability, felony records and spells of incarceration, substance abuse, and homelessness. All but one had less than a bachelor's degree, which was part of the selection criteria for inclusion in the study, and two-fifths (nineteen) had either dropped out of high school or completed a GED. When comparing employment status by race, ten of the seventeen White men were employed at the time of the interview, three of these in OTB jobs, and four had stable employment histories. Of the twenty-eight men of color, sixteen were employed, three in OTB jobs, and eight had stable employment histories. The prevalence of CLS involvement among the White men in the sample is the most likely explanation for the lack of a racial gap in employment, which we might expect would be wider because of systemic racism and felony penalties in hiring.

Although minimum wage retail or food service jobs were common early in the Frankford men's employment trajectories, some, particularly those who were White, started working alongside their parents in the construction or restaurant industries as teenagers. Their early and sponsored introduction to career-building fields gave them a durable competitive advantage into adulthood. They developed the skills and connections needed to get jobs without searching or interviewing, and often despite having criminal records. One-third of the White men (five of seventeen) had family members who helped them get jobs in the construction or food industry at some point, whereas less than one in ten of men of color (three of twenty-eight) got such jobs through their relatives.

The most troublesome question in our interviews involved creating an itemized monthly budget of expenses and sources of income.[36] For some men, seeing all their expenses in relation to their income was an anxiety-producing, even traumatic experience, for it revealed that their expenses exceeded their incomes, sometimes by a factor of two. Although their earnings from all forms of work varied widely, the crucial factor in making ends meet was their ability to share financial burdens with families, friends, or romantic partners or to receive support from local and federal assistance programs.

Housing was the men's leading expenditure. Although one-fifth did not pay any rent, those who did spent an average of 30 percent of their total earnings on rent. This is at the top of the recommended housing to income ratio specified in federal guidelines. Anyone who pays over 30 percent is "cost burdened," and those who pay more than half of their income on rent are "severely cost burdened."[37] Since the vast majority of the men in this sample were in the 25–34 age range in 2014–19, they experienced the effects of the mortgage lending crisis, the Great Recession, and the ongoing housing crisis acutely. The housing stock in Frankford is old and deteriorating, and residents pay disproportionately high rents for substandard apartments.

What these men spent on food depended on who they lived with and how much food assistance they received under the Supplemental Nutrition Assistance Program (SNAP), the federal program colloquially known as "food stamps," which now takes the form of debit cards. On average, food accounted for 18 percent of their total monthly expenditures. Many of the Frankford men got by because they shared food expenses with family members and were not custodial fathers. Other men lived in recovery houses where food was provided, sometimes in exchange for a portion of residents' SNAP benefits. Food programs run by the faith community in Frankford alleviated some of the men's hunger through hot meals or food banks. Still, a number of men we interviewed experienced food insecurity, sometimes skipping meals because they had no food, or didn't know where their next meal was coming from.

Over two-fifths of the men reported making regular monthly contributions to family members. (Only two men reported paying child support, which is not included here.)[38] Family financial obligations were a substantial weight on many of the men we interviewed. Those who were even modestly successful at earning money reported that their close relatives relied on them to stay afloat. Some considered moving away to reduce the impact of these obligations, which they had difficulty meeting without going broke themselves.

Just one-fifth of the Frankford men reported having assets or sources of wealth such as inheritances, which are important because they serve as a safety net against financial shocks and volatile earnings. Cars allowed men to escape Frankford's "drama," reducing the likelihood that they would find trouble with the police or peers. More importantly, they allowed men easy access to the suburbs, where jobs were more plentiful and paid more. The men often described cars as the embodiment of adulthood because they confer the freedom to come and go as one pleases and not have to depend on others for a ride or on the vagaries of the Southeastern Pennsylvania Transportation Authority (SEPTA), Philadelphia's expensive public transit system. A couple of men had inherited houses from grandparents or parents. As long as the mortgage was either paid in full or not in arrears, homeownership reduced monthly housing costs for individuals and served as a crucial safety net during spells of joblessness or financial crises. Two or three men mentioned owning investment properties, which they had inherited from family members or purchased at low cost at a sheriff's sale to rehab and rent out. This type of asset relies heavily on social capital, including knowledge of where and when sales are held, how to leverage existing programs to assemble a down payment, and home equity financing for capital improvements.

Mirroring wider US trends, the Frankford men reported carrying substantial debt. Two-fifths (nineteen of forty-five) of the men owed money to the CLS, in the form of fines and fees for court or supervision costs. Five owed at least $10,000, and two owed $20,000 or more for skipping bail. Some mentioned forfeiting assets such as cars, houses, or businesses because of their involvement in drug sales. Legal financial obligations (LFOs) are a heavy and growing burden for those involved in the system, deepening the social inequalities caused by mass incarceration and extended supervision.[39] The privatization of legal functions and the rise of offender-funded remedies mean that individuals must pay restitution to the survivor or a fund for victims; fees for court appearances and probation supervision; and the cost of drug tests, mandatory treatment, and even nights in jail. Under the threat of reincarceration, those returning from jails and prisons or on probation supervision feel immense pressure to satisfy the requirements of this debt. The inability to pay off their LFO debts can keep them under supervision indefinitely.[40]

The second most common form of debt is medical, typically incurred when men without health insurance coverage visit emergency rooms. One-fifth of the Frankford men reported health debt ranging from $400 to $100,000, which they were unable to pay. About half of the sample had health insurance, the vast majority of which was provided through Medicaid. Credit card debt was the third most commonly mentioned form of debt, with eight men reporting they were carrying a balance ranging from $347 to $10,000. That more men did not report credit card debt reflects their lack of credit, rather than their ability to pay the balance in full every month. Carrying a balance with a high rate of interest is troublesome, but a lack of credit is also problematic. Employers and landlords regularly treat credit scores as an indicator of reliability; those without a credit record may not be eligible for loans and may need to have someone else set up their utilities. Moreover, those who lack access to regulated forms of credit must often rely on predatory systems such as payday loan companies.

INTERPRETIVE PERSPECTIVES

The interpretation of these findings was guided by multiple perspectives. My overall goal is to situate human agency and identity construction in the cultural contexts of racialized adult masculinity. I see these as developed in response to economic forces, including the CLS.

My training as an urban ethnographer is grounded in symbolic interactionism, which focuses on nonverbal and verbal interactions between individuals that produce shared meanings. One starting point for this perspective is the classical pronouncement by William Thomas and Dorothy Swaine Thomas that "what men perceive as real is real in its consequences."[41] Subjective perceptions are the basis for human action, even when they may differ from supposedly objective "facts." Symbolic interactionists reject the positivistic assumption that social "reality" can be uncovered by a neutral, outside observer.[42] Instead, we study reality as it is perceived by participants, conveyed through interaction with the researcher, and ultimately filtered through the analyst's lens.

Symbolic interactionism provides a framework for understanding identity construction. The self does not exist outside social relationships; individuals form a sense of identity by imagining how they are perceived by others.[43] If students believe that their teachers view them as intelligent, for example, they are likely to see themselves in that way. Moreover, this self-conception leads them to perform in ways that are consistent with intelligence, such as studying harder, which reinforces the teacher's perception and reflects back on the student. Here, the term *performance* does not suggest insincerity, but rather that all of our interactions with others are designed to present ourselves as credible.[44]

The Frankford men worked to manage a number of stigmas that could damage their identities, including unemployment; homelessness;

histories of addiction; disabilities; felony records; and *racial-criminal stigma*, the assumption that men of color are inherently dangerous, regardless of their social class status or actual behavior. Stigma management involves signaling to others that one's character is inconsistent with negative stereotypes by presenting *disidentifiers*, visible symbols such as clothing and comportment, and counternarratives that challenge the validity of stigmatic labels.[45] Moreover, many of the men we interviewed, especially men of color, engaged in prosocial activities, serving as informal mentors and volunteering at soup kitchens and food pantries. These bids for redemption were ways of challenging racial-criminal stigma, reinforcing claims to goodness through acts of generosity.

The life course and developmental perspective has shaped this study from its inception. This model focuses on the order and timing of events and stages unfolding over the life span and assumes that prior experiences influence but do not necessarily determine later ones. Human agency, the time and place in which development occurs, and *linked lives*, or the interdependence of relationships with others as they unfold over the life span, are core principles of life course studies.[46] Cohort studies, such as Glen Elder's *Children of the Great Depression*, examine the effects of growing up at a particular confluence of historical events, as the present study does for millennials.[47]

Psychologist Erik Erikson's theory of personality development posits that the self and society interact to produce age-specific internal crises that must be resolved to develop virtues, such as purpose or competency, and to pass to the next stage, resulting in healthy psychosocial development.[48] Erikson proposed that men between the ages of 18 and 40 should be developing the virtue of love by working to resolve the conflict between intimacy and isolation. Although this tension is indeed a central preoccupation of the Frankford men, their trajectories pose a challenge to Erikson's linear model by also exhibiting great concern with generativity, which is typically associated with people aged 40 to 65. They are also still struggling with some of the crises associated with earlier life stages, including industry versus inferiority, which he found was typically resolved by age 12, and identity versus confusion, which was typically resolved by age 18. The complexity and unevenness of the Frankford men's development registers the impact of economic social changes that have made it more difficult for millennial men to chart their courses into adulthood in the same ways and at the same pace as those in earlier generations. In fact, it is fair to say that they are working to resolve many of these crises and contradictions simultaneously as they arise.

The life course perspective has also radically changed criminology, with the development of a variety of theories explaining *desistance*, or the termination of or reduction in criminal offending as individuals mature.[49] These explanations range in their emphasis on individual motivation or structural factors, including marriage, parenthood, or employment, as potential "turning points" that facilitate a law-abiding trajectory. All of these perspectives agree that desistance is the norm for all but 6–8 percent of the population, who continue offending well into and throughout adulthood. A remarkable finding of this study is that most of the Frankford men desisted from offending despite rarely reaching these milestones and living in a place and time where contact with law enforcement was so pervasive. A substantial number were never engaged in law-breaking or system contact at all.

Critical race theory (CRT) has recently made headlines as numerous school districts around the nation have been barred from teaching the subject, which is often a cover for a blanket prohibition of teaching about racial inequality. What is especially troubling to extreme conservatives is that CRT views White supremacy as a contemporary and central feature of mainstream American society, not confined to the past or to the ideological fringe.[50] CRT directs us away from a focus on individual forms of racist treatment and argues that systemic racism is embedded in all our social institutions, including schools, the labor market, health care, housing and neighborhoods, citizenship, and the legal system. Moreover, CRT often aims to show how these institutions intersect to make racism harder to see and address. Guided by this perspective, which has been brought home by mass protests against endemic, state-sanctioned violence against people of color, I have come to see the CLS as a sort of "shell corporation" that launders racism to make outcomes appear color-blind.[51] Although it is no longer legal or socially acceptable to discriminate on the basis of race, it is perfectly legal to restrict the rights of those convicted or even accused of breaking the law. In defining the behavior of Black, indigenous, and other people of color as illegal or saturating their communities with surveillance, the United States is able to achieve the same outcomes that were produced in the past by slavery and Jim Crow, while creating plausible deniability that the process has anything to do with race.

The analysis used in this book integrates principles of CRT with the model of intersectionality developed by Black feminists.[52] The intersectional framework replaces additive treatments of marginalized identities, for example, describing Black women as doubly disadvantaged, with a lens that examines overlapping structural positions along intersecting axes of oppression, such as race, gender, class, sexual orientation, gender expression, and ability. This paradigm allows us to recognize that less educated men are both privileged on the basis of their gender and disadvantaged by their social class. Moreover, intersectionality helps us understand how White men's racial privilege operates, even when their economic position resembles that of men of color. Feminist theory also reminds us that regardless of these men's increasingly vulnerable positions in relation to the women in their lives and to other men, they still benefit from patriarchy.[53] Despite the shifting ground that many men in US society are navigating, including the assumption of selected gender performances that we typically associate as feminine (such as caring and caregiving), most research concludes that these are changes in the *expression* of systems of power and inequality but ultimately do not challenge the patriarchal gender order.[54]

Although my analysis in this text is focused on microlevel concerns around gendered techniques of identity construction, this process cannot be understood as separate from gender as a macrolevel, historically specific configuration of relational power between women and men—*and* between men with structural access to hegemonic masculinities and those who are relegated to subordinated or marginalized forms of masculinity.[55] This model suggests that masculinities are constructed along axes of racial privilege and subordination. In considering Black (and Latino) men's construction of masculinities, it is critical to avoid the trap of what Black feminists Freedon Blume Oeur and Saida Grundy call "the zero-sum seesaw logic," whereby if "Black men [are] down . . . Black women are up."[56] The men's perspectives shared here—most of which were conveyed in interviews with White women and are idealized as are *any* presentations of self—may obscure the struggles faced by women of color, including interpersonal and structural violence. In short, we cannot be seduced by men's claims to define masculinity in care-centered ways because we were not in their kitchens and bedrooms to see the ways that they very likely also borrowed from conservative gender ideologies to subordinate the women in their lives.[57]

The centrality of economic institutions to this book's analysis and conclusions is consistent with sociological approaches that map the social and cultural features of late capitalism, including neoliberal policies, economic insecurity, and the rise of the risk society. This perspective rejects the manifest function of the CLS to produce public safety and redirects us to its true but hidden function, which is to target those at highest risk of falling through the cracks in an increasingly precarious economy; frame them as posing a public safety risk; and construct technologies of control that further marginalize, segregate, pathologize, criminalize, incarcerate, surveil, exploit, and exclude them.

The ever-expanding carceral apparatus is a significant component of the US economy. This system, which directly employs 2.8 million Americans, or more than 1.5 percent of the total workforce, has become a steady source of jobs, not only for police, probation, and corrections officers, but also for countless others who work in industries supplying food, supplies, and services to prisons and correctional or supervisory agencies.[58] "Incarceration-as-economic-development" has been a major strategy in rural areas that were hollowed out when factories closed in the 1970s, despite its lack of success in saving these depressed places. Finally, the system generates profit through innumerable predatory practices, ranging from prison labor to civil asset forfeiture and municipal fines to private companies with contracts to collect fees from system-involved individuals who often pay for the privilege of incarceration or supervision and then pay interest on their overdue balance.

The desire to control an increasingly uncertain future is a primary feature of the *risk society*, a modern form of social organization concerned with managing threats to safety and security, including environmental hazards, health, and financial crises.[59] Reducing unpredictability through information has become a societal preoccupation. Every choice we make is infused with risk, whether buying food, choosing where to live, or selecting an occupation. Social class stratifies exposure to risks by offering a greater variety of options, including the purchasing power to mitigate some risks. Moreover, whereas US social policy historically took a collective approach to mediating risk through New Deal policies such as the Social Security Act, contemporary society is more likely to privatize risk, making it the responsibility of the individual to face and address the risks posed by nature, business cycles, global health pandemics, or the police.

The CLS's manifest function is to provide security to leverage against the risk inherent in a society with crime. As a social institution, it relies on citizens' trust, which is garnered by *predictability*, or the assurance that procedures will be carried out reliably and actions will be routine or consistent.[60] This assumption breaks down when racial-spatial disparities in police response are so visible, when agents of the system routinely violate the law, and when brutality against citizens is common. The result is that the system that is ostensibly intended to *decrease* risk actually *produces* uncertainty.

The men in this study are risk averse and frame many of their decisions to minimize risk. Men of color reduce their interactions with police and with others who might victimize them by staying in the house and restricting their social networks. They view criminal activity as posing the kinds of risk that only adolescents can tolerate. Relying on others is generally considered risky because their support could disappear or, worse, they could bring additional financial risks or demands into the exchange.[61] Risk discourses misidentify men of color in particular as *posing*, rather than *absorbing*, the greatest degree of risk from the CLS and economic retrenchment.

LISTENING TO MARGINALIZED MILLENNIAL MEN

Chapter 2 describes Frankford as an ideal place to study the lived experiences of crime and "justice." Philadelphia is both a national leader in progressive reform of the legal system and a site of deeply problematic relationships between citizens of color and the police. This setting shapes men's survival strategies, employment trajectories, access to local resources, use of social ties, and constructions of adulthood and masculinity. It explores the world that has been created by the US implicit policy of dealing with the failure of the educational, economic, and social system to enable young men from impoverished backgrounds, especially young men of color, to attain adult manhood by criminalizing those who suffer most intensely from the problems that societal failure creates.

Given their social and economic vulnerability, it is particularly significant that the Frankford men have largely desisted from offending. In chapter 3 I examine the mechanisms supporting desistance, particularly in the absence of structural turning points emphasized by criminologists.[62] Most important, these men's subjective perceptions of offending are inconsistent with their constructions of adult masculinity.[63] Models of positive Black manhood foster *racial literacy*, a set of tools for mitigating the negative effects of racism and discrimination and providing a pathway forward.[64] I contrast the Frankford men with the younger men whom I followed in *Falling Back*, arguing that they prefer stable, adult relationships and roles that are inconsistent with crime and the risks it presents.[65] The effort required to desist as these men move from their midtwenties into their midthirties diminishes over time because they are less tied to male peer groups and increasingly attuned to the expectations of romantic partners. Michael Rocque's theory of maturation as desistance provides an integrative framework.[66] The remaining chapters follow the men as they manage the tension between hypervisibility to the police and feared invisibility to others.

Chapter 4 demonstrates that avoiding or mitigating trouble, which these men call "drama," is a focal concern and an organizing framework for their daily routines and interactions.[67] Trouble can come in many forms, including attention from the authorities, falling back into old patterns of criminal offending or drug use, and violent victimization. The majority of men of color in Frankford stayed in their houses and avoided public spaces and interactions in order to decrease their risk of death or incarceration. Network avoidance often meant a complete lack of engagement in their community, in civic or service organizations, and even in getting to know their neighbors. This strategy exemplifies "responsibilization," whereby men assumed the state's concern with targeting their own risk as potentially violent men, leading to their removal from the public sphere and recreation of the features of carceral spaces at home.

Within the context of economic instability, racial caste, and the "stickiness" of criminal system labels, young men struggle to craft identities that cast themselves in a positive light. Chapter 5 focuses on the effort made by men of color to contest group-based stigma.[68] They seek to reassure others that they do not fit the stereotypes of violent Black men, often by presenting what Erving Goffman called "disidentifiers" that challenge others' negative perceptions.[69] As they develop, men of color repeatedly encounter predictions of failure directed at them by outsiders who represent major social institutions, including expectations that they will engage in criminal activity, violence, irresponsible fatherhood, and dependency.[70] This chapter examines redemption bids and projects as a way of making good. Redemption, which has been highlighted as an effective means of desisting from criminal behavior, is a central meaning-making activity of men in Frankford—*even among those with no criminal history*.[71] I show that redemption is consistent with their construction of masculine, adult, racial, and place-based identities. Redemption narratives most often turn on performances of good personhood, on acts of generosity and generativity.[72] Because they must be witnessed and reflected back as believable, men seek out suitable audiences for their acts of giving back. To redeem themselves, these men require social ties—the same ties that they perceive as increasing their risk of "drama."

Deep and durable social ties are critical to human development. Family members, romantic partners, and children can be consistent sources of material and emotional support. Family and romantic relationships can also be toxic or traumatic, hinder healthy adult development and social mobility, and come with troublesome reciprocal obligations.[73] Chapter 6 describes the personal ties that the Frankford men formed and sustained with their families of origin, intimate relationships and marriage, and fatherhood. For many of them, forging closer ties involved forgiving parents who had not been there for them during their childhoods. Despite the pulls of individualism and isolation, millennial men in Frankford value durable social ties and strive to maintain them, even when this places their own progress in jeopardy. While men define their ideal romantic partners in emotional terms, they worry that their own contributions to relationships will be assessed solely in economic terms and that they may consequently be found lacking or be deemed irrelevant.

Chapter 7 explores how the Frankford men constructed the achievement of these milestones. Most regarded them as separate processes;

adulthood happens more or less naturally with age, while masculinity involves more effort and may ultimately be elusive. In short, they have felt like adults for many years but reported that they have only recently begun to—or do not yet—feel like "a real man." Moreover, they tended to think that once adulthood had been attained, it was a permanent state, while masculinity was something that needed to be accomplished consistently and was a status that could be lost.[74] The Frankford men were conscious of and did their best to distance themselves from the numerous negative images of men who are deadbeat dads, unemployed bums, leeches, or immoral, violent offenders. With limited ability to provide for their loved ones financially, they constructed definitions of masculinity that they could attain, namely caring for and caring about others. Moreover, they called attention to the effort and consistency needed to do gender in this way, in the same fashion that feminist scholars have historically done to highlight the invisible nature of care work.

The conclusion reflects on how we can support and facilitate marginalized men's transition to adult masculinity in their own eyes and in the eyes of others. Doing so requires us to shed the dominant neoliberal framework of "atomistic individualism."[75] The Frankford men need and desire to form meaningful social connections. Although a handful of the most vulnerable men are going it alone, the vast majority are striving to build durable social ties. Their efforts can be supported by shoring up the human and social capital that already exists in their seemingly disorganized community.[76] Criminal injustice and the increasingly precarious labor market are the salient issues facing this and future generations.[77] Current criminal legal reforms, however promising they appear, will likely adapt and persist as means of controlling the poor, reproducing racial caste, and inhibiting collective solutions to social problems.[78] They exacerbate rather than mitigate the situation. I discuss emerging research on justice reinvestment, improving the built environment and social infrastructure, and the importance of local nonprofit organizations, then review several alternate frameworks from which we can redefine "justice."[79]

2 Philadelphia as a Site of Shifting Ground

[Frankford is] diverse, it's pretty working class, it's kind of gritty, I don't know at the same time it feels like a community. People know each other, neighbors talk to each other and shit like that. So even with the crime and stuff like that it's still relatively friendly community to live here.

—Chase, 27, White, in recovery

INTRODUCTION

Philadelphia, like many other American cities, has suffered grievously from the intersection of an expanding criminal legal apparatus and shrinking economic opportunities. In *Falling Back*, I offered a detailed description of the city's social, economic, and political-legal landscape.[1] A decade later, Philadelphia remains an ideal place to study the experiences of men who are traversing the shifting grounds of these social structures and cultural expectations within them. This chapter embeds these men's survival strategies, patterns of offending, employment trajectories, use of local resources and social ties, and constructions of adulthood and masculinity within the local context. It ends with an exploration of Frankford, the neighborhood where the men lived.

Pervasive poverty is Philadelphia's most salient feature, reflected in its status as the poorest large city in the nation. Although the most recent census data predates the COVID-19 pandemic, 2019 figures show that almost one-quarter (23.3%) of the city's residents were living below the poverty line, with Latinx Philadelphians making up the largest group living in poverty.[2] Although poverty has decreased since 2005, half of poor

Philadelphians live in deep poverty, with incomes that are below $12,300 for a household of four.[3] The Affordable Care Act of 2010 resulted in dramatically increased enrollment in Medicaid to 667,000 Philadelphians by 2017. Over 107,000 received Supplementary Security Income, 92 percent of whom qualified because of a disability.

Poverty and affluence coexist in fairly close proximity, with only five miles separating the poorest community in the city—Fairhill, in the northeast—from the richest, Graduate Hospital, in Center City. These stark differences are sometimes found on a block-by-block basis and lead to widely varying daily experiences and long-term health and well-being depending on where residents live. Each of the five neighborhoods where I've lived in Philadelphia over the years has its own distinctive commercial, cultural, and environmental climate, with widely disparate resources, densities, ways of getting along in public, and leafy green or littered streets. All underwent gentrification while I lived there. These inequities translate to a twenty-year difference in life expectancy between zip code 19132 in North Philadelphia, where residents live on average to age 68, and 19106 in Society Hill, Center City, where they live to 88.[4]

The most recent census data reports that 60.9 percent of Philadelphians of working age are in the labor force.[5] Leading industries in Philadelphia include education and health care, with 237,000 jobs; government (107,000); professional and business services (101,000); and trade, transportation, and utilities (90,000).[6] Importantly, each of these sectors requires an education that goes beyond high school. In Frankford, the neighborhood from which this book's sample is drawn, two in five residents aged 16 and over are not in the labor force. Among those who are working, the largest number are doing direct service in the educational services, health-care, and social assistance sector.[7]

Underlying these stark contrasts in well-being across Philadelphia neighborhoods is the level and intractability of racial residential hypersegregation.[8] Although neighborhood racial composition has shifted substantially in the last two decades, spurred by gentrification and the establishment of a largely but not exclusively Vietnamese and Mexican immigrant corridor along Washington Avenue in South Philadelphia, neighborhood reconfigurations have ultimately reinforced existing segregation patterns.[9] The city's policy of ten-year tax abatement on new construction has contributed to middle-class White migration into neighborhoods such as Kensington, which is the most impoverished and high-crime community in the city and the epicenter of the city's opioid epidemic. Some community members in Frankford I interviewed mentioned that they were hoping for gentrification to move north and east to revitalize the community and counteract a sharp decline in housing values. Others, of course, would likely be priced out and forced to move if gentrification affected the community.

THE POLITICAL-LEGAL ORDER IN PHILADELPHIA AND PENNSYLVANIA

Philadelphia is a progressive local jurisdiction within a commonwealth long dominated by Republicans. The issue of reforming the CLS became more salient in Philadelphia during the 2016 presidential campaign, in which crime was a major focus of the Republican nominee for the first time in decades. Larry Krasner, "one of the most . . . maybe *the* most, progressive DAs in the country" won in a landslide victory over his Republican opponent in November 2017.[10] Krasner, a civil rights attorney who represented the Occupy and Black Lives Matter movements, ran on a platform of police accountability, ending cash bail, and promising never to seek the death penalty, and was staunchly opposed by the city's police union. He began his term by firing thirty-one prosecutors in an attempt to change the culture inside the district attorney's (DA's) office, and he hired several former public defenders to play key roles, including Robert Listenbee, the former head of the Philadelphia Juvenile Defenders Association and chief of the Office of Juvenile Justice and Delinquency Prevention.

Krasner's election hastened several legal reforms that were already in motion under Mayor James Kenney's administration. Earlier that year, City Council approved the formation of the Special Committee on Criminal Justice Reform to examine the "unsustainable and rapid growth of the adult corrections population" and "the impact that current laws have on Philadelphia communities."[11] The city was awarded a $3.5 million grant through the MacArthur Safety and Justice Challenge Network to reduce the number of people in jail, largely by addressing the problem of cash bail.[12] The effort resulted in an almost 42 percent reduction in the jail population between July 2015 and October 2021.[13]

The city decriminalized the possession of small amounts of cannabis in 2014, treating carrying and smoking in public as a civil offense punishable by fines. A report by the Vera Institute of Justice has shown, however, that despite steeply declining arrests overall, racial disparities in marijuana arrests have remained stable in Philadelphia and actually increased for disorderly conduct, one of the most highly discretionary charges.[14] Pennsylvania opened up cannabis dispensaries for medical use in 2018, which are now easily accessible to individuals with the means to get a doctor's prescription and a medical marijuana card. In the November 2021 elections, in which Larry Krasner was reelected as DA, Philadelphia voters approved a referendum urging lawmakers in Harrisburg to legalize recreational use of cannabis by adults, a nonbinding but symbolic message.[15] Today, many Philadelphians drive over the Delaware River into New Jersey to visit dispensaries there or buy from illegal but nevertheless fairly low-visibility storefronts in the city.

Philadelphia's local officials have taken a multipronged public health approach to the opioid epidemic, emphasizing prevention and education, treatment, overdose prevention and harm reduction, diversion of persons identified with substance use disorder (SUD) away from the legal system, and additional support for formerly incarcerated individuals living with addiction.[16] In 2020 public health officials distributed 60,000 doses of the overdose reversal drug Naloxone and trained three thousand citizens to use it, encouraging bystanders to intervene in the absence of first responders. Overdose deaths (86% of which were attributable to opioids) peaked in 2017 and again in 2020, likely the result of contamination by fentanyl, as well as increased social isolation during the pandemic. Although overdose deaths were found in nearly every community, Kensington, adjacent to Frankford to the south and west, is the epicenter. In January 2018 officials announced that Philadelphia would become the first city in the nation to implement safe injection sites to address the opioid epidemic.[17] But South Philadelphia residents objected to the location of the program, and in 2021 a federal court ruled that the plan violated the 1986 "crack statute," scuttling the program.[18]

Philadelphia's progress toward reform has been largely limited by the Republican hold on the Pennsylvania legislature (although Democrats took the House in the 2022 cycle). In probation and parole, whose parameters are set by the commonwealth, reform has been stymied. As rap artist Meek Mill's case revealed, Pennsylvania's statutes mandate no limit to community supervision terms, leading to lengthy probation sentences, particularly as they can be "stacked" one after the other.[19] As a result, Pennsylvania's rates of community supervision are going up as the trends nationally and in nearby states are declining. Although one in fifty-five adults in the United States is on probation or parole supervision, the figures in Philadelphia are one in twenty-three Philadelphians and one in fourteen Black adults.[20] Philadelphia's supervision rate is the highest of any large city and twelve times that of New York City. Moreover, those on supervision still face incarceration for failing drug tests for marijuana, even after its decriminalization. Altogether, violation of the technical conditions of probation contributes to 45 percent of Pennsylvania state prison admissions.[21]

Pennsylvania maintains and enforces many regressive laws that were developed during the superpredator scare of the 1990s, which funneled large numbers of juvenile lawbreakers into the adult system, under one of the country's "deadliest" DAs, Lynne Abraham, who served for almost two decades starting in 1991. For example, Pennsylvania's criminal code specifies no minimum age for adult charges for homicide and defines "murder" broadly to include being present during the course of a felony that results in a victim's death. Further, when the US Supreme Court decided in *Miller v. Alabama* (2016) that mandatory life without parole sentences for juvenile offenders were unconstitutional, the Pennsylvania Supreme Court decided that it would not retroactively apply the law to individuals who had been sentenced prior to *Miller*. It took another four years, under *Montgomery v. Louisiana* (2016), for the Supreme Court to overrule this decision. Only then did Pennsylvania begin resentencing hearings for the more than five hundred juvenile "lifers," many of whom had already spent three or four decades in prison. The majority were from Philadelphia.

Although Pennsylvania has a robust online criminal records system that provides easy access to the public, it also leads the country in its adoption of the Clean Slate Law in 2018, which automatically seals criminal records for summary offenses and misdemeanors when there has been no new conviction in ten years and, importantly, for cases in which charges have been dropped or a defendant is found not guilty.[22] By early 2022 an estimated ten million cases had been sealed, which has the potential to dramatically mitigate the harms of a criminal record. Moreover, a growing number of nonprofit and legal aid organizations in Philadelphia assist citizens with petitions to expunge such information from their criminal records.

During the pandemic lockdown in early 2020, with school buildings closed and nonprofit programs running on shoestring budgets for disappearing clientele, gun violence began to soar. Philadelphia Police Department data on homicides (91% of which were attributable to guns) reveals a dramatic increase from a recent low of 248 in 2014 to 499 in 2020 and a record high of 557 in 2021.[23] Similar spikes in lethal and nonlethal gun violence were seen in many other US cities, with eleven other cities breaking records in 2021.[24] Criminologists have pointed to the economic and social strains of the pandemic and White fear associated with racial justice movements to help explain this phenomenon, although the numbers of legally purchased and "ghost" or homemade guns on the street have also increased, as have reports of retaliatory violence.[25]

Local government officials and stakeholders from community-based organizations, universities, and hospitals have engaged in heated, sometimes acrimonious debates about the causes of Philadelphia's gun violence and the most effective policy solutions. Two competing discursive frames, one focused on community *health* and the other on community *safety*, characterized these discussions.[26] The first framework identified the root cause of street violence in structural racism and deprivation and argued for holistic, community-based resources to combat these problems. The second emphasized law enforcement strategies to track, surveil, and deter gun violence. Ultimately, the Philadelphia Roadmap to Safer Communities incorporated both orientations.[27]

POLICE-COMMUNITY RELATIONS IN PHILADELPHIA

In the wake of the Ferguson protests in 2014, the beleaguered Philadelphia Police Department was hobbled by difficulties in recruiting new officers and well-publicized scandals leading to federal prosecution of six narcotics officers charged with organizing a criminal terror ring involving kidnapping and robbery. Under the new leadership of Chief Richard Ross, the department attempted to clean up its image and come into compliance with the recommendations of President Obama's 2015 Task Force on 21st Century Policing, the first of which was aimed at building "trust and legitimacy" between officers and citizens. The department embraced community policing, data-driven strategies, enhanced use of technology, and public accountability for police-citizen encounters.

Relations between residents and the police nevertheless continued to suffer from a lack of trust and legitimacy. Shortly after taking office in 2018, DA Krasner released a "do not call" list of twenty-nine officers with substantiated patterns of "testilying" or lying during court testimony; their presence on the public list disqualified them from being called in future cases. The DA's office established the Conviction Integrity Unit the same year, which to date has exonerated twenty wrongly convicted Philadelphians—all but two of whom were Black—in cases that were replete with both police and prosecutorial wrongdoing such as "withholding exculpatory evidence, coercing false confessions, or committing perjury."[28] Since 2018 the city government has paid out $34 million to just six people who were exonerated, with at least twenty more eligible to or planning to file civil lawsuits.[29]

In mid-2019 the Plain View Project, a nonprofit group of attorneys, compiled a database of Facebook posts and comments made by more than three hundred active police officers that the group determined "undermine[d] the public trust and confidence in the police." These "appeared to endorse violence, racism, and bigotry."[30] "In some of these posts, officers commented that apprehended suspects—often Black men—'should be dead' or 'should have more lumps on his head.' In other Facebook conversations, officers advocated shooting looters on sight and using cars to run over protestors. Numerous posts deemed Islam 'a cult, not a religion' and referred to Muslims as 'savages' and 'goat-humpers.' And in still others, officers appeared to joke about beating and raping women."[31] An independent review conducted by local media outlets found that almost half of the officers in the database had at least one civilian complaint record, and some had a "laundry list."[32] After an investigation was completed, fifteen officers were slated to be terminated, but eleven retired before being fired, and one was promoted.

Police commissioner Ross resigned abruptly in 2019 after he was implicated in covering up sexual assault and harassment inside the department. In 2020, a month before the COVID-19 pandemic closed down much of the city, Danielle Outlaw was sworn in as the new commissioner. The first Black woman in the position, Outlaw was met with skepticism among local community members because of her public comments as former chief of police in Portland, Oregon, about protesters who "whine and complain" about being assaulted by the police.[33] This concern about her ability to address historically antagonistic police-community relations in Philadelphia was amplified during the racial justice protests of summer 2020 in the wake of George Floyd's killing by police in Minneapolis. After days of protests against police brutality in Center City and West Philadelphia, which included incidents of breaking storefront windows and setting police cars on fire, Outlaw called for peaceful protesters blocking Interstate 676 to be tear gassed. Photos and videos of panicked demonstrators trying to escape toxic fumes by scaling steep embankments and being shot by rubber bullets were widely circulated, and both Outlaw and Mayor Kenney later apologized for the decision. A report commissioned by the City Controller's Office described the incident as the "most aggressive police response to community unrest" since the MOVE bombing of 1985, in which an entire city block of West Philadelphia was leveled and eleven residents were killed.[34]

In late October 2020 protests were ignited again after police shot and killed Walter Wallace Jr., a 27-year-old Black man with a history of mental health problems.[35] His mother, who was well known to dispatchers, called the police to help defuse a situation in which her son had picked up a knife and was out in the street in their Cobbs Creek neighborhood. Protesters questioned why less lethal force such as tasers had not been employed, and days of marches and physical altercations with police ensued. During the chaos, Rickia Young, a 28-year-old Black home health-care aide, got lost while driving home and made an illegal U-turn. Footage shows at least fifteen officers swarmed her SUV, broke her windows, dragged her and her 16-year-old nephew out of the vehicle, and beat them both in front of her two-year-old son. To add insult to injury, the police took her toddler son, and the Fraternal Order of Police posted a photo on social media of his being "rescued" by an officer, claiming that he was barefoot and lost during the violent protests. They wrote: "We are the Thin Blue Line. And WE ARE the only thing standing between Order and Anarchy." After public outrage at the lie, the post was taken down the next day.[36] The city provided a $2 million settlement before the mother could file a lawsuit.

During this period of collective anger, several city councilmembers proclaimed that it was time to reduce police funding. In Philadelphia, as in Minneapolis, "defund the police" remained a slogan but was not reflected in appropriations.[37] The Philadelphia City Council ultimately reduced the police budget by $33 million by denying them a requested $19 million increase and shifting $14 million for crossing guards and civilian, unarmed traffic enforcement officers to another department.[38] By the time the next annual budget was decided in 2021, the crisis of gun violence took priority, and the budget discussion was dominated by antiviolence initiatives.[39]

In October 2021 the City Council passed a first-of-its-kind driving equality law, designed to eliminate negative interactions with police, citing research that shows that Black and Brown drivers are disproportionately stopped for minor traffic infractions as a pretext to searches for guns and drugs. Under this policy, drivers now receive citations in the mail for expired registration or inspection or broken taillights. The bills' sponsor, Councilmember Isaiah Thomas, stated: "I am humbled by every person who told my office of the humiliation and trauma experienced in some of these traffic stops. To many people who look like me, a traffic stop is a rite of passage—we pick out cars, we determine routes, we plan our social interactions around the fact that it is likely that we will be pulled over by the police."[40] Accompanying the bill was a mandate for a public, searchable database of traffic stops needed to evaluate the initiative.

FRANKFORD

It's a sticky summer evening in June 2016, and the doors are open in the community room of St. Mark's Church. A collective of faith-based leaders and residents concerned about gun violence has convened, and one of its few young members (in her twenties) shows off several logo designs for its new group, Frankford Forward. The Pulse nightclub massacre is on everyone's minds, despite the ongoing violence in the blocks surrounding the building. The deacon has arranged to have the church bells toll once for each of the fifty victims, including the shooter. Pat Smiley, the group's founder, says, "We learned today that there are times when you can just witness. We always think that we have to be doing something and that puts pressure on us. Presence is real important." We sit in silence, most with heads bowed. It takes a long time to ring the bell fifty times.

Frankford, located in the lower northeast section of Philadelphia, is an impoverished, racially diverse community with high rates of crime and violence and, importantly, a reputation as a "high reentry" community. I selected Frankford as the site for this study because these characteristics make it an ideal setting to explore the lived experiences of men in a place and time of contracting economic opportunities and a vastly expanding criminal legal apparatus. Just as I have suggested that millennials are the "canaries in the coalmine" because they are the first cohort to come of age during the late capitalist economic-carceral configuration we see today, Frankford is a prime indicator of the effects of these current trends because of its exposure to them in their most extreme form (see table 1 in the appendix). Sociologist Robert Zussman describes case studies like this one set in Frankford thus: "Successful case studies look at extremes, unusual circumstances, and analytically clear examples, all of which are important not because they are representative but because they show a process or a problem in particularly clear relief."[41]

At the midpoint of the study, the 19124 zip code, which roughly mirrors the boundaries of Frankford, had over 69,000 residents: 42 percent Black, one-third White, and 38 percent Hispanic of any race.[42] As table 1 shows, Frankford's rate of violence was nearly double that for Philadelphia as a whole and almost five times the national rate. More than one-third of Frankford households are below the federally established poverty line, compared to one-quarter in Philadelphia and one-seventh nationally. Unemployment, median salaries, and the proportion of renter-occupied houses all follow the same pattern. Frankford residents are just as likely as other Philadelphians but less likely than Americans in general not to have a high school diploma.

The 15th Police District, which contains Frankford, is by far the busiest in the city as measured by 911 calls.[43] Frankford also contributes to and absorbs a disproportionate number of prisoners from jails and state prisons.[44] A recent report shows that the 19124 zip code has the fourth highest rate of admissions to prisons citywide. Almost sixteen hundred persons released from prison in 2015 resided in Frankford.[45] As sociologist Andrea Leverentz demonstrates, neighborhood context is an important but understudied feature of the reentry experience.[46]

In Frankford, economic opportunities are declining and the quality of life is deteriorating. An analysis of key indicators identified Frankford as one of seven Philadelphia communities "facing the most challenges" compared to all other neighborhoods.[47] The income of residents fell by 11 percent between 2009 and 2014, population shrank by 5.5 percent over the same period, and home prices plummeted by 26 percent between 2011 and 2015, compared to a city-wide *increase* of 6.6 percent. Although official crime rates in Frankford declined by 13 percent between 2009 and 2014, this was significantly less than the citywide decline of 19 percent.

Frankford's dwindling business base led to a major decline in key social institutions during the last decade. The local YMCA and Salvation Army closed, as did the Police Athletic League program and the Frankford Group Ministry, which served at-risk youth. The Frankford Community Development Corporation teetered on the brink of bankruptcy until it was revived in 2014. Both Catholic churches in the community were closed by the diocese without notice in 2013. The community contains fifty churches, if we count storefront venues, which help to meet the rising need for food and shelter.

In Frankford the police captain and rank-and-file officers took community policing and public accountability seriously, holding monthly meetings at Aria Hospital to discuss crime trends and develop partnerships with citizens to address a wide variety of problems related to crime and public order. In particular, the lieutenant who ran the meetings between 2015 and 2018 was extremely responsive to citizens' reports of trouble and regularly urged them to report officers who remained in their patrol vehicles throughout their shift or who failed to treat them with respect.

Residents who attended community meetings with the police often did so at their own peril, sharing stories of direct intimidation and threats made by drug sellers. One told a story of a next-door neighbor whose home was firebombed after she called the police; another reported that her neighbor moved after being "choked out" by a drug seller. As drug violence intensified, many long-term residents left, but many remain because they cannot move or are unwilling to cede the neighborhood. One resident told me, "I feel like I'm living in Escape from New York," a film about a dystopian future in which New York City has been turned into a maximum-security prison and the inmates run the island.

The neighborhood's most distinctive physical feature is the Market-Frankford El tracks, which run above Frankford Avenue and end at Frankford Terminal, the transportation hub that serves as the end of the line for this major thoroughfare and a place where commuters transfer to buses going east-west. Women and children dressed in work attire and school uniforms stream down the stairwell at regular intervals. Panhandlers brave the wind tunnels rushing up Frankford Avenue, and small groups of young men engage in barely disguised hand-to-hand drug sales. Two of the busiest drug corners in the city are within two blocks of the terminal. Although professionals who are just passing through to their home communities in Oxford Circle (west) or Bridesburg (east) keep to themselves, listening to earbuds to discourage small talk, younger women may be found flirting and exchanging numbers while they wait.

Below the tracks is a mix of small businesses serving low-income customers: check-cashing and prepaid wireless stores; bodegas; and shops for individual servings of beer, wine, and liquor as long as it is consumed indoors. Aria Hospital can be viewed from the terminal, and as one continues to walk south, they would pass St. Mark's Episcopal Church, where most interviews for this study were held, and the public library and public benefits office. Until the 1960s, Frankford Avenue was the place where residents (including my mother-in-law) shopped. After the Roosevelt Mall opened in 1964, many businesses moved out and left unoccupied shells in their place. During the day, the commercial corridor under the El is frequented by a diverse array of residents and others passing through the area. At night, Frankford Avenue is mostly unoccupied, except for drug sellers, sex workers, or people who are visibly drunk or high. During my fieldwork, residents used the buddy system and graciously accompanied me to my car after police-community meetings; anytime I was on Frankford Avenue, I walked with my head "on swivel," my keys in my hand, and no more than $20 in my wallet in case I was mugged. Following the interaction order of the sidewalk outlined by Elijah Anderson in *Street-wise*, I looked people in the eye as I passed, giving a quick nod, and keeping it moving.[48] The secret to moving about public space in areas where street crime is prevalent is to signal that you are aware of your surroundings but not overly interested in whatever you see.

Frankford Avenue serves as a rough boundary between east and west Frankford. As longtime resident and editor of the *Frankford Gazette* Bob Smiley described during my first meeting with him, the east side is historically Black and is probably most notable for the Whitehall Apartments—a public housing complex with a playground and community center in an interior courtyard—and several African American churches, including Second Baptist Church, which hosts numerous community events. This side of Frankford Avenue is more stable, and the men in the study who grew up here described long-lasting, tight friendships with the other kids from the block as well as elder "old heads" (male and female) who looked out for and occasionally admonished them. Driving around this area, one would see small groups of young men hanging out just outside corner stores; kids on bikes; and the occasional homespun memorial to a victim of gun violence, including teddy bears, deflated balloons, and votive candles.

The west side of Frankford, with the exception of Northwood, is more transient and the site of most well-known halfway and recovery houses for individuals returning from jail or prison and/or recovering from addiction. This side is also more racially diverse than the east side, with White and Hispanic as well as Black residents. Key institutions in this area include the Frankford Friends Quaker School; Frankford High School; the Historical Society; and the well-kept Overington Park, where sidewalk sales are sometimes held. St. Joachim, the historic Catholic church, was closed by the diocese in 2013 and was the center of much local activity to keep up the grounds and an unsuccessful petition to restore it. Walking around this section of the neighborhood, one would notice lower land density, with more empty, fenced-off lots than on the other side of Frankford Avenue.

The Northwood section of west Frankford abuts Roosevelt Boulevard and two large cemeteries. This middle-class enclave is protected by its own civic association; an active town watch; and deed restrictions allowing only single-family, owner-occupied houses and forbidding corner stores, apartment complexes, and commercial property. Walking through this area, one would see modest single-level homes with well-kept lawns with tastefully painted gated enclosures. Northwood is racially diverse, with working and retired residents from a variety of occupations. I attended many civic association meetings here, which were more likely to focus on slowing down speeders along Castor Avenue and addressing visible signs of disorder such as abandoned cars than on crime. When residents did discuss criminal activity, it was often in the context of defending the neighborhood's border with Frankford and keeping the "bad element" out. They relied heavily on coordinated calls to the police and 311 (the nonemergency reporting line) and private cameras outside their homes to provide a sense of safety.

Frankford is home to a bustling drug trade and associated gun violence that is frequently in the news and contributes to the stigma surrounding the community. Several drug sellers I have interviewed in other areas of the city say that the neighborhood is one of the last places in the city to make a decent living selling drugs and that racial diversity expands the variety of available drugs, which are normally limited by neighborhood because of ethnic niches. The Frankford Terminal offers convenient access for outsiders looking to buy drugs or sex, and the physical presence and noise of the El tracks make illegal transactions less visible to the police. On one of my first days of field research, Father Jon Clodfelter of St. Mark's Church took me on a driving tour of the community; our first stop was a few blocks south of the church, where news vans had gathered to interview neighbors about Megan Doto, a pregnant 26-year-old woman who had just been fatally shot while sitting on the stoop of her boyfriend's house. Jon reluctantly agreed to an interview and pointed out that hers was the fourth such shooting in that area in as many weeks.

Abandoned houses serve as places to stash drugs or are home to squatters, who often live without heat or hot water. Absentee landlords who are registered in Florida and New York State are unresponsive to neighbors' complaints and fines from the city's Licenses and Inspections Office. Entrepreneurs who scour obituaries in the newspaper and identify unoccupied houses break and replace existing locks and attempt to illegally hook up houses to water and gas. Then they sublet the houses to others. The housing stock, much of it too large for single families, is well suited to a cottage industry of mostly unregulated halfway and treatment houses.[49] These are interspersed with single-family homes, causing residents to complain about absorbing a disproportionate share of the city's service needs and the relationship of these houses to criminal activity. The locality, which used to have factories and a busy armory, has a lax zoning code, which also allows for drug treatment clinics to locate there. Residents note that at one residential intersection it is a daily occurrence to see thirty-plus people lined up outside a suboxone treatment clinic; at the end of the day, their cigarette butts and plastic soda bottles line the gutters. Residents' children must pass the adults in this line every day to go to school.

Frankford is a historic community whose long-term residents take pride in keeping their blocks clean and engaging in service through faith institutions and other community-based organizations. They remember the past fondly and feel like they are in a losing battle against larger social forces. As the Smileys wrote in their compilation of the neighborhood's stories, "They range from Frankford as an idyllic 'Mayberry' to Frankford as a dystopian 21st century slum."[50] During my years of field research, I was heartened by how much the residents who attended meetings gave to their community and the compassion they expressed toward others who were suffering. The religious leaders alone were responsible for feeding and housing the hungry and helping those they found sleeping on their steps into recovery programs. Yet they realized that their resources were inadequate to meet the need and worried that their meetings were rarely attended by young people who could take up the task. In many ways they represent the promise of community social cohesion as well as the fears stemming from an increasingly isolated world.

3 Leaving Crime Behind in the Process of Maturation

My girlfriend will leave me if I get locked up. [And]
I wouldn't hear the end of it from my mom or sisters.
When I was younger, I really didn't care, but now I see
that it's bigger than just me.

—Yusef, 28, Black

Yusef, a devout Muslim with a high school diploma and a few college credits, had lived in Frankford for sixteen years; his mother had moved his family here from North Philadelphia to get away from the violence there, although he notes that it followed them. He still lived with his mom and sisters, ages 14 and 16, although he also played an active role in his girlfriend's kids' daily routines. He referred to his girlfriend as his wife and her girls (ages 10 and 13) as his stepdaughters.

When Yusef was 16, three of his male cousins were the fatal victims of gun violence, which he describes as a turning point in his life. He turned to the "wrong crowd" and began dealing drugs and carrying a gun for protection. His own dad, who had a drinking problem, wasn't a part of his life during his childhood. His mother, with whom he had a close relationship, had a bachelor's degree and had worked for SEPTA for fifteen years. Despite her apparent stability, Yusef's family had an extensive history of involvement in drug sales and violence and regular contact with the CLS. He said: "I have family members currently in jail for just about every crime: some family who were molesters, some people who shot people, some people who robbed people, some people who sold drugs. They got all different types of cases, some have lists of stuff that they've been in and out of jail for."

He started getting into drug sales "real heavy" at 19 or 20 years old, after flunking out of community college. Burger King wouldn't rehire him, and his mom wasn't going to help him out, so he "had to do something." Yusef's low point in life was at age 25, when he was on his deathbed from walking pneumonia. "I was so heavy in selling drugs that I didn't even care about dying at the time, I really didn't. . . . I would die with a pocket full of money in my hand and that's all that matters. . . . [H]ow I looked at life, I could die in my sleep, go to sleep tonight and not wake up in the morning. Anything can happen. I live for the day and plan for tomorrow but tomorrow's not a promise." During this point in his interview, he went from a bubbly narrating style to sinking down into his hoodie and going sullen.

He continued to sell drugs until two years prior to our interview. When we asked him why he stopped, he gave all the credit to the women in his life, as reflected in the epigraph to this chapter. In contrast to the isolation and lack of hope for the future he had experienced a couple of years before, he identified the high point of his life as meeting his girlfriend, whom he said changed his life forever. At 38, she was ten years older than Yusef.

> She showed me that trapping [selling drugs] is a choice. Going outside and selling drugs is a choice, you don't have to do that if you don't want to [she told him]. If you want to be a real man, real men support their families, real men don't keep going back and forth to jail, that's not a real man. You keep going back and forth to jail putting your family in situations and now you're forcing your wife that you say you love to go out there and fend for herself and fend for them kids without you. If you would have been out here and working and striving to look for a job you could be out here raising your [fictive] kids.

When we followed up with Yusef three months later, he had completed his certification as a home health aide and was working thirty-two hours a week with three clients, looking for a second job, and saving money to move "anywhere but Frankford" with his girlfriend and her kids. It has been six years since his last arrest.

INTRODUCTION

Despite playing marginal roles in the economy and living in a heavily sur-veilled community, most of the Frankford men were law-abiding. This chapter examines why and how these men constructed identities and ac-tivities that they viewed as moral and productive, defying others' predic-tions and common stereotypes.

I situate this examination within the criminological literature on offend-ing over the life course, which attempts to explain why law-breaking peaks in the teens and steeply declines in the midtwenties.[1] Much of this research has focused on "turning points" such as marriage and employment that spark a change toward conventional activities and relationships.[2] How-ever, as marriage and employment rates have declined among millennial men, some have wondered whether crime will continue to fall with age.[3] Alternative "hooks for change," such as cohabitation or parenthood, may be more meaningful in the contemporary demographic context.[4]

With this in mind, we might be surprised to find that ten of the forty-five Frankford men avoided anything more serious than low-level adolescent law-breaking and had no official contact with the adult CLS. Using methods described in the appendix, I classified just over half (twenty-three) as de-sisting, and roughly one-quarter (nine to twelve) as persisting in criminal offending. I analyze the narratives of desisting and persisting men, with a focus on their subjective perceptions of offending and personal change over time. I conclude by comparing stories from the younger men studied in my previous book, *Falling Back*, to those from the adult men in Frankford.[5]

DESISTING MEN

When the Frankford men discussed their histories of criminal offending, particularly any activity resembling a career, it most often involved drug sales, as it did for Yusef. Drug selling is a ubiquitous activity in Philadel-phia and most other urban centers and is described by both scholars and drug sellers as a strategy used by marginalized men (and some women) to make ends meet in the absence of steady employment that provides a living wage.[6] In Philadelphia, where the drug market is not organized by large, well-known gangs such as the Crips and the Bloods, individuals who can identify a supplier, a customer base, and a venue for sales can participate. Profits for street-level drug sellers are low, however, and are rarely enough to get by on.[7]

The Frankford men outlined many reasons why selling drugs was an undesirable strategy for making ends meet. Some described the harms the drug game caused to their families and communities as a reason for not wanting to be part of it. They often took a moral stance that was embedded in their definitions of masculinity: a "real man" gave to his family and community instead of taking from them. Their cognitive frameworks and reference groups are grounded in the maturation process, when durable social ties lead men to recognize that their actions have consequences for others. Several of the desisting narratives I explore here were articulated by men who still fall into the persisting category. Instead of viewing these statements as lacking authenticity, we can see them as a form of "desistance talk" that supports a slow-down or cessation of offending that had not been completed at the time these men were interviewed.[8] The articulation of these narratives among men from both groups should be interpreted as an acknowledgment that continued offending is inconsistent with their core values and their desired presentation of self.

Because the most well-established turning points—marriage and employment—were relatively rare among the Frankford men, they were more likely to identify other turning points, including incarceration and fatherhood, as responsible for their changing worldview. Consistent with prior research, some described incarceration as offering time to reflect on their past actions.[9] Kareem, a Black and Asian 26-year-old, realized how his actions affected his loved ones in conversations with his "cellie" in jail. Similarly, Cory, a Black 29-year-old who was unemployed but had dreams of becoming a truck driver, told us that during his period of incarceration he had a lot of time to think. He realized that his actions were "poisoning" people like his mother and hurting the community. Throughout his interview, he said repeatedly, "It's easy to do bad. It's really hard to do good." While inside, he took a life skills course and the teacher helped him think about alternatives. He realized that he had accomplished nothing in his life and became ashamed of his past actions. Cory didn't believe that selling drugs was a good job: "Everything about it, from the substance that's destroying somebody in some type of form, some type of way. So when you do it, you just think about the money, you don't think about the person themself, so you're not actually looking at the person." When he was incarcerated, he began thinking about the damage he had done. He didn't like talking about his "criminal career," asking, "How can you have pride in doing wrong?"

Many men identified fatherhood as a turning point that led them to desist from crime.[10] Marvin, a Black 24-year-old stay-at-home father with a tattooing and hair cutting shop in his basement, said, "As soon as my daughter came, I had to stop" adolescent delinquency. "I had to cut off a lot of things." Jelani, a 33-year-old Black-Latino father of three, had been married for thirteen years and was very involved in his church. He said that his kids were supportive of his recovery from addiction: "I want my children's lives to be better than mine. I tell them that I used to do drugs and sell drugs. I tell them to stay away from that. Be a leader; don't be a follower. Look, you see what I went through, be better, be better than me." Isaac, a 36-year-old biracial father with a stable romantic relationship, engaged in convincing desistance talk. It had been just over a year since his last drink: "I lived that lifestyle years ago, I been through them phases, it's not worth it in the long run. 'Cause you end up losing everything. That's what happens when you play in the streets." When asked how he knew when someone had become a real adult, he said:

> I guess when you're mentally mature and start doing things differently. Sometimes it takes people a long time. Shit, it took me—I'm like 36—took me to 36 before I started changing my mind set. I got discipline now, it's not, like, you know I can think something, I don't have to react. Running the streets. . . . I destroyed myself doing that. Chasing girls and chasing money were two of the worst things I could have did in life, I think, cause I just went to the extreme with both of them. I wasn't really thinking about consequences back then.

Not all men who engaged in fatherhood-based desistance talk, however, were able to avoid further contact with the police.

PERSISTING MEN

Depending on how persisting men are counted, there were between nine and twelve in this set of men. Those who continued to be involved in the

CLS were often vulnerable in multiple ways, afflicted by housing and food insecurity, serious mental illness, trauma histories, and cognitive or physical disabilities. They were more likely than their desisting counterparts to be living on the margins of society and more exposed to the community's problems, especially violence. Their lack of resources led them to engage in low-level offending such as retail theft, and their fear of violence prompted them to engage in protective behaviors, such as carrying a gun. At times, their vulnerability alone brought them into conflict with law enforcement. For example, Vincent, a 30-year-old Black man who suffered from severe mental illness, was arrested for disorderly conduct and spent thirty days in jail after cursing out a police officer. Andre, a Black 32-year-old, had a list of arrests for misdemeanor charges related to his homelessness. His street begging had resulted in charges of obstructing a highway, and he had been charged with retail theft and selling individual cigarettes, called "loosies."

Three patterns were apparent in the persisting men's narratives. First, the turning points they identified were very similar to those of desisting men. They described fatherhood, for example, as a motivating factor for behavioral change. Grant, a 27-year-old Black stay-at-home dad, reported drug sales but said he wanted to stop: "If you want to stand out here, you'll stand out here [sell drugs], but some people get tired of it. I got tired of it so now I'm making moves." Grant had just returned from a year's stint in jail and never wanted to go back. "I need to be there for my three sons" (aged 9, 6, and 5). "They look up to me so I have to lead by example."

Brady, a 33-year-old White food truck vendor, reported that he felt like an adult for the first time when was when he was twenty-one and his daughter was born: "You never know when you're a real adult. . . . I feel like a kid sometimes still. I feel like I could do more, be more responsible. [But] without my daughters, I would probably be in a worse place, selling drugs maybe. My daughters made me grow up." Later in the interview, he said, "A real man provides for his family—keeps a roof over their head, makes sure family has what they need. An adult is an adult, but a man is someone who does what he has to do to support his family." Brady's narrative reflects the complicated relationship that fatherhood has to desistance.[11] Although it supplies a rationale for desistance and leads many to embrace an adult identity, it also creates new financial obligations. Brady was supporting his family with his food truck until a new ordinance limited his hours and substantially reduced his income. At the time of our interview, he reported being under a great deal of stress and having regular conflicts with his kids' mother. His arrests since his interview had all been for marijuana possession, which could indicate regular use or signal that he had returned to drug sales, but he was doing it carefully enough to avoid "intent to deliver" charges. It is also worth noting that possession would not have been a criminal charge if he had been within Philadelphia city limits.

Alex, a 35-year-old Latino father, reported that the birth of his first child signaled that it was time for him to stop selling drugs and stealing cars, although his peer group did not easily let him go: "Yeah! Everybody's calling me a pussy and a bitch, I'm like, yeah it's alright. They're like, what happened to you? I'm like, life . . . life changes people [chuckles]. I don't want my son selling drugs, I don't want my son getting shot, I don't want him doing any of that." More than any other man in this study, Alex framed his identity around fatherhood. He claimed to have given up predatory offending when his children were born, which was consistent with his official court records. Yet he reported using violence to defend his children, beating up his son's school principal and assaulting two parents whose child was in a schoolyard fight with his daughter. His case poses a real challenge to identifying desistance, because his role as father spurred the end of one criminal career and the start of another, even though thus far he had not been charged with assault and battery.

The second pattern that is visible when comparing narratives of desisting and persisting is that while the former tends to emphasize the moral nature of offending and the negative impact it has on families and communities, the latter are more likely to describe a "feared self" and focus on the loss of freedom associated with continued offending.[12] In contrast to the desisting men, none of the persisters described a cognitive transformation, or a changed self.[13] Instead, they often referred to being "tired" of criminal offending and being arrested and fearful of being reincarcerated.[14] Although they expressed a desire to stop offending and becoming system involved, this desire was not enough to result in lasting behavioral change or a decrease in their visibility and vulnerability to contact with law enforcement agents. In contrast to Ray Paternoster and Shawn Bushway's findings on the power of the "feared self," these men's fear did not enable them to leave offending behind.

For example, Cam, a 23-year-old Black-Latino father on probation supervision, reported slowing down because he knew he would get caught.
He noted that he used to move weight, or buy drugs in large quantities
and break them down for sales, but now he sold only to support his own
habit. Stallworth, a Black 28-year-old man who was also on probation,
told us: "As bad as I want to hustle for the money, I want to get my charges
expunged soon and stay out of trouble for at least next five years. As bad
as I want to hustle, I am more afraid of going back to jail. I don't want that
life; I can't take it no more." Colin, a White 28-year-old who lived with his
mother, similarly reported, "I just got tired of the lifestyle; the money's
good but I can't keep going to jail."

Another final distinction is that persisting men were less likely to report feeling like a "real man" than their desisting counterparts. As we will
see later, men very often distinguished adulthood and manhood, with
the former being achieved by taking care of oneself and the latter by taking care of others. This may be why it made sense to Alex to stop selling
drugs and stealing cars but compelled him to violence when his kids were
threatened. Similarly, Mateo, a 29-year-old Latino man in recovery, told
us, "An adult is not going to go out and sell drugs to provide cause it's in-
sanity, [but] a man will, cause [manhood is achieved] by any means, you
dig?" Randall, a 27-year-old White man in recovery, reported that "I'm an
adult right now but not a real man because I'm doing what I have to be
doing, but not taking care of my responsibilities." Vincent, the 30-year-old
father who was jailed after cursing out an officer, told us, "I feel like a fucking failure." This pattern is consistent with prior research that finds that
desistance is a marker of adult manhood, which often equates offending
with "boy's stuff" or juvenile pursuits.[15]

DIFFERENCES BETWEEN DESISTING
AND PERSISTING MEN

The single clearest factor that distinguished desisting and persisting men
was their degree of structural and social stability. The "stability index"
(0–5) is an additive measure of stable social bonds and circumstances,
such as housing and employment.[16] Stability scores for persisting men

were lower than those of desisting men or those who were not involved in offending (persisting = 1.77, desisting = 2.86, never involved = 3.63). It is important to realize that instability can be a consequence as well as a cause of criminal offending and legal system involvement.

Stable men were less likely to engage in desistance talk during their interviews because desistance was a less deliberate and effortful process. This finding is consistent with the "cognitive transformation" theory, which posits that "given a relatively 'advantaged' set of circumstances, the cognitive transformations and agentic moves we describe are hardly necessary; under conditions of sufficiently extreme disadvantage, they are unlikely to be nearly enough."[17]

Twelve men reported stable employment, meaning they had either been in the same job for more than a year or were serially employed with little down time between jobs. Those who were stably employed were less likely than their counterparts to persist in criminal offending (8% vs. 33%).[18] Similarly, the sixteen men who reported being in a stable romantic relationship were less likely to persist (18% vs. 32%). The twenty-five men who had been incarcerated as adults were three times as likely to persist as those who had not (36% vs. 12%). Despite the fact that men's narratives often identify a spell of incarceration as a "time out" that helped them embrace positive change, a robust literature has demonstrated that incarceration is a significant negative turning point that diminishes legitimate life chances, thereby making future criminal activity more likely.[19] Educational attainment was also associated with persistence in crime: 32 percent of men with less than a high school degree, 25 percent of men with a diploma, and 17 percent of men with some college credits were classified as persisting.

MATURATION

Because of the variation in both outcomes and mechanisms supporting desistance among the Frankford men, I carried out an additional analysis that provides a unique view into the life courses and offending trajectories of similarly situated men. I compare and contrast findings from my previous work on incarcerated young men of color to those from the Frankford study.[20] Both samples are millennials, born 1981–96, and both represent marginalized Philadelphia men with limited educational credentials and unemployment or underemployment. The men in *Falling Back*, who included fifteen Black and Latino men aged 17 to 19 when I began following them in 2004, were incarcerated as juveniles. The Frankford men varied in their experiences of legal contact; many mentioned having had contact with the juvenile authorities and being confined as adolescents, and many also had had contact on the adult criminal side. Most men in both samples were striving to desist from offending behavior related to drug use and sales. A side-by-side comparison of their desistance processes allows us to see how they differed at two stages of the life course: emerging adulthood (ages 18–25) and early adulthood (ages 25–34).

The emerging adults in my earlier study struggled mightily to avoid "falling back" into their old offending patterns and coming into further contact with the legal system. Almost all articulated a strong motivation to use their spell of incarceration as a positive turning point.[21] Most deliberately engaged "hooks for change" such as employment, romantic relationships, postsecondary education, and fatherhood, but they found that they could not sustain their grip on these hooks for very long.[22] Job opportunities came and went as the young men realized their precarious positions in the labor market and had to rationalize low-wage, often degrading work with the masculine qualities of their former careers as drug sellers.

Their ties with romantic partners and children were characterized by "drama," or extreme volatility marked by infidelity, jealousy, manipulation, and even violence. The women in their lives had the upper hand because they held the lease on shared living space and received steady, although meager, income through various forms of public assistance. When men failed to contribute to the household or to otherwise meet the demands of a mature relationship, they were kicked out and had to find temporary places to live until they could earn their way back in. Adult status was tenuous, as they had to reestablish the trust they had lost with members of their families of origin during their days as drug sellers. Fatherhood presented new financial obligations that they were generally unprepared to meet because of their precarious positions in the labor market. With fragile claims to regular contact with their children because of shaky relationships with their children's mothers, they often "fell back" in an unintended way, returning to old patterns of drug sales to address short-term material needs.

The Frankford men, who were older at the time we interviewed them, less often engaged in desistance talk, perhaps because they had already committed to nonoffending. Avoiding involvement in criminal actions was part of a package of adult behaviors that also included establishing a legal way of earning an (often minimal) income, stable housing, and durable social ties.[23] They equated drug selling with jobs at McDonald's: as a form of work for adolescents and not befitting the expectations of adult men. Their constructions of masculinity, which were often moral in nature, defined their progress and growth in terms of leaving all that "drama" behind and developing routines that kept them off the radar and away from the risks associated with the police and the CLS. These men saw fatherhood and other forms of generativity, such as civic engagement or caring for youth or elders, as a way of constructing a positive sense of masculinity.[24] Particularly for Black men, this sense of masculine identity helped them actively counter negative stereotypes or expectations that they would be jobless and incarcerated, a drain on the system and on their families and communities. Their commitment to prosocial roles as spouses or partners and fathers or mentors was deepened as others in their social circle reinforced their success.[25] Ultimately, they did not experience the same ambivalence about returning to the drug game or other forms of offending as the men in *Falling Back*. They did not discuss their "love for the streets" or say that "the drug game was calling them." As they accomplished mature adulthood, desistance typically fell into place without the need for a daily recommitment to nonoffending, to pull off a convincing performance, or conscious deliberation.

Comparative case studies of younger men from the *Falling Back* and adult men in Frankford illustrate this package of identities, values, and actions. Each of these case studies was selected because it represents an "ideal type" of the concerns and circumstances among emerging adult and young adult men. I conclude by introducing Rocque's model of "maturation" as a coherent organizing framework for the interrelated set of processes that involve both internal change and growth and the establishment of stable, prosocial social ties.[26] I argue that maturity is the engine that drives transformation in all the key domains analyzed in this book.

SINCERE, AN EMERGING ADULT

Sincere was 18 when I met him at Mountain Ridge Academy. Even then, he aspired to become a father, telling me, "I want to see a part of me that's never been bad." Sincere had been arrested at age 16 and "placed" at a therapeutic facility for drug sellers that focused on changing "criminal thinking errors." I met him several months before he completed treatment and was released to Philadelphia, and he became very involved in my study, providing me with a great deal of insight into street life in the city.

Sincere was incarcerated for almost two years. During that time he developed a sense of maturity that he believed would lead to better choices after he returned home:

> When I first got locked up, I was sixteen and I'm eighteen now, and time do mature you. . . . It was like weed was my best friend and wasn't nothing in the world going to change that. Now all that's changed. Freedom is my best friend now. I'm trying to get it back. If that was that kind of person, I could return to all those negative behaviors I was involved in, but me being here and away from home for almost eighteen months. . . . It's not worth it, me doing all that stuff I was doing out there.

This "desistance talk" was in part a reflection of the therapeutic discourse inside juvenile facilities, which encourages young people to view their incarceration as a positive turning point in their lives and to view inconsequential achievements such as achieving behavioral milestones as substitutes for real steps toward upward social mobility.[27]

Shortly after returning home, Sincere's long-term girlfriend, Marta, became pregnant, and he eagerly embraced the new identity of father. He moved in with Marta and they lived as if they were already married, in part because their mothers were best friends. Their relationship was tumultuous, characterized by what he described as "BMD," or "baby's mama drama." They fought, broke up, and reunited more times than I could count. When Marta got fed up with Sincere's inability or unwillingness to contribute to the household's finances or heard about his flirtations with other women, she banished him from the apartment, forcing him to stay with his mother or sisters. Marta received public assistance and disability income (SSD) and held the lease on their apartment, so she wielded a great deal of power in their relationship. This was a difficult pill for Sincere to swallow, since his Christian religious education had taught him that women were inferior and should be subordinate to men ("because Eve came from Adam"). When he felt powerless in every other way, he lashed out with violence toward Marta.

Sincere made some half-hearted attempts at finding work but did not embrace employment as a vehicle for adulthood until the women in his life—his mother, sisters, Marta, and Marta's mother—ganged up on him for failing to be an economic provider for his young family. Then he embarked on enough job searching to keep their concerns at bay for a while. When Sincere Jr. was born, his new family experienced a period of intense bonding and optimism about the future. Before long, however, financial crises arose, and Sincere felt more pressure to generate some income. Although he no longer spent most of his time with the male peer group that he had hung out with before he was incarcerated and became a father, he retained contacts with his old community of drug sellers in case in he needed to activate them at a moment's notice.

Wanting to avoid arrest and another period of incarceration, he returned to drug selling on a contingent basis, selling only enough to meet financial exigencies and to people whom he trusted. (I later learned that this was known as "dibbing and dabbing" in drug sales to meet short-term needs.) Sincere was vulnerable to get-rich-quick schemes, at one point purchasing materials that were purportedly going to help him become a "flipper," someone who buys houses, fixes them up, and sells them for a substantial profit. At one point, he received a $25,000 settlement award for a car accident he had been in many years earlier and blew through it in a matter of weeks as he generously treated all the significant people in his life to small luxuries that they could normally not afford. This may have been the single best opportunity in his life—at least as he could conceive of it then—to feel the masculine pride of providing for others.

Fatherhood was a role that Sincere eagerly embraced, but it entailed contradictory pushes and pulls in relation to desistance from drug selling. On the one hand, paternal involvement in his new son's life allowed him to manage the stigma of being a drug seller and reinvent himself as a "family man." Using a measuring stick based on his own father's lack of involvement in his life, as well as the absentee fathers he saw in his community,

he felt pride in defying stereotypes of Black fathers and potentially breaking the cycle of an absence of male role models for Black boys. On the
other hand, with his young family barely subsisting on public assistance,
fatherhood generated increasing demands for quick solutions to economic
crises, such as being notified that the heat would be cut off or running out
of diapers before the end of the month. At the same time, Sincere was receiving conflicting messages about the need for him to get a job. Marta
and his mother derided him for his inability to contribute to the economic
stability of the family; meanwhile, Marta wanted him to stay home to help
her with the baby (as well as her own daughter from a previous relationship) and stay away from the lures of other women. He met these contradictory demands by spending most of his day engaged in family-oriented
activities but did not consistently feel like his performance as paternal
caregiver was sufficient to be considered a grown man by anyone else. He
was emasculated both in relation to his male peer group because he was
engaged in traditionally women's work of caring for home and children,
and by Marta and his mother for failing to fulfill the provider role.

Sincere's method of "dibbing and dabbing" was effective in the sense
that it allowed him to navigate the conflicting pressures to "be there" for
his family and to provide for them economically.[28] It also was a preferable
method of retaining some control over his finances, since it didn't generate
a pay stub that could be immediately garnished by Marta. Selling drugs
was a way of constructing masculine dignity by doing something he knew
he was good at, providing rare feelings of mastery and competence. He successfully avoided arrest (other than a summary offense for public urination)
despite using drug sales as a semi-regular means of making ends meet.

KEITH, AN ADULT

Keith, a Black 27-year-old, earned a GED while incarcerated at a juvenile
facility at age 17. Born and raised in North Philadelphia, he moved between North Carolina; Las Vegas, where he was competing as a semipro-
fessional boxer; and Philly during his late teens and early twenties. He was
on his own a lot when he was growing up; he remarked that in retrospect,
his mother was single and "didn't really know how to be a mother." His

first arrest at 17 was for drug sales. "I got arrested again [at 19], this time for more serious charges, . . . armed robbery and aggravated assault." "At the time I was young and I had something to prove and, um, it was like somebody did something to my mother and I felt like I had to do something back and the only way that I knew how to do something back was through violence. So I did what I did, I ended up getting arrested and I spent like a year in jail for that."

After release from jail, he "got on the straight and narrow" for a couple of years while working on his boxing career in Las Vegas. When he returned to Philadelphia, "The next thing you know, I catch another case . . . but this time it's more serious than the last charge I caught. This one is an attempted murder, and so I spent like a year in jail for that. Like every time I come here, I get in some trouble. Like, I love my city but every time when I left for the most part I been alright but as soon as I come back, I get dragged into some shit."

While he was in jail on the attempted murder charge, Keith shared a cell with his uncle and the two of them got into trouble, leading him to spend some time in solitary confinement. "While I'm in the hole, I got a lot of time to think and I got a lot of time to read 'cause I couldn't watch any TV. *So I'm just reading and thinking and I'm elevating my mind and I'm like, man, I gotta make some changes. So I make the changes that I need to make mentally within myself first and then I get released.* . . . I come home on house arrest, doing everything I need to do." In response to the question, "What did you read?" he said:

> I read a book by Maya Angelou's son called *Standing at the Scratch Line*, mainly about a man and his family and how his whole life he was all about the fight, but also about family.[29] *About how a man grows as he has a family. And it helped me to mature. I looked at life a little differently once I read that.* Not just your family that you're born into but the one you create-like your children and leaving on that legacy to them. So I looked at that. I also read *The 48 Laws of Power* by Robert Greene.[30] And I read a lot of Islamic literature.

When we interviewed him, Keith was wearing an electronic monitoring bracelet, living with his girlfriend, and following a strict routine prescribed by Islamic prayer and his work schedule as a grill chef. He was awaiting the outcome of his trial for the attempted murder charge, which we confirmed was removed from his record when the Clean Slate Law went into effect. When asked to talk about his subjective perceptions of drug sales and other forms of offending, he told us that the meager profits from drug sales are no better than one could make in a legal job and that he enjoys being able to work without constantly worrying about trouble: "I know dudes that's hustling. They prolly making 600 dollars a week . . . and it's like, you could just do that at a job. They got a car, it ain't even real fly [laughs], it's like a old Buick or whatever, just souped it up. And they spending they money on designer belts and stuff and don't really got no money after that. . . . I got friends that sell drugs but that job ain't good cause you gonna be in jail or bailing yourself out." In response to the question, "So what's been your favorite job to date?" he said: "Probably the one I'm at now. 'Cause everybody's just . . . they let me do my job and that's it. And I feel like uh, I don't know, *maybe it's at the point where I'm at in life right now.* . . . I feel like I'm doing my job, nobody giving me trouble about it, and that's it, I cruise through the day." Similarly, when he came in contact with the police, he had no worries: "Well, now I interact with them, like anytime I see them I wave and stuff. I didn't used to be like that, though." When asked, "What changed?" he replied: "Working, number one, that helped change it, and when I started like living a non-criminal life, that's one thing that changed it, 'cause now it's like I don't got nothing to hide."

Keith took a moral view of his past behavior, referring to himself as formerly being "a bad man" and "doing a lot of dumb stuff." This moral thread in his narrative was supported by his involvement in Islam, and when we asked if he had picked this up in jail, he laughed, saying, "I'm not one of those guys. Nah, I been Muslim my whole life."

As his comments about how his reading affected him suggest, Keith used his time in solitary confinement as an opportunity for reflection and engaged in a cognitive transformation whereby he "elevated his mind" and decided he needed to "make some changes." He embraced what some psychologists refer to as a "growth mindset," in which intelligence is not viewed as fixed and all experience is viewed as an opportunity for learning.[31] Now that he was out of jail, he sought out people who could help him grow as a person. When we asked him what he looked for in a romantic relationship, he told us: "Communication is definitely key, communication, understanding, like being understanding . . . being able to grow with each other and mature with each other and the want to learn from each other and mature with each other and the want to see each other to the next level and . . . wanting better for that person than what they want for themself and that person wanting better for you than what you want for yourself."

Having recently learned that he was going to be the father of a daughter had "changed [his] life significantly." "At first I was [freaking out] 'cause I was like, damn I'm having a girl, but like it's good though, because it's better for me, I think, like 'cause now I got somebody. If it was a boy it would be good too, but with a boy it's like alright, I just gotta be a role model, but with a girl it's a little more tedious because it's like I gotta watch a lot with a girl." As his commitment to being a family man deepened, he left his male peer group behind, viewing them as hindering his personal growth: "Like I used to have people who I considered best friends, but like nobody is really there for you like that. . . . A lot of people in my life I feel like I surpassed them and it's not even like I want to look down on them like I'm better than them but it's like if I stay where you're at, then I'm going to be holding myself back and I can't do that."

This growth mindset was also visible in his definition of a "real man" and what he saw as his future: "Hmm, that's a deep question. . . . 'Cause a real man isn't afraid of change. A real adult, you can be responsible, you can be mature but it don't necessarily mean that you not afraid of change but a real man is willing to change, yeah." Similarly, when asked what he thought the next five years would bring for him, he replied: "Growth. . . . The growth is part of the baby [coming], though, but mainly I'll sum it up in one word: it's growth, maturity, and knowledge."

Keith was neither married to the mother of his child, whom he had been with for three years, nor stably employed. His job had started about six weeks prior to our interview. But he engaged both incarceration and fatherhood as hooks for change. These changes were deliberate and conscious—"I made the changes I needed to make within myself"—and were supported by a negative view of his old behavior—being a "bad man" and the futility of selling drugs to make ends meet—and a preference for stability and a lack of "drama" at work and in interactions with the police. He embraced the "tedious" nature of parenting a girl as a form of informal social control; saying that he needed to "watch a lot" implied that he would be "watching" his own behavior as well as her own. He carefully culled his circle of friends, identified support for growth as his primary criterion for a partner, and made personal growth central to his definition of masculinity. He saw himself not only as a changed person, but above all as an adult.

AN INTEGRATIVE FRAMEWORK
FOR UNDERSTANDING MATURATION

Criminologist Michael Rocque has developed a conceptual framework based on the idea that aging is a robust predictor of desistance from crime and elaborates on the underlying processes supporting this pattern.[32] He delineates five domains of maturation: (1) cognitive/neurological, that is, brain development; (2) psychosocial/personality, including the integration of different components of the personality; (3) identity/cognitive transformation, including the crystallization of identity, or "discovering one's true self"; (4) citizenship or civic, such as voting, community service, volunteer work, and concern about the community; and (5) social roles, the markers of adulthood such as becoming an intimate partner, a parent, and a working contributor to the family and society. Taken together, Rocque suggests, these domains reconcile what seem like competing theories of the processes underlying desistance, bringing together biological, psychological, agentic, and structural forces into a coherent story of how maturation proceeds at the level of the self.

Maturation helps us to understand the variation in desistance trajectories between the men studied in *Falling Back*, for whom desistance was largely an unsuccessful struggle, and the Frankford men, for whom desistance appeared to be part of a larger set of attitudes, values, social relations, and activities consistent with adulthood.[33] Using Rocque's framework, I highlight features that differentiate the emerging adults' orientation toward desistance from the young adults' trajectory, acknowledging that there is much variation within these two groups:

(1) a preference for stability, or an absence of "drama";

(2) generativity: a concern with community, giving back, serving as a role model;

(3) coherent identity: a sense of a core self that is not derailed by peers—
the ability to resist stigma, construct masculinity, and balance hopes for
the future with wisdom based on past experience;

(4) development of a moral self: a consistent sense of right and wrong,
orienting choices around religious values and recognizing the harm to
others caused by offending;

(5) durable social ties that deepen commitments, as a partner, father, or
family member and increase reciprocal obligations, within which
messages about appropriate adult and masculine roles and behavior
are communicated—a reduction in individualism and increase in
collectivism; and

(6) routines that are centered around the needs of others, such as caring
and providing.

As Rocque observes, maturation is not an inevitable consequence of aging, and levels of maturity vary significantly among persons of the same chronological age. Structural circumstances and cultural norms shape societal and familial expectations for the adoption of adult roles.[34] For example, the men who were living in Frankford as part of the recovery community were explicitly given a temporary "time out" from expectations that they should be employed or develop stable romantic ties while they focused on self-improvement and were not expected to prioritize others. Nevertheless, the power of social ties in supporting desistance is critical. A confluence of values and actions accompanies the maturation process, supporting a worldview that acknowledges the person's effects on others and choices made in the interests of others. The analysis presented here supports the idea that desistance is a central part of adulthood and generally requires less deliberation and effort as the maturation process proceeds.[35]

4 Isolation as a Way of Avoiding Trouble and Managing Risk

> You can talk to someone and then get put up on the wall by the cops and the dude might have four bags on him and the cops say "looks like y'all have four bags on you." [I'm thinking] What you mean *y'all*? ... If you shake somebody's hand you can get caught up in the mix, get raided by the cops with them. You can just walk up and start talking to someone and someone walks up to shoot at him and you get caught in the crossfire.
>
> —Grant, 27, Black, describing the random nature of trouble in Frankford

David, a 26-year-old Black "preacher's kid," lived with his parents in the middle-class Northwood section of Frankford. Deeply creative, he wrote and produced R&B music and designed T-shirts, which he sold at trade shows. David had a high degree of Black consciousness, which infused his descriptions of his daily activities as well as his dreams for the future. He told us that his twenty-fifth birthday felt like a milestone: "I was praying every day in my twenties, Lord get me to 21, God get me to 22, because I know out here, I mean, not just to help me live, but make sure I'm not locked up, make sure I'm not caught on something stupid. So when I made it to 25 and I didn't have a criminal record and I wasn't shot at least a couple of times, I was like dang, thank you. I celebrated so hard that night." When I asked, "Do you feel like you're in the clear now?" he laughed. "No, it's like, now, get me to 50. 'Cause I seen it happen to the best of us where, no record, no past situations or anything and still got locked up for something stupid. I have a little bit of a sigh of relief . . . but even still I know I still got to keep my hands clean and I have to cross all my t's and dot all my i's because I could still be in the system tomorrow."

David's insistence that he must be extremely careful to avoid being incarcerated or shot is especially profound because in actuarial terms he was at low risk of either one: he had no criminal record, had never engaged in illegal activities, had chosen friends who were not involved in crime or recreational drug use, lived in the safest section of Frankford, was the son of a well-known pastor, and was friendly with the police officers who lived on his block. We might imagine that someone like him would not spend much time thinking about risk, but he reported that he worried about it a lot, particularly when compared to his White friends.

AVOIDING TROUBLE

Staying out of trouble, often referred to as "drama," was an important measure of success in David's eyes. The pervasive scrutiny of men, especially men of color, by police, security cameras, and passers-by requires them to maintain a low profile while navigating public space.[1] In communities where street drug sales are visible, men must negotiate interactions with groups of other men on the corner who are engaged in high-profile criminal activity. These men are objects of attention from the authorities and are targets for bursts of gun violence. Men who want to avoid trouble take note of places and times in their community when it seems most likely to occur. The men on some blocks are involved in "beefs" with those from other blocks, so everyone has to watch out. As they grow older, they must decide which male friendships to retain, based on whether their peers are engaged in productive and safe activities or are likely to expose them to risk. Avoiding drama, then, requires no small amount of work and often involves skillful deployment of street knowledge.

Yet trouble is unpredictable, rendering all these carefully orchestrated efforts useless. Under the prevailing policy of proactive policing, any man who "fits the description" may find himself the target of police questioning and pat downs.[2] Managing one's emotions and learning the regular routine of "submissive civility" reduce the likelihood that interactions with authorities will result in arrest or brutality but do not guarantee safety.[3]

Men share stories with one another about the random and unjust nature of Philadelphia's CLS. Other violent events, particularly drive-by shootings, are even less predictable, and everyone moves about public spaces with the knowledge that "bullets don't have names."

Drama is a situation of conflict with the authorities and/or other persons that inevitably spills over from its initial participants to their families, friends, and other relationships and may bring them into contact with law enforcement even if it doesn't begin there. The term *drama* evokes an expenditure of emotionality or a rollercoaster of ups and downs that creates chronic stress, but it also suggests a loud or demonstrative performance that draws the unwanted attention of others. The *Urban Dictionary* notes: "People who engage in 'drama' will usually attempt to drag other people into their dramatic state, as a way of gaining attention or making their own lives more exciting."[4] These individuals could be other men engaged in street-level drug sales and associated defensive posturing, children's mothers who use custody or visitation as cudgels in ongoing romantic disputes, or family members who put private business out there for everyone to see. Men in these situations sometimes respond by saying "you['re] drawin'," which means the person is drawing unwanted attention.[5]

Men who use the term *drama* to describe unpredictable forms of trouble they must navigate on a regular basis view it as an immature and risky way of relating to the world.[6] When men say they "don't have time for drama," they mean that they are trying to be productive citizens, to have a predictable daily existence engaged in prosocial adult activities such as work, monogamy, and caring for family. Drama introduced in the course of interactions or relationships poses a threat of dragging them down, or backward into adolescent pursuits, and to create disruption when what they seek is stability and to stay off the radar. It may also represent a risk to those they care about, not just to themselves. Although the term *drama* is not unique to men in Frankford, it was only used by men of color during our interviews. As will be apparent, the concern with drama is strongly linked to their status as Black and Brown men and their vulnerable positions vis-à-vis the CLS.

This chapter examines the varieties of drama that concern young men in Frankford and analyzes the ways they organize their daily routines and interactions with others to mitigate the ever-present possibility that trouble might arise and do them harm. Almost all of the men of color we interviewed in Frankford stayed in their houses and avoided public spaces in order to avoid risky situations and people. Their practice of network avoidance often meant a complete lack of engagement in their community, in civic or service organizations, and even in getting to know their neighbors.[7] Men using this strategy spent long stretches of time indoors playing video games or in virtual communication on social media. Network avoidance is a raced and gendered adaptation to the expansion of the criminal legal apparatus and the unpredictable nature of men's interactions with its agents and enforcers. Network avoidance effectively erases young men of color from the public sphere in the same way that incarceration removes them from their communities, with considerable costs to the men themselves and their neighborhood.

DEGREES OF DRAMA

Frankford is a demonstrably risky place. The dangers posed by others could not clearly be distinguished from the dangers posed by the police; in many instances, they tended to compound one another. Avoiding risk of any type is a focal concern for the men of color we interviewed.[8] They described types of drama that entailed variable, and often unpredictable, levels of trouble. Some risky situations were unavoidable and even routine, but they could escalate or explode in the blink of an eye.

Every single respondent we interviewed in Frankford reported seeing police on a daily basis, and many said they interacted with them frequently. These men described being routinely stopped, questioned, and frisked, whether they were on foot or driving their cars. Many recounted incidents of brutality at the hands of the police, including being "slammed," "power drilled," or "broadsided." While a full treatment of these interactions is beyond the scope of this book, a constant police presence is the first condition that underlies men's concern with risk. Patrol cars circulating through the neighborhood, public transit officers stationed at the Frankford Terminal, and surveillance cameras in businesses—many of which are connected to the main police monitoring feed through the SafeCam program—are a constant reminder to men that they are being watched.[9] The reach of the system also extends inside homes when residents, particularly mothers, selectively engage the police as protection, despite their general cynicism toward the institution of policing.[10]

The decoupling of criminal behavior and arrest in the era of proactive policing leads to uncertainty about the potential outcomes of interactions with the police, as underscored by Nasir, a 30-year-old Black Muslim:

> I was wrongfully arrested. I was in the Tap room minding my business— I don't drink nor smoke, I was playing pool—but there was something going on, you know this area there's always something, someone got shot, murdered, robbed or whatever, they come and you know raid the bar, people's throwing things, there's a gun on the floor, they come and beat the crap out of me, put the gun on me, lied and said, "I seen him [meaning me] throw a gun." I proved that it was a lie, [with] cameras and stuff and witnesses, and they came to trial and they apologized. They didn't see me throw the gun, so to this day I have a lawsuit against the city and everything. I was in [prison] four years for that.

Residents of inner-city communities in Philadelphia share stories of false charges and imprisonment, dirty cops, and huge cash settlements, which form a body of folk knowledge of how the system operates. Nasir's claim to have been imprisoned for four years on a trumped-up charge is consistent with his clean court record (although he was on parole when we interviewed him, it was lifted when his case was cleared). It also jibes with the city's case volume and total settlements data for malicious prosecution, false arrest, false imprisonment, and overturned convictions claims, which totaled almost $40 million between 2010 and 2019.[11]

Similarly, Roderick, a 28-year-old Black-Latino home health aide who reported no history of criminal activity or previous system contact, told us about being falsely accused of extortion when he tried to be a good Samaritan by returning a lost phone:

> I was outside of the bus terminal downtown and I found a phone on the ground. I noticed that the person wasn't from Philly so I wanted to give it back. The person texted and said that they would give me $100 for the phone. I went to meet him and all of these cops surrounded me and arrested me and looked at the texts. They looked at the guy [the phone's owner] and said "I thought you said he was extorting you," and he claimed that I was,

but the cops said that since he was the one who offered the money initially it wasn't extortion, so they un-arrested me. But then a chief came and told the cops to arrest me anyway because it was the end of the month. My mom had to bail me out. I had to go to court and everything. It was horrible.

The feeling of constant risk is especially palpable for those who are being formally supervised in the community. Over forty thousand, or one in twenty-three, Philadelphians, including one in fourteen African American residents of the city, are under supervision by probation or parole.[12] Pennsylvania laws allow these terms of supervision to go on for decades instead of being time limited, as they are in thirty-one other states.[13] Avoiding trouble while on supervision means meeting an average of eighteen to twenty conditions *per day*, especially avoiding drug use and contact with other individuals engaged in offending or currently on parole or probation supervision.[14] Of course, meeting this condition is effectively impossible in a high-reentry community such as Frankford, where hundreds of individuals arrive from jails and prisons each year and where a disproportionate number of halfway and recovery houses are located.

At the deep end of the risks named by the men we interviewed are incarceration and violent death. They often describe them as twin fates, perhaps because men of color often hear regular predictions that they will end up "in the cemetery or penitentiary."[15] These extremely negative expectations born of the moral panic about "superpredators" have been so fully internalized by millennial men of color that defying them has become the yardstick by which many measure their own success.[16] Yusef, the desisting man featured in the opening of the last chapter, reflected: "I look at my life and pat myself on the back. There are not many 28-year-olds who are still alive and kicking. Most are either dead or in jail, so I applaud myself."

Isaac, a 27-year-old biracial narrator, reported: "Shit, my success would just be not being in jail [chuckles]. I feel successful 'cause I'm not in there, I'm out here, you know, going to work every day. It's better than being there." Indeed, as would be expected in a high-reentry community, twenty-six of the forty-five men in this study had been incarcerated in jail and/or prison, and another three had been in juvenile facilities or spent a few hours in jail before being released. Thus, their fears about reincarceration were typically grounded in personal or close vicarious experience.

The risk of relapsing into criminal activity and substance abuse also concerned some of the men we interviewed. Here, they defined *themselves* as the source of the risk they feared, internalizing the legal system's messages about social control as self-control.[17] Chapter 3 makes clear that not relapsing into an old pattern of behavior demands that men resist their desire to avoid people and places that expose them to risk; instead, they must form and maintain durable social ties and venture out to engage in the labor market, renegotiating their identities to be consistent with the ideal of a productive, law-abiding adult man. Strategies for avoiding trouble that are based on disengaging from social networks and community groups are counterproductive when men are struggling with these issues.

NAVIGATING TROUBLESOME SPACES AND PEOPLE

Growing up in an impoverished neighborhood with a high rate of violence requires careful attention to one's presentation of self in public staging areas such as sidewalks and street corners. Sociologist Elijah Anderson has argued that an important component of the "code of the street" is knowledge about how to interact with men on the corner, particularly those engaged in behavior that could signal risk.[18] Regulating eye contact, posture, pace, and greetings prevents trouble by signaling that one is street savvy—that is, not an ideal target for victimization—but not interested in extended engagement. Several of the men we interviewed discussed how they negotiated with men in public as they moved about Frankford and other parts of the city.

For example, Wesley, a 26-year-old Black-Latino military veteran, said he used a standard greeting—"How you doing, brother?"—as he passed the drug sellers on his way to the corner store. He explained that this was meant to signal, "I'm one of you, but I'm not into that." He elaborated: "I don't really know anyone around my home and don't really try to. Associating with the wrong people can get you into trouble." He told us about being stopped by an unmarked police car one day when he was coming home from work. When they searched him, they found a small bag of marijuana in the pocket of a jacket he had borrowed from a friend. He planned to fight the charge and represent himself at his upcoming hearing; even though it was only a misdemeanor, he refused to plead guilty to something he did not do and recognized the stain it could leave on his record, even in a jurisdiction where possession of marijuana had been decriminalized. His efforts paid off, as the charge was cleared.

Christian, a 26-year-old Black information technology professional, said that he did not feel that his crime-free status eliminated his risk of arrest: "You can be in the wrong place at the wrong time. I know people who've gotten arrested for being next to people who are drug dealers, everyone get problems with the whole bunch 'cause no one wants to point the finger at everyone, so all takes the blame." Angel, a 33-year-old Latino husband and father, described his interactions with the men on one of the most active blocks in the neighborhood: "I usually have slacks on, I have my book bag, I'm minding my business, I'm by myself. If I do say 'whatsup' to the guys on the corner, it's like a dap [fist-bump] real fast and I'm gone." Despite the fact that he deliberately dressed to signal his law-abiding status, he estimated his current risk of arrest as a 3 on a scale of 1 to 10. "If someone want to be a complete jerk, then at that point, they can come and arrest me."

Yusef, who was trying to put his criminal history behind him, identified the bars in Frankford as a site for drama and chose to go to his uncle's speakeasy in North Philadelphia instead. He told us, "I don't want the drama or to deal with all the male testosterone stuff." His reference to performances of masculinity is telling. The Frankford men wanted to engage with other men as part of "doing gender" but had to balance that need with the unpredictability that hangs over these interactions.[19] Yusef enjoyed the male socialization that bars offered but also recognized them as hypermasculine spaces where fights could easily break out and draw the attention of the authorities. He managed this risk by leaving Frankford, where the drama was more pervasive, and going to a smaller, more exclusive setting run by a family member who would have his back if trouble arose.

Similarly, Alex, a 35-year-old Latino father, regarded bars as particularly troublesome: "I don't go to bars. I used to go to a lot of bars but I stopped that a long time ago . . . when I was what, 22 or 23. Every time I went, there was always a situation, an issue. I got tired of it. Even my little brother. . . . We all go, start drinking, they become incredible Hulk, next thing I know everybody taking off and I'm stuck in the middle of a situation and everybody's gone, like what the hell is going on?"

By contrast, men who try to avoid the visibly risky men in their community may have their manhood called into question. For example, David, who told us about celebrating his twenty-fifth birthday, reported that others "think I can't take care of myself" because "I keep my nose clean," which threatened his projection of manhood and put him at risk of being victimized by those who viewed him as vulnerable. Similarly, Nelson and his family had been harassed by the drug sellers on the corner. With asthma and a host of other health problems, Nelson was a prime target of taunts and threats when he stepped out of his house. He had been "sucker punched" in the face while coming back from the store. He did his best to avoid these interactions, viewing it as safer to stay in the house and play video games.

NETWORK AVOIDANCE

The primary means of avoiding risky situations in Frankford involves network avoidance, a deliberate restriction of social ties that are regarded as increasing the likelihood of trouble. Network avoidance is grounded in young men's perception that their own risk of being caught up in neighborhood drama cannot be fully mitigated by their adult status and law-abiding behavior. Men of color are especially aware of the dangers they face because of their race. Those who engaged in network avoidance described "staying in the house," "keeping a tight circle" of trusted friends and family, and avoiding relationships with individuals who could trigger the criminal legal apparatus.

Staying in the House

Approximately half of the men in the Frankford study reported "staying in the house" as a strategy for avoiding drama. They remain indoors for long stretches of their waking hours, reducing their exposure to people and situations that could result in trouble. Several said, "I don't really go outside," or "I don't really walk around anymore." Their homes are simultaneously shelters and prisons.

Lewis, a 30-year-old Black narrator who had relocated to Frankford ten years earlier from New Orleans after Hurricane Katrina, reported: "I pretty much don't leave the house unless I am picking up a check [from work]. It's a very horrible neighborhood to just be out, lingering around. There are lots of drugs, people smoking crack at the bus stop, they crap, urinate, and eat right next to each other. Even people who have houses will still [urinate] in the alleyway."

Nasir, whose story about being incarcerated on false charges was recounted earlier and who was still on parole supervision at the time of the interview, explained that he reduced his risk of rearrest by sticking to a strict routine and avoiding going out at night: "I drive, I go to the gym at a certain time every day, I go in the house, I'm never on the streets at 10:30, 11 o'clock at night. I'm in the house by 10, [or] earlier than that sometimes. I don't hang out on corners, I rarely stand outside, unless I'm in the park or I'm running."

Being on community supervision certainly contributes to the sense of risk and unpredictability posed by the CLS.[20] Nevertheless, the Frankford men who were on probation or parole at the time of their interviews were no more likely than unsupervised men to report engaging in network avoidance, and no one specifically mentioned avoiding only former criminal associates because it was a condition of supervision.

Brady, a 33-year-old White food cart owner, reported "sticking to myself" and not "liking people." Although he regularly accompanied his children to the nearby park, he generally tried to keep the kids in the house and did not participate in any community events or services. Several other studies have shown that residents in high-violence communities "don't go outside" and restrict their children's outdoor activities.[21] The Frankford men, however, were just as likely to identify contact with the CLS as posing an untenable risk to their lives and freedom as they were to mention interpersonal, street-level forms of drama as a source of danger that required them to restrict their movements.[22] Moreover, our field observations in public spaces in Frankford suggest that younger men draw on this strategy more often than women or older men do, perhaps because they have more forms of risk to avoid. As the next chapter explains, men under 40, particularly men of color, are subjected to racial-criminal stigma, which results in heightened scrutiny by the police, shop owners, and passersby. In their experience, the CLS has no apparent logic or legitimacy; simply going about one's business is not enough to avoid being caught up in aggressive law enforcement, as Angel articulated so clearly.

Men without jobs often express a heightened need to manage trouble, since they have too many hours to fill. When we asked these men about their daily routines, they described spending long hours playing video games, screening YouTube videos, watching movies, listening to music, and scrolling through social media feeds—all pursuits that might sound more typical of adolescents than adults. Social media was an important means of connecting with friends and family members. For those isolated men, social media also offered the possibility of creating new relationships, many of which remained largely online. This pattern underscores men's sincere desire to create and maintain bonds with others even while remaining physically alone and off the radar.

Keeping a Tight Circle

During our interviews, we asked each man to name his three closest friends. Perhaps more than any other question, this item revealed their limited social networks. Several had trouble naming three friends; others could not name even one friend, while some named their sisters and mother instead. "Keeping a tight circle" meant extending trust to only a small handful of people who had demonstrated their trustworthiness over a long period of time. Men using this strategy were able to leverage some of the support functions of a social network without running the risk of trouble. Trust and betrayal are prominent themes in their life stories, and nearly every respondent said that a good friend had betrayed them in the past. This reluctance to trust is part of the neoliberal ethos of individualism and self-determination that views social relations as carrying a risk of even further economic instability.[23]

David, whose story opens this chapter, kept a tight circle of friends and had systematically cut out those who introduced risk, including those who smoked weed. He explained that as he matured, he "closed up" his circle of friends. When we asked what he did with his friends, he said that they watched UFC or basketball, played video games, read and organized comic books, listened to and recorded music, and wrote. He liked to surround himself with creative energy.

Avoiding Relationships with Troublesome People

Men's vulnerable position in relation to mass incarceration and supervision can be leveraged by intimates during romantic conflict.[24] For some men, this fact makes romantic relationships with women—particularly those who are prone to "drama"—a risky proposition. Some men view women, particularly their children's mothers, as manipulating "the system" to their personal advantage. For example, Cam, 23, told us that he avoided seeing his daughter because he and her mother always argued when he went over to their house to visit, and he was afraid that she might call the police.

Lewis, 30, was charged with attempted murder after a fight with his child's mother. He told us they had sex, followed by an altercation that became physical. Afterward, she accused him of sexually assaulting her and trying to kill her and her unborn child, who was presumably from another relationship. "I couldn't believe she said such a thing," he exclaimed. Despite being pressured by the prosecutor to plead guilty in exchange for a light sentence, he maintained his innocence and was eventually cleared of all charges.

Bryan, a 31-year-old Black father, told us that his children's mother had a restraining order against him.[25] He once tried to bring them some money on Father's Day, but her family called the police on him. Although he and his ex were not abiding by the restraining order and continued seeing each other on and off for awhile, he complained that she "picks and chooses" when she wanted to invoke its prohibition against contact.

Bryan's mother was also a source of drama. She had been addicted to crack cocaine throughout his life and eventually lost custody of him because of her erratic and violent behavior and the poor conditions in their household. He reported that she still placed him in risky situations. For example, when he met her at a bar at 7:00 a.m. after she had been out drinking all night, she ended up getting him into a fight with some other guy who took a stool to the back of Bryan's head. "I didn't want anything to do with it. I was just trying to chill with my head down and get drunk, but my mom brought me into it."

Nasir also discussed the imperative of engaging in violence with other men in order to protect women. He felt trapped by compulsory heteronormative masculinity: "The female out here [who is] in everybody face, you don't need to deal with her, 'cause eventually she'll have a problem and she'll run to you and you'll have to fight or whatever. Somebody might beat you up or shoot you . . . and listen, [the men] are hurting the females too, they're killing them! It's crazy, ain't it?"

Men who had lived in Frankford for a long time had to manage relationships within neighborhood networks they feared could lead to trouble. For example, Andre, a 32-year-old Black narrator from East Frankford, described the tight-knit nature of his community as a problem: "I've learned it's best to work outside of Frankford because [I] know everybody in Frankford and most of the people that [I] know are into the BS, the drugs, and that'll bring you down in terms of your record and you won't be able to get a job. . . . And coming back from work in Frankford, you'll end up indulging in things you don't want to." Andre reported that when he first moved to Frankford there was someone selling drugs on his block who wanted Andre to hustle for him. When he refused, they ended up getting into a fight, and the man knocked his front tooth out. "The guy is now in prison for near twenty years for killing somebody else, so the karma came back on him." Andre was quietly saving money to move out of the neighborhood because of the intolerable level of risk it presented.

Yusef, who talked about going to his uncle's speakeasy in a different neighborhood, reported that his dense network of friends and family in the area could not mitigate trouble: "Over the years . . . all of the civilized people started moving out of Frankford, slowly but gradually more negativity started popping up, and it's like North Philly now! You got people shooting each other, stealing, crime all over the place. . . . Kids are busting up people's cars and being disrespectful to adults, people robbing and killing, doing whatever to make some money, breaking in homes and cars, tampering with cars, lots of drama and he-say–she-say. You'll be stressed out cause you might not never have a peaceful day in Frankford." Yusef described trying to avoid areas where he knew there was a lot of violence, but it moved "around Frankford. . . . These days most people are getting killed over nothing, and the innocent person is getting killed." So he was "trying to stay out the way and not be in someone's situation."

RACE AND RISK OF DRAMA

Concerns about drama and network avoidance were much more common among the Black or Latino men in the study, and many identified their status as minoritized men as drawing unwanted and unwarranted attention from the police. As noted previously, nineteen of the twenty-three men who worried about trouble and sixteen of the twenty-one who employed network avoidance were men of color. Nationally, men of color are disproportionately targeted by police for questioning and frisking, and it is no different in Frankford. First-person accounts of these encounters highlight the degree of fear generated by the unpredictable nature of these interactions. For example, in *Just Mercy*, Brian Stevenson recounts that despite his status as a Harvard-trained attorney, his first reaction to a police stop was to flee. Lewis, a 30-year-old Black man, reported being pulled over in his car three to four times per year for the last decade.[26] He responded in a way he hoped would be interpreted as nonthreatening: "I know my size. I keep my hands on the wheel, don't look at the police in the face. I don't give him a reason to feel intimidated. He has a badge and gun; I have skin and bones."

Lewis's reference to the "skin and bones" he brought into every police interaction underscores the legitimate terror that persons of color experience during routine encounters. It reflects his recognition of his subordinate status when measured against the state's power to end his life or take away his freedom, and it references the embodied nature of these relations. Lewis was engaged in "submissive civility," or "a method of self-preservation enacted in social situations where power relations are asymmetrical, and the dominant party can administer sanctions. The strategy, used in interactions with police and other powerful outsiders, is to deliberately overconform to social norms."[27]

When comparing the daily activities of Frankford men by race, it is clear that White respondents were more likely to enjoy freedom to move about the neighborhood without fear. Some, like Nick, a 33-year-old active opioid user, engaged in high-profile behavior without a second thought. He earned income through junking, which, at the most innocent end of the spectrum, involved walking around daily and picking through trash on people's sidewalks or in dumpsters behind businesses. He also self-reported destruction of property and multiple break-ins during these scrapping activities. Unlike many others featured in this chapter, he enjoyed taking walks around the community for exercise. His peer group included other active drug users who got high together, including his former "cellie" (cellmate) and others he described as "not very upstanding citizens."

Chase, a 27-year-old White man who grew up in Northwest Philadelphia but came to Frankford for recovery, said that Frankford "feels like home now." While he saw the police every day, he rarely interacted with them and believed his current chances of arrest were "pretty low." "I'm not engaging in illegal activities generally, so I think I'm pretty safe." His daily round of activities brought him to the bus stop at the Frankford terminal area, which he used to visit his best friend and parents in Germantown and go to work in Port Richmond to the south. His story highlights the privilege that is afforded many White men to move comfortably around public space without attracting unwanted attention by the police or needing to engage in interactional acrobatics with groups of men on the corner. This freedom is even more remarkable when we consider that Frankford is not his "home turf." It is also instructive that he feels at home in a variety of neighborhoods in the city, many of which are "White spaces" and thereby informally off-limits to others.[28] Many men of color stated that when they venture outside of Frankford they feel exposed and lack a cognitive roadmap for navigating space without encountering potential problems.[29]

NEGATIVE CASES

Examination of negative cases, or those that run counter to the researcher's working hypothesis, is an analytic tool designed to serve as a check on overly simplistic generalizations from qualitative research findings.[30] I first examine the four White men who worried about trouble to determine if they shared any characteristics that distinguished them from their White counterparts. Then I turn to the five White men who used network avoidance, using the same technique. I conclude that drama and network avoidance are generally coupled for men of color and decoupled among White men in Frankford. Black and Latino men appeared to engage in network avoidance as a result of a concern with trouble, whereas White men were unlikely to express either, but when they did, those engaging in network avoidance did not appear to do so because of a concern with drama.

The four White men who expressed an overriding concern with avoiding trouble were Luke, Oren, Declan, and Kurt. Three (all but Oren) had disabilities or mental health issues that were externalizing in nature and thereby drew the attention of the police. All four men also had had significant, negative personal experiences in the CLS that made them feel vulnerable and fearful of any further contact. Luke, 32, had spent five years in prison, including sixteen months in solitary confinement. He presented with what seemed like significant trauma and paranoia, noting that the interview questions were invasive and he normally wasn't "social" with strangers. He also mentioned being under the care of a psychiatrist and on medication, but that his diagnosis had changed so much, he couldn't even name it. Although he saw police all the time, he reported never interacting with them "unless they're cuffing me" and had "literally, never" had a positive interaction with law enforcement. His main focus in life was "avoiding [prison] walls," and he was terrified about the potential for interactions with his child's mother to go wrong: "I'm scared to death she gon' hit the button, 'cause it's nothing for a chick. . . . [L]ike right now, real rap, if you were like, '911, he hit me,' they gonna come book me. You don't even need to have a mark, they be like, alright, let the judge figure it out, they don't give a fuck. And my baby mama is not above that, so. . . . It's just a dicey situation."

Declan, 33, had suffered from a traumatic brain injury and was aware of the risk of getting into trouble because his disability made him slur his speech and appear to be drunk or high. He explained that his behavior could make him a victim of predatory crimes such as robbery or draw the attention of the police. When asked what definition of success he applied to his own life, he replied: "Not getting arrested. [laughs] No, my own life, the goal of success I'm shooting for is a job, a wife, a house, all that stuff, but the one I have now is just to make it through a day without getting shot or arrested."

Kurt, 31, also had a disability that was visible during social interactions in public that made him vulnerable to police scrutiny. He self-reported having Asperger's syndrome, which caused an inability to read social cues. He also reported seeing police "a couple times an hour." He had recently been arrested and charged with criminal mischief after an altercation with another man: "I was having some kind of space issue with a gentleman. He was in my personal space, and I did not see. . . . [I was] not evaluating it in the correct thinking capacity. So I'm reacting to this man, so I lunge my body to where he is out of my way or space and I damaged this window. I damaged the window and I guess the people that maybe witnessed would not have felt that that was within the right mind."

Oren, 31, did not have a disability, but expressed a concern with random trouble associated with the police that was grounded in his experience of being incarcerated in his late teens: "I'm not trying to get arrested for nothing. If I get too close to a cop I know I'm backing up and I'm walking the other way cause I don't want to be locked up ever again. I don't want to be around..I don't want to do that shit ever again. . . . It was just dirty and nasty I don't want to be there again."

Importantly, none of these four engaged in network avoidance or worried about how members of their social networks could draw unwanted attention from the police. Their concerns about trouble led them to avoid law enforcement, not to limit their movement, their engagement with neighbors, or their ties to friends and family.

Further, none of the five White men who practiced network avoidance expressed particular concerns with trouble or drama, leading me to conclude that perceptions of trouble and responses were decoupled for White men. These men all reported mistrusting and therefore avoiding contact with their neighbors (e.g., "keeping to myself")—but not necessarily other people or the police—because of mistrust and suspicion about their motives. Three of the men were in recovery (two were living in a recovery house), and a fourth was actively using and kept his socializing to a small group of fellow users. Those in recovery reported engaging in community service activities as part of their program. Randall, 27, said that his avoidance of neighbors was due to the stigma of being "an addict," and he said the neighbors gave him "types of looks." All of these men reported feeling free to move around the neighborhood or go to other areas of the city for recreation or work. Of the seventeen White men in the sample, eight were both concerned with trouble and engaged in network avoidance. By contrast, of the twenty-eight men of color, twenty were found in both categories.

IMPLICATIONS

Avoiding drama takes considerable skill and effort in Frankford. Many risk-filled circumstances await young men, and the forms of trouble include arrest, court involvement and a criminal record, incarceration, violent victimization, and death. Risk is a game of probabilities that takes skilled observation and analysis to play successfully. Yet as in gambling, risk cannot be eliminated because of its unpredictable nature, whether it is a stray bullet, a false charge, or a law enforcement stop gone wrong. The only way men find to eliminate risk is to remove themselves from the public sphere altogether, "staying in the house" and cutting off contact with others who introduce the possibility of drama. The result is the deepest of ironies: men of color "avoid [prison] walls" by recreating social and physical confinement in their own homes and community.[31]

We may ask whether withdrawing from the public sphere and spending long hours indoors on their phones or laptops is unique to men in highly surveilled communities such as Frankford. Many parents lament their adolescent children's preoccupation with social media. So what is different about these young men's behavior? The social context of increased isolation and virtual connection-making does play a role in network avoidance as the adaptation of choice.[32] Nevertheless, the racial and gender differences observed here indicate that more is at work. Staying in the house and keeping a tight social circle may be a functional adaptation to the stigma of not having a job or fulfilling hegemonic masculine roles. But more to the point, the men themselves identify the CLS as a pervasive presence leading them to define their world in terms of risk.

The harmful consequences of worrying about trouble or drama and of network avoidance are myriad. The vigilance needed to avoid trouble creates an environment of unrelenting stress, which takes up cognitive bandwidth, has negative health effects, and reduces life expectancy. David, the "preacher's kid," reported: "That's why we [Black people] die so young, all the diabetes, high blood pressure, this that and a third, because we're stressed out more than the average person." David's observation is consistent with recent research on the adverse health effects of personal and vicarious police contact, which is strongest for Black and Hispanic individuals.[33]

Network avoidance limits the development and maintenance of social ties, which are critical for healthy human development and serve as a safety net for the economically precarious.[34] It prevents the accumulation of social capital, which is fostered by a large network of weak social ties.[35] Moreover, it forces individuals to manage the risks they fear alone, instead of as part of a collective. As Sarah Brayne points out, avoiding surveilling institutions such as banks or hospitals can result in increased financial or health insecurity.[36] If this reluctance extends to avoiding social service agencies, men lose opportunities for job training or other educational credentials that could mitigate their disconnection from the labor market. Moreover, limiting geographic mobility to a small radius where risks are more predictable also prevents men from traveling to unfamiliar spaces where employment opportunities are more numerous or lucrative.[37]

Many of the Frankford men discussed distancing themselves from family members and romantic partners to mitigate their potential for drama. Kevin Roy's study of low-income fathers finds that avoiding dangerous spatial and social terrain limits both the amount of time and the types of parenting activities that men feel safe enough to engage in, which has trickle-down effects on children and mothers.[38] Moreover, he concludes that some of the mistrust between African American men and women is rooted in the uncertainty and risk posed by potential romantic partners' social networks and the trouble introduced when traveling into their neighborhoods. Choosing to limit or avoid social ties is especially problematic for African American men, who already have fewer social ties than their White counterparts, because of both the isolating impacts of racial residential segregation and the disproportionate effects of incarceration on this group.[39]

When practiced systematically, network avoidance likely has deleterious effects on whole communities. Young men of color are simply missing from the public sphere in Frankford, including typically masculine spaces such as barber shops and bars. Their lack of a visible presence and participation in the community and their dearth of connections to others are likely to hinder efforts by neighbors to control crime through collective efficacy.[40] Much of the discussion at civic association meetings was about the risks posed by and to young men of color, yet they were most likely to be missing from these conversations that disproportionately affect them.[41]

Finally, network avoidance diminishes the citizenship of those who practice it, reducing their ability to fully participate in society and extending the negative effects of mass incarceration and the expansion of the criminal legal apparatus.[42] Mistrust of social institutions and avoidance of public space reduces community engagement, political participation, organizing, protesting, and capacity building, activities that build stronger social infrastructures and are engines of social and personal change.[43] The lost potential of men who engage in network avoidance instead of forging connections is profound. As I detail in the book's conclusion, these men could be cultivated and celebrated as assets to their communities, serving as teachers, counselors, and credible mentors.

A critical analysis of this adaptation might lead us to surmise that the neoliberal project has reached its logical conclusion. If the goal was to effect the erasure and annihilation of Black and Brown men, who have been constructed as dangerous, in a manner that is consistent with contemporary color-blind racial ideology, what could be more effective than creating a social situation in which they confine and isolate *themselves*, seemingly by choice? Risk discourse, originally applied to young men of color by labeling them "superpredators," has been internalized by the very same men who were it targets, leading them to define themselves and their worlds in terms of risk.[44] This is a form of responsibilization, when individuals take on the state's function of social control.[45] Yet these men's focus was on *self*-control, not on recognizing the ways in which their behavior was shaped in reaction to an expansion of state power into their communities, routines, and social relations.

5 Stigma, Generativity, and Redemption

I'm always saying something to these young kids and they listen to me too, they'll be like "yo man" they might pull me over in the street and . . . they be happy to see me and that make me feel good sometimes. I always give them something 'cause these other bulls, they just givin' them just the worst of the worst. Like I use to encourage kids to do something that they like, like one kid that was always on a bike. . . . I pulled him over, I said, "yo you ride that bike pretty good," he was like, "yeah I know." I said, "well look, every time I see you ridin' your bike I'm gonna give you a dollar" and I would do that. But then after a while I'd act like I didn't see him 'cause he was cleaning me out [laughing]. I used to do that so that was my way of encouraging them, you know what I mean?

—Nasir, 34, Black

Kareem was a 26-year-old Black and Korean man and lifelong resident of Frankford. While earning mediocre but passing grades in high school, he was among a group of boys who skipped classes and began selling marijuana and eventually cocaine. After graduation, his drug sales career took off and he began to accumulate shoeboxes of cash under his bed. As a drug seller, he was making "more money than I've ever seen with any of them jobs." "I'm really not a bad person, just money hungry," he commented, and then explained: "Everybody want to be around you, you making money, you can do what you want, get what you want, it felt good. Instead of going to class, working. . . . I was helping my family with bills, feeling like a man." Here, he engaged a traditional definition of masculinity as a provider and, even when recounting illegal activities, focused on caring for and giving back to others.

Eventually Kareem's luck ran out. He was arrested several times in the following two years. He spent just under a year in jail and began to re-think his decisions. "Me and my cellie, he was older, we used to be talking to each other about what we could do better, like, when we get out of this situation, like our girls and our family [were] out there with nothing... without us." Through ongoing interactions with his cellmate, who was around 30, he became concerned about the consequences of his actions for others.

Kareem, who was 23 by the time of his release, cemented his commitment to going straight. With a felony record, he struggled to find legal work and lost his college scholarship. He began mentoring the young men he coached on his alma mater's football team, talking to them about avoiding his mistakes and learning from his failures. Using his substantial social capital in the community, he connected them to job opportunities. Eventually he began his own community program for boys in Frankford, designed to help them work through the challenges they regularly faced, instill a sense of racial consciousness, and find a path to entrepreneurship. With his own money, he formed a nonprofit organization and launched a slick website to draw the attention of funders. His work was recognized by a community-based social service agency, which hired him as its volunteer coordinator. At the time of the study, Kareem was 35 years old, had re-mained arrest-free for more than a decade, and was fulfilling his dream of becoming a community activist and leader. He had a strong sense of gen-erativity in relation to his community, its youth, and his family. Moreover, he both practiced racial uplift and taught racial literacy, or the knowledge and understanding of systemic racism used to help mitigate its effects.[1] He was teaching them racially and gender-specific lessons.

Kareem's story demonstrates how he redeemed himself and repaired his identity after incarceration by giving back, gradually turning his ser-vice to others into a personally rewarding career. He was a go-to resource in the community, which filled him with visible pride. His self-described "mistakes" and "failures" were transformed into salutary lessons for the boys he mentored, rebuilding his own narrative and reinforcing his trajectory from drug sales and incarceration to a constructive adult life. Kareem was a "wounded healer" or a "credible messenger," uniquely situated to influence youth because he shared their experiences.[2] In turn, his redemption narrative as a straight-talking Black male role model was affirmed by others in the community, helping to strengthen his new identity.

Although Kareem's generative activities certainly contributed to the end of his criminal career, acts of redemption were also common among men who had no history of criminal offending. Because men of color are presumed to have a criminal history regardless of their past behavior, many engage in the same performances of "making good" as those who were actively engaged in the work of desistance.[3] This chapter draws on research and theory on stigma to examine the function of redemptive acts that were so commonly found in narratives of the Frankford men. I begin by examining stigma theory, introducing the concept of racial-criminal stigma, and establishing some experiences of stigma that shaped men's sense of self. I then compare the generative and redemptive activities these men employed and demonstrate their role in constructing coherent masculine adult and racial identities.

STIGMA, GENERATIVITY, AND REDEMPTION

Managing spoiled identities involves a dynamic interplay of self and society, whereby the discredited individual presents disidentifiers, or signals challenging negative perceptions.[4] To the extent that this performance is credible to others, it becomes more fully internalized by the individual, whose belief then strengthens future performances and is eventually realized as part of the core self.[5] Narrative criminology has detailed this process for individuals who are working to desist from offending or substance use.[6] Redemption scripts are narratives that allow individuals to present themselves as essentially good, and they typically center on generativity, or acts of giving back to future generations or their communities.[7] In helping others, these "wounded healers" or "credible messengers" can counter stigma by nurturing a self that is positive and productive.

Although all individuals who are marked by a criminal record must manage stigma associated with system involvement, boys of color encounter criminalization of their behavior as early as preschool, where they are often labeled as oppositional troublemakers, and throughout their development they encounter widespread expectations of violence and untrustworthiness.[8] To grow up as a man of color in the United States requires navigating *racial-criminal stigma* resulting from pervasive images and narratives that Black and Brown men are essentially violent, hypersexual, and in need of control.[9] To develop a positive masculine adult sense of self, Black and Brown men must resist internalizing racial-criminal stigma, as well as a host of other negative predictions about their potential as fathers, romantic partners, employees, and productive citizens.[10]

Although the particular forms of racial stigma that these men navigate are newly defined in the era of the superpredator scare, the ideas undergirding them are persistent. Of Black men, bell hooks writes:

> Seen as animals, brutes, natural born rapists, and murderers, black men have had no real dramatic say when it comes to the way they are represented. They have made few interventions on the stereotype. As a consequence they are victimized by stereotypes that were first articulated in the nineteenth century but hold sway over the minds and imaginations of citizens of this nation in the present day. Black males who refuse categorization are rare, *for the price of visibility in the contemporary world of white supremacy is that black male identity be defined in relation to the stereotype whether by embodying it or seeking to be other than it.* At the center of the way black male selfhood is constructed in white-supremacist capitalist patriarchy is the image of the brute—untamed, uncivilized, unthinking, and unfeeling.[11]

Although some men we interviewed internalized stigma throughout their life course, it was far more common for them to describe their efforts to resist these labels and to craft counternarratives of redemption.[12] In this analysis, *redemption* is a conscious, deliberate activity designed to restore one's standing in the eyes of society writ large or of specific groups of significant others against whom one measures oneself. Redemption is not a state, but a process of reclaiming and reframing one's identity in opposition to stereotypical labels or negative predictions. Redemption has a moral connotation grounded in the essential goodness of the self. It has sometimes been portrayed as an almost religious conversion undergone by individuals who have overcome their own past, but it is most successfully and durably accomplished through interaction with others.[13]

RACIAL-CRIMINAL STIGMA

Men of color described a variety of venues in which they experienced racial-criminal stigma, or being criminalized for their skin color, at school, at work, and in their interactions with police, Angel, a 33-year-old Latino, recounted his experiences in Catholic school. As one of only a few students of color, he faced stigma and racial profiling that started in grade school:

> That was a nightmare—I literally got picked on every day by the teachers. Every day because I was Puerto Rican and I came from the hood. There was a period in sixth grade where I was searched every week and I thought it was normal so I'm like, okay, I guess they do this to other kids. I didn't tell my grandparents; I didn't tell my mom. And finally, I was like, "I don't ever see any other kids in here. Like why you guys always searching me?" They're like, "Well, somebody told us you had a knife." "What do you mean, a knife! I don't have a knife!" And then I told my mom and [she] cussed everybody out.

But racist slurs from educators did not stop there:

> The next year in seventh grade my English teacher called me a "Spic." . . . I'm like, "You called me a what!?" . . . So, I called my mom again and she came up there again and the teacher started crying and my mom was like "I don't want to see your tears, wipe them away, I don't care about those things," and my grandfather didn't pay [tuition] for the rest of that semester. And then in eighth grade another teacher told me that by the time I was 16, I was going to drop out and I was going to become a junkie.

Angel, who had no criminal record, recounted that he regularly wore dress slacks to signal to police, and to other men who presented possible negative interactional entanglements, that he was a productive citizen on his way to work.

Several Black men—but, interestingly, none of the non-Black Hispanic men—emphasized that they "didn't want to become a statistic."[14] They were conscious of White peoples' hostile images of young Black men and had been subject to numerous negative predictions about their futures. A statistic is a summary measure, meant to reduce large numbers and report averages. Black (and presumably all) men don't want to be lumped together; they want to be seen as individuals and apprehended as full human beings. The men in the study wanted to be understood and related to based on their personal conduct, for their goodness, generosity, and other aspects of their character. They dreamed of disproving negative stereotypes and "beating the odds," which many accomplished through redemption bids and projects built on generative activity.

MANAGING STIGMA THROUGH REDEMPTION BIDS

I distinguish between redemption bids and redemption projects. *Redemption bids* are short-term assertions of self that run counter to stigmatic treatment or labeling. These are the small moral victories we all celebrate when someone puts us down, and then or later we prove them wrong.

Consider Lewis, a 30-year-old Black man who had experienced repeated, blatant racial profiling while driving in Philadelphia. Once a police officer even taunted Lewis by boasting that he specifically looked to pull over Black men. He found one experience especially terrifying and humiliating. An officer stopped his car because its registration was expired. He recounted the events in staccato fashion: "Had my seatbelt on. He's got sunglasses on, he's the man. Jumped out of his car with his gun drawn, with his partner. I tell my son everything's going to be okay. Son, watch your father. You okay. Cop runs to the window. If anybody move, I'm going to shoot somebody. [I've got] hands on the wheel, not saying anything, not doing anything." Lewis was cuffed and put in the back of the cruiser while the officer ran his name through the database and his five-year-old son sat alone in the backseat, crying. Right after this incident, Lewis took care of the paperwork and paid the fines.

When he faced the same situation again, he felt vindicated because it ended differently. "When I go back to [the] neighborhood, I get pulled over by same officer. I looked for that same cop, just so I can wipe that dumb smirk off his face. From that moment on, I love handing him everything legit. When a man make you feel like they can squash you in front of you children, hurt me, hurt my son, arrest me. Never will I let that happen again. . . . Now I say, I like it when cops pull a Black man over thinking he's going to lock them up and has to let them go."

Lewis's story highlights important aspects of redemption bids. First, the bid was most meaningful when it was witnessed by the same officer who had pulled his gun on Lewis and threatened to lock him up, although he reported feeling triumphant every time he is pulled over and proves the officers wrong. Second, his redemption bid was grounded in his resistance to a form of stigma that was aimed at both his racial identity and his masculinity, which was diminished when the police "squashed" him in front of his son. It is also worth noting that Lewis also experienced racial stigma at his workplace, where he was let go from the nursing facility where he worked and the police were called after he was falsely accused of having a weapon. "Why would I bring a firearm to my job? . . . Those White folk don't play, they take me forever away, forever away!" The stigma of racial exclusion and criminal stereotyping is often experienced throughout the life course and in multiple settings, cumulatively creating a spoiled identity that can be mitigated through redemption bids.

Redemption bids are related to but distinct from "campaigns for respect," which Elijah Anderson discusses in his work on inner-city Black men. These campaigns treat respect as a zero-sum game in which young Black men compete with one another. Since respect is a scarce commodity among marginalized youth in impoverished neighborhoods, they move about public space "looking for a fight" in order to take respect away from others.[15] Redemption bids, by contrast, are grounded in a desire for human dignity, which cannot be achieved at the expense of others.[16]

Redemption bids were made in the course of interviews.[17] Men frequently made moral claims regarding the harms of crime and violence. For example, Mateo, a 29-year-old Latino, explained why he would never burgle someone's home but had, in the past, broken into businesses to steal: "I'm a criminal, but I got morals." Nasir, a 34-year-old Black boxer, emphasized the human toll of violence: "I'm not violent even though I like to box and I know it but I'd rather use my head because that's the last resort, and I really believe that, that's the last resort because that amounts to trouble, that amounts to people getting hurt, that amounts to, you know, people going to court, people going to funerals, it's just bad. So you never supposed to think like that." Christian, a 26-year-old Black father, admitted, "I got dared to throw this brick into someone's windshield and I . . . was like oh yeah! But thinking about it now I'm like oh man that sucks. . . . One of the stupidest things I did and I feel so bad for it; if I could go back and pay for it I would."

Of the twenty-eight men of color in this sample, eighteen had made redemption bids, including five men who had no criminal involvement or record and another three men who had reported offending in the past but had no record. By comparison, five of seventeen White men had made redemption bids. All five reported experiencing stigma from noncriminal sources, like being underemployed (Anthony), homeless and in recovery (TJ, Jason), living with mental illness (Luke), or having visible disabilities such as a traumatic brain injury (Declan).

The audience for redemption bids is diffuse: it could be comprised of family members, teachers, employers, police and probation officers, and even journalists and researchers like ourselves. Several men viewed participating in our study as a way of giving back and hoped that the final product would be one that reflected well on the community and on Black men specifically. David, the 26-year-old "preacher's kid," reported:

> Not just speaking for myself, but speaking for all these young Black males, it's good that you're telling this story and you need to find more . . . not just the ones that have been in and out of the system, but the *positive* Black men who are trying to stay above water. It's a lot more of us out there, but they don't get spoken about as much because there's so much hate put on them. *There's more of a stigma for us than it is for the guys that has been in and out of gangs and stuff, because we're trying so much harder. . . .* That's why I felt it was so important to talk to you, because you're telling so many great stories about Black men in our community, so that their eyes are opened, so that they *see* us. Cause we're like exhibits at the zoo or something to them.

Here David, a Black man with no history of criminal activity, asserted that he felt racial stigma, which is connected to community stigma. It is notable also that David engaged in generativity by leading his local church's youth group.

REDEMPTION PROJECTS AND GENERATIVITY

Redemption projects, in contrast to bids, are longer-term efforts to crystallize a new identity in the face of stigma and labeling.[18] The primary means of crafting a redemption project is through "generativity," which psychologist Dan McAdams defines as "an adult's concern for or commitment to promoting the welfare and development of future generations. . . . Generativity is about parenting, teaching, mentoring, leading, providing for others, caring for and nurturing young people or those in need, working hard to make things better for the future, aiming to leave a positive legacy."[19] The majority, or twenty of the twenty-eight, men of color reported some form of generativity, most frequently mentioning their informal mentoring of neighborhood children (see table 2 in the appendix).

A criminal history was not a necessary precursor for redemptive generativity. Christian, who recounted his regret at throwing a brick through a window, redeemed himself in two senses. He was expelled from high school and sent to an alternative school for kids with disciplinary problems. He attended eight days before dropping out, saying that the schoolwork was designed "for idiots" and the building was set up "like a jail." His family then sent him off to a wealthy suburb in New Jersey to live with an uncle, who enrolled him in a better school and supervised his studies. He excelled academically and was exposed to opportunities for more privileged students. By leaving Frankford, he disproved teachers' and administrators' predictions of failure. He was keenly aware that his peers who remained in the city did not enjoy these advantages; indeed, the system was stacked against all Black youth. "I kind of felt as though I kind of like out-beat" the system, "cheat it a little bit. I was able to graduate on time even though I did all that. And then my friends are still like feeling the burden" of an impoverished school. "So that kind of made me feel a little bit good about myself." His assertion that he "beat," or even "cheated" the system implies that he viewed it as deliberately designed to fail and eject Black youth, leading to their incarceration and exclusion from legal employment. Christian had earned an associate's degree and certifications needed to become a computer systems technician, which he described as his "passion."

Christian was also a father and acted as a mentor to neighborhood kids. "I think fatherhood means to be trying to teach, it doesn't even have to be just my daughter, just the younger generation, . . . every child, it's like 'each one teach one.'" This maxim is common in the African American community. "I try to teach her to be better than what I was. I know all the things I know I did wrong so I try to teach the same things to her but opposite." He served as an informal credible messenger to encourage the next generation to stay in school. "I ask them, how you doing in school, to show them I care about school, and just like tell them to keep doing this. . . . I try to be the voice of reason to get them to understand . . . the older perspective."

Angel, whose schoolteacher predicted he would become a "junkie," was now a stably married father and had built his redemption on family, faith, and community. He and his family had moved to Frankford to attend a new church and to seek better job opportunities. During our field research at civic association and violence prevention meetings, he was often the only man under age 40 in the room. He loved his community and saw the drug activity on his block as an opportunity to do informal outreach on his front stoop. "We've made relationships in the area, we come to community meetings. . . . We've had drug dealers sitting on our porch, and we've argued with people and all while still making positive moves."

Generativity is described by social psychologist Erik Erikson as a stage of human development associated with middle adulthood, which usually occurs between ages 40 and 65. According to Erikson, as we age, individuals develop a concern with "making a mark" on the world that will live on after our death. Successfully doing so leads to feelings of usefulness and the development of the attribute of care.[20] The narratives of generativity shared by the Frankford men, however, indicate that it may be enacted by those aged 25 to 34, much earlier in life than Erikson suggested. Moreover, it may be evident even among men who, because of economic and racial disadvantage, have not successfully or fully passed through earlier stages of psychosocial development. The Frankford men navigated these conflicts and dilemmas simultaneously, not linearly, and their success in one area often depended on how well others were resolved.

WHITE MEN, STIGMA, AND REDEMPTIVE GENERATIVITY

Of the seventeen White men in the study, ten reported helping with block clean-up or serving meals at the church, and five of them did so as part of their recovery house programs. Recovering men also employed narratives with a redemptive arc, striving to present themselves as changed people. However, few mentioned experiencing stigma, perhaps because the opioid epidemic has been largely framed as a public health problem.[21] Importantly, nine of the seventeen White men and nine of fourteen recovering men were employed, which is consistent with traditional definitions of masculinity and therefore not a source of shame. Moreover, despite felony records being common among recovering men, they made above-average wages in the building trades.

A handful of White men presented narratives that centered on stigma. Declan, 33, had been permanently disabled by a traumatic brain injury when he was 17. He had "burned a lot of bridges" with his previous peer group because of his violent rages. He admitted to being racist prior to his accident but had found that afterward, when his White friends disappeared, "Black people was just embracing me and I was like, these are my people, dog." Unable to work in a formal position because of his disability, Declan began volunteering for an AIDS organization in Center City. "At first I was weirded out cause it's a lot of gay people up there and I was like eh, it just made me feel uncomfortable, but then I was like, they're great people, I'm cool with it. Like the one guy used to always hit on me, which you know at first I was like eh, and then I started to become flattered by it, I was like I'm not gay, but thank you [laughs]." Finding a community of people who accepted his limitations without judgment was a profound experience for Declan. He felt deeply misunderstood whenever he went out in public, afraid of getting into trouble with the police because of his slurred speech and memory problems and aware that others might draw negative conclusions about him. In finding a new peer group of marginalized others, he had transformed his disability into an opportunity to prove himself and be regarded as a good person. It is worth noting that Declan, who was White but whose stigma was visible during social interactions, found acceptance within intersecting stigmatized groups, including members of the lesbian, gay, bisexual, trans, and queer (LGBTQ) community, those living with AIDS, and Black men.

The four men featured here engaged in generativity in different ways, but each took the core attribute of a stigmatic experience and transformed it by inverting it, constructing a credible redemptive performance as a good person. I do not mean "performance" to suggest that it is anything other than genuine, but rather that it requires others to endorse it in order to be believable both to them and to oneself. Declan, who was

White, chose to engage outside the community, while Kareem, Christian, and Angel conducted their redemption projects in Frankford. This pattern could reflect the fact that White men were less likely than their counterparts to be from the community, or that White men felt safer traveling in "White spaces."[22]

GENERATIVITY AND ADULT MASCULINITY

The development of a caring identity is age graded and normed, meaning that there are increased societal expectations for caring activities as individuals move into adulthood. Being more focused on others than on oneself is a sign of maturity, which significant others expect from adult social relationships. A lack of maturity, as evidenced by an adolescent-like focus on the self to the exclusion of others, can result in social sanctions, such as expressions of disappointment from parents, older relatives, or guardians or rejection by desired romantic partners. Consider what this means in light of the previous chapter's findings on how carefully many men avoid persons or situations they perceive as bringing immature drama. There are built-in reward structures for the kinds of generativity we have seen among the Frankford men. They are a sign of mature adulthood, a valued quality among peer, family, and romantic networks. Giving back to others engenders respect from others and confers a sense of dignity, which may both be woefully absent in other realms.

For Black men in particular, generativity is a long-established means of constructing masculinity, particularly when it promotes racial uplift among Black boys.[23] One of the earliest ethnographic studies of a Black community described the "race man," an archetype of Black masculinity who distinguished himself by leadership and stewardship in his community.[24] Today's race men include men like Kareem, who engaged in street-level violence prevention and prison reform.

Care is a deeply gendered concept, typically associated with feminine attributes and linked to women's primary responsibility for nurturing children and stereotypically female occupations such as teaching or nursing. Yet many Frankford men described their own masculinity in "softer" terms that are built upon generative activities. For example, they often defined a "real man" as someone who takes care of his family and is not afraid to be vulnerable.[25] Engaging in generative activities is a means of constructing a mature masculine identity, an age-graded performance of manhood that rests on connections to social institutions such as family and community and is actively distinguished from juvenile masculinity.[26]

RACE, STIGMA, AND GENERATIVITY

Redemption bids and projects are achieved through acts of selflessness, giving back to one's family and community and assisting vulnerable groups or the next generation. The credible performance of redemption, conducted before an audience and resulting in positive appraisals, supports the construction of a positive adult masculine identity in the face of stigma.

The negative effects of stigmatic labels are so well-established that we might be tempted to conclude that the "self-fulfilling prophecy" that labeling often produces is a deterministic process that unfolds when individuals internalize negative predictions and begin to assess themselves as bound to fail. Yet recent scholarship on men of color suggests that some navigate and resist stigma, and that these strategies may have positive transformational potential. Victor Rios's study of young Latino boys who were caught up in the "youth control complex" included a number who engaged in political resistance movements as they got older.[27] This activism provided a positive sense of identity, as well as opportunities for social mobility. Moreover, Nikki Jones found that young Black men in the Fillmore neighborhood of San Francisco engaged in redemptive projects as a pathway to desistance.[28]

Just as in the last chapter, where it was almost always men of color who took steps to avoid drama, we see here that generative activities and redemption bids and projects were disproportionately undertaken by African American men who were resisting racial stigma and stereotyping. The imagery of the superpredator that framed their cohort's coming-of-age experiences linked Black men to crime and violence in the minds of White Americans. We see evidence of this daily, such as when Ahmaud Arbery, a Black man taking a jog through a Georgia neighborhood, was murdered by two White men who reported that they thought he was a burglar, and when Amy Cooper called 911 to report that Christian Cooper was threatening her life when he asked her to leash her dog in Central Park in order not to frighten the birds he was watching. Just as men of color consciously signal their lack of ill intent to passersby on the street by not walking too close to women or by crossing the street to avoid them, these same men are engaged in projects of giving back in order to signal to others, and ultimately themselves, that they are not bad people, despite how others might see them because of their race.[29]

Men who were not African American or Latino also mentioned stigmatizing experiences. Since many of the White men we interviewed were part of the substance abuse recovery community in Frankford, they had to deal with being labeled "addicts," which carries highly negative attributions, such as being untrustworthy, weak-willed, or prone to relapse. These men felt the need to redeem themselves by atoning for the mistakes they had made in the past, as well as to present consistently "sober" behavior over an extended period of time before significant others were willing to believe their performance.[30] This is a personal journey, although group support helps immensely.

The nature of ascribed, group-based racial stigma is categorically different. It casts its reach over an entire class of persons, regardless of their behavior or moral character. Racial stigma presumes guilt and is ineradicable. It denies its targets' very right to exist, to human dignity or citizenship. It can be sneaky, allowing those with social class status markers to feel that they can move freely around White spaces until that privilege is suddenly rescinded in what Elijah Anderson calls the n-word moment.[31] And it is experienced vicariously, for example, when racist incidents are circulated on social media and viewers are reminded of their place in society.

Redemption, then, is not simply taken on behalf of the self, but also on behalf of the entire racial group to which inferior attributes are applied. In *The Chosen Ones*, Nikki Jones argues that the redemption of Black men is a social activity.[32] I agree and go a step further to suggest that it is a *collective* activity. When the Frankford men detail their generative activities, they are crafting a redemption narrative for all Black men. The power of group-based stigma is that it applies to all, so one man's counternarrative has the potential to call into question the entire characterization of their race and gender, as David exemplified when he discussed the need to tell stories about the "positive Black men who are trying to stay above water."

We may ask why generativity, and not some other means of constructing a positive identity, is so important to redemption and self-respect for men of color. I suggest that, first, it is a trope and tradition that is widely shared within communities of color. Indeed, narrative psychologist Dan McAdams remarks that "some of the most redemptive texts in the American tradition may be found in the African American heritage and in the life stories of highly generative black adults."[33] The "each one, teach one" philosophy espoused by Christian is an African American proverb whose historical origin is unclear, but which many believe came from the idea of enslaved persons teaching literacy to others as a form of resistance.

Calls for generativity are supported within faith traditions, as well as consistent with less organized but nonetheless spiritual orientations of working-class men.[34] In Frankford, the churches are a major locus of social service delivery, with volunteers organizing hot meals and showers for those without housing and school supply drives for local families. Moreover, giving back is a major tenet of twelve-step programs, which are abundant in this community. In short, Frankford is a "social service hub" where generative activities are visible and important threads in the social fabric.[35] The positive influence of these programs on the daily lives not only of those who are served by them but also of others in the vicinity runs counter to the metanarratives that neighborhoods with dense networks of social service are unhealthy places.

Taken together, this analysis contextualizes a paradox that sociologist Freeden Blume Oeur articulates aptly.[36] Black men have conflicting needs to be *anonymous* in public, as the chapter on avoiding trouble argues, and at the same time *to be seen* by others, that is, to be recognized as human and as men.[37] They respond to the expansion of the criminal legal apparatus by "going underground" and, for example, wear hoodies to make themselves indistinguishable from others as a means of survival.[38] They strategically reduce their interactions with people who present a risk of attracting attention from the police. At the same time, they need social interactions with peers, family members, coworkers, and members of the public in order to present a performance of good personhood, to be recognized as contributing to society.

6 Durable Social Ties, Linked Lives, and Adult Masculinities

> I raised myself for real, [my mom] worked two jobs so she's
> really hurt about that, she still vent over that, she be like "yo
> I swear to God I'm sorry for everything I did to you, I'm
> sorry for not being there when you needed me[."] . . . I had
> tried out for basketball and I had made it to the champion-
> ship like I took the whole team, me and two other people
> took it to the championship three years in a row and she
> ain't make not one game. My dad ain't make not one game,
> you get what I'm saying?
>
> —Grant, 27, Black narrator

INTRODUCTION

So far, I have presented an apparent contradiction, which is that men in Frankford who were concerned about (further) exposure to the CLS carefully limited their social ties using network avoidance. For men of color, network avoidance was an adaptation to drama, or exposure to surveillance and scrutiny by the police or other agents of the CLS. Black and Latino men we interviewed in Frankford expressed concern that social ties to women, particularly their children's mothers, as well as friends and family members could activate unwanted attention by the authorities.

At the same time, these men also *built and relied on* social ties to manage various forms of stigma through acts of redemptive generativity, or giving back through mentoring, volunteerism, or paid service work in the nonprofit sector. This chapter analyzes the construction of durable ties with families of origin, romantic partners, and children within the structural constraints of economic marginalization and vulnerability to system involvement. What characterizes these relationships is intimacy and connectedness versus isolation. Here, I explore whether and how men without a college degree who grew up amid White fear of the Black male "superpredator" perceive durable social ties as desirable or attainable and what kinds of financial and emotional contributions they want to make—and are *able* to make—in these relationships. I also examine what durable ties do to help men who are on shifting structural and cultural ground craft positive masculine adult identities.

This analysis is grounded in a long sociological tradition addressing family formation, reciprocity, and extended or fictive kin networks that are critical to survival in marginalized communities.[1] It draws on Elder's concept of "linked lives," which he suggests are the most important aspect of the human life course.[2] It also extends more recent work that examines the effects of system involvement on family members, which has focused largely on women's burden in "holding down" the home situation while their male counterparts are incarcerated.[3]

With some exceptions, the Frankford men strove to form deep and durable ties, which represented hope for the future and the goals of permanence and progress for those who were economically unstable. I begin by discussing relationships with families of origin, which were often grounded in damaging pasts that men tried to reconcile and forgive as adults. Many men still relied on their parents and extended kin network to make ends meet or as a conduit of support during substance use recovery, although some provided financial assistance to their elders. Reciprocity norms bind marginalized men to their families of origin, which can expose them to unwanted drama or attention by outsiders or continued emotional abuse or conflict, which their vulnerability prevents them from avoiding.

Connections with families of origin, romantic partners, and children also enabled men to construct *caring masculinities*, or gender practices that rely on "positive emotion, interdependence, and relationality" rather than domination.[4] In the relationship marketplace, these men have little to offer in the way of economic support for the families they create and sustain. Caring allows men to provide for others in a way that doesn't rely on financial contributions. It helps men understand themselves as morally good despite their inability to fulfill more traditional "provider" gender roles.

FAMILIES OF ORIGIN

The vast majority of men we interviewed in Frankford mentioned one or more types of durable social ties. Almost all identified close adult relationships with members of their family of origin, including grandmothers, aunts, uncles, and cousins, and eleven still lived at home with family members, usually mothers. The development of these relationships was often marked by serious and multiple adversities, including trauma, physical and emotional abuse, abandonment, separation, mental health and substance abuse problems, and tragedy. That so many men are still so close to members of their extended kin networks as adults is partly driven by their unstable economic and living situations, including their vulnerability to CLS involvement. Financial interdependence with family members meant that many regularly traversed emotional minefields, either being needed by or needing the help of parents who were not good to them as children and sometimes not good for them as adults. They mostly did this without formal therapeutic supports.

Prevalence and Nature of Family Ties

Mothers were the most frequently mentioned as continued and frequent presences in their lives, and the men under 30 years of age were often still co-residing with them. When asked who in their families they were closest to and whom they would go to for help, they most often said their mothers. Regular check-ins with their mothers by phone or text were a common part of their daily routines. Men often spoke lovingly about the emotional support they continued to receive from their mothers well into adulthood. Luke, a 32-year-old White man with significant trauma after his stint in solitary confinement, said: "I speak to [my mom] damn near every day. She's not great with texting but I shoot her a little text, hell I'm a mama's boy, I make no bones about it, love you mom, xoxo, heart face, that's my mom. Always my whole life been in my corner. I could go fuckin punch Trump in face, she'd be like, 'that wasn't Luke'. . . . Always, right or wrong, she never ever doubted me." Luke's description of his mother's unwavering support is heartwarming, but these strong bonds are often formed in the face of substantial hardship. Approximately half of the men discussed their mothers' long-term substance abuse, which they said presented a major obstacle to "being a mom" and forced them to take on adult responsibilities during their childhood or teen years. Nevertheless, with some exceptions, the Frankford men were remarkably forgiving and understanding of their mothers' limitations. Christian, 26, the Black IT professional, whose mother left him to pay the mortgage on the family house, said, "My mom was dealt a tough card so it's not her fault that I'm getting leftovers from that."

Similarly, Keith the 27-year-old Black narrator featured in the desistance chapter, told us:

> It was hard for her cause she didn't really know how to be a mother, she had me when she was 19–20. . . . So she was trying to raise me [as a teenager] along with three other children with no help, no child support – none of our fathers [paid] child support. And she also had a drug addiction problem. So it was kind of hard for her to navigate through that, so, you know, me, I just took to whatever I could find, whatever influences I could find. . . . My mom, she tried her best, to do the best that she could do, it was kind of hard for her cause she didn't know what she was doing at the time. *So I kind of helped her grow as a mother.*

This theme of mutual or reciprocal relationships between parents and children in the context of urban poverty was also apparent when men talked about relationships with their own children.

Fathers were a much more fraught topic as we unpacked family dynamics with the men. Many left fathers out of their narratives altogether and, when probed, seemed unwilling to say more than that their dads weren't part of their lives. Approximately half of their fathers were dead, incarcerated, or totally absent. This fact was particularly consequential for how eagerly the men who had children embraced their own fatherhood. The men we interviewed were deeply affected by this absence, especially when their fathers were still in contact but chose not to be involved. Andre, the 32-year-old Black narrator who was saving money to leave Frankford, said: "My dad wasn't there like that—it was kind of hard—I didn't get a connection with my dad until after high school when I was 21–22. He wasn't there when I was younger, he didn't teach me how to ride a bike, talk to a girl, socialize and be a man. I had to really learn most of that stuff on my own, or my older cousins taught me. Why even have a dad, if you wasn't even there?" Despite the profound sense of disappointment Andre felt toward his father, he still had reconciled with him in his midtwenties when his father had had a stroke, leading to an "epiphany" about the importance of being in his son's life. Andre is still working through his father's explanation for his absence. "I'm your only son, so what's up? What was the situation? He lost his mom, he lost his brother and only had one brother left and just was lost. . . . I can understand losing your mom and brother back-to-back. But I looked at it like we made up for that—when your mom and brother died, I was born, when my grandma died, my sister was born." Consistent with Andre's narrative, men generally felt that an older male influence was needed to teach boys how to become men.

Sickness and death was a major theme in our conversations with men. Of course, the death of grandparents, aunts, uncles, and occasionally parents is a part of any transition to adulthood. In the context of profound neighborhood disadvantage found in Frankford, however, early death by gun violence, drug overdose, or chronic health problems was widespread. Trauma caused by witnessing death or losing real or fictive siblings or cousins was pervasive.

Death was by far the most common response to the question about major events in their family histories. Men with otherwise tough, masculine facades often wept when discussing the death of family members with us, and only a few had access to therapeutic resources to work through their grief. When asked about significant events in his family's history, Nasir, the 34-year-old Black Muslim who was wrongfully arrested at the Taproom, told us about his mother's death from diabetes and cancer when he was 15 years old. "I watched her break down and they'd [amputate] stuff and then it became normal just seeing it every day, then the doctor would come and take the bandage off and she got all of this missing [fingers], just to see it and it was white and black and they wrap it up. First she had legs, now they're gone." Chase a White 27-year-old who grew up in a middle-class section of Philadelphia, described his childhood home as a volatile place because of his mother's mental illness:

> My mom and my dad live in the same neighborhood but they're not together. So I grew up mostly with my mom and she has her own mental issues – she's like really volatile, she's mellowed out a lot since I was younger but back then she was kind of crazy—abusive and stuff, so there was always a lot of fighting in the house—it was just me and her too—my sisters were all

out by the time I came around. So it was a lot of conflict between me and her—she would kick me out a lot, even before I was using drugs, she was just really mentally unstable—she's got some legitimate mental problems.

When asked, "Is she medicated now?" Chase responded: "Uh, I think so, she's a lot better cause she's getting older or because there's no kids in the house, I don't know, but we're actually on really good terms now. When I was a kid it was not so much. Yeah, so that was always going on. So when I was a teenager I started being out of the house a lot more to get away from that and I started getting into drugs a little bit more, getting into trouble—never anything really serious but like fighting, just stupid stuff." Like Andre, Chase adopted a compassionate view of his mother's violent behavior toward him and reported being close to both his mother and father now that he is an adult.

A small number of men had cut all ties to their family members after serious betrayals. Men who reported this pattern were significantly more likely to be actively suffering from severe mental health problems and homelessness. Their untethered existence on the margins of society was tied up with their tumultuous childhoods and their lack of durable social ties as adults. An especially memorable example was Bryan, a 34-year-old Black narrator with more than twenty official contacts with the CLS by the time we interviewed him, was recovering from an addiction and appeared to be severely paranoid. He avoided going out in public because he believed unspecified people were planning to kill him. When we asked him to name his three closest friends, he replied proudly, "Bryan, Bryan, and Bryan." He told us that he learned early in life to rely only on himself and to be in control of his own life. His family members, including seven or eight siblings (he couldn't be sure), were deeply involved in crime, and he had been the victim of serious family violence as a child. He struggled with housing and food security. "Most everything I'm going through is because of my family. If it wasn't for them I wouldn't be going through the things I go through now," he told us. He also reported being quite lonely and was hoping to be on more solid financial ground in the future so that he could build "solidarity" with others, such as a wife. In the meantime, though, he was suspicious about the motives of the women he "talks to" and would have liked to have a roommate but feared that they might steal from him.

Others worried that family members might drag them back into trouble with the law, even if they were unwilling to cut ties altogether. Nasir (34, Black), who was working hard on turning his life around after a long criminal career and stint in prison, had given the interviewer the impression that he had little contact with his family of origin. She asked: "You're not that close with your biological brothers and sisters?" He responded:

> Uh, not really. I see one of them, actually one of them smokes crack in Frankford, I see him all the time, he asks me for money. I don't give it to him but I, like I talk to him all the time, he's my older brother, I talk to him all the time, he suffers with that addiction. And then my other brother, we're okay, we're okay, I don't trust him too much, when I went to jail for those four years he was trying, behind my back, talk to my daughter's mother in some type of way [in a romantic way], and then I stopped trusting him, but he's the one I could say I talk to more or less.

So far, I have presented the affective terrain that the Frankford men navigated in relation to their families of origin. In the next section I elaborate on the economic interdependence that keeps families together, even when they contain so much emotional baggage.

Financial Interdependence

Families of origin often play a critical role in constructing safety nets for their adult children, especially for the men under 30 years old. Parents, siblings, and extended family members provide basic material needs such as housing and food as well as short- and long-term childcare. Moreover, as we saw with Andre, these needs are often mutual, with the more stable men providing physical care to elderly family members and financial support for parents who were aging or chronically ill or substance dependent.

Some men were carried by family members in times of desperate need. For example, Andre told us in graphic detail about witnessing his baby's mom get killed by a car. His father died a couple of days later. Reeling from trauma and loss, he visited his children, who had been placed in the custody of their late mother's mother, who was addicted to crack. "I came back to Germantown and saw both of my kids in the stroller and they were dirty, like Flintstones feet. When I saw them, I unsnapped them from the stroller and took them and got on the bus with them. I went down to my sister's and my grandma took us in and helped us." The grandmother got custody of the kids, put them in school, and raised them until her own death.

Family members, mostly women, provided housing and other material support for men after the latter's release from prison.[5] The instability created by incarceration is well documented, and the critical role of housing in reducing the likelihood of future confinement is clear. It is worth pausing to consider the profound burden this places on impoverished families, particularly in the context of the shrinking welfare state. In communities such as Frankford, many elders are running de facto prisoner reentry programs with no funding or financial support. This task follows their emotional and financial investments in supporting the men while they were incarcerated, as well as the inflated costs of phone calls, visits, and commissary items designed to mitigate the conditions of confinement.

Consistent with the extension of children's dual roles as supported and supporters into adulthood, the Frankford men commonly reported that financial contributions flowed both ways. As noted previously, Christian was left to shoulder the burden of the mortgage on the family home when his mother, who battled long-term substance abuse, went to live with her own parents. Kareem, age 26, cared for his mother, who had recently survived a suicide attempt, and his 79-year-old father, who had had a stroke and was in an assisted living facility. Kareem listed his father's Social Security income as part of his own income, even as he mentioned contributing $300 per month to the family. Nelson, the 26-year-old Black Boy Scout who lived with his mother and sister, covered most of his family's financial needs using his Social Security disability check. Meanwhile, they were almost the only people he saw in person, since his carefully limited interactions outside his house often involved bullying and even violence.

As we reviewed their expenses and sources of income, twenty-one of forty-five men reported providing regular contributions to family members or romantic partners, ranging from very small contributions, which might pay for something "extra" or help when a person was broke, to substantial sums, which might cover a significant portion of the rent or food budget ($10 to $800 monthly). Nine reported receiving regular contributions from their family members with similar ranges, and six reported regular contributions from romantic partners. Given their shaky financial situations, I am inclined to be cautious about these claims, as they may well be influenced by the norm that adult men are supposed to support others rather than be supported by them. By these standards, it is remarkable that some men acknowledged financial assistance they received from family members and partners.

Malcolm's narrative demonstrates that, even though a man regards his family as a drain, he will continue to meet the responsibilities that have fallen to him. When this 33-year-old Black gay-identified man was asked to recount significant events in his family's history, he recalled:

> A couple years ago I went and bought a little scratch-off lottery [ticket]. I was sitting there scanning it twice and I couldn't believe it said what it said, it said I won a thousand dollars. At the time I was living with my mom. I told her and as soon as I told her and as soon as I got it is as fast as it went. I gave her half to help with bills, then I gave her boyfriend 50 bucks for taking me to go cash it. So, it leaves me with not much. Then she went and told my younger sister and she was like, can I borrow such and such for her older son for school. I was like, damn, I should have kept my mouth shut.
>
> This is another thing I had an issue with growing up. My mom would get stuff in our name and not pay the bill and it's like, *at the time she felt as though [she was] my child.* One time she got the cable bill in my name and I didn't know until I saw the bill. I said wait, I didn't get this. She said oh yeah, I was going to tell you about that. I was like, don't you need a signature to get that? Then I learned that she would tell me to get credit cards in my name so she can have money at the time to do what she wanted to do to make ends meet.

Interestingly, Malcolm still lived with his mother at the time we interviewed him. Although he explained their arrangement as stemming from the need for him to care for her during radiation for breast cancer, he would be unlikely to survive on his own making $250 per month doing HIV outreach and testing for a nonprofit organization.

Others reported feeling betrayed by family members who cut ties to get their own financial situations together. Mateo, the 29-year-old Latino who gave out "blessing bags" to homeless people with addictions, told us: "We used to be so family oriented – they grew up and got these good jobs and got sticks up their ass like their shit don't stink. I don't understand and that's the dilemma I love them all and that's the thing—I don't know, like, it bothers me. You were so family oriented. What's going on? Everybody's so selfish now. But I still can't conform to that, I can't turn into that." Mateo had access to a therapist because he was in recovery. Working through some of his family issues, he began to see how unhealthy patterns reproduced themselves in his romantic relationships:

> Mom? Who? [laughing] She lives [close by]. She just texted me. It's funny you said that. I won't reply. The thing is like she's my mother so I guess she feel like I owe her something, which I do, and I gave you that for years, through allll that bullshit with the family and the things you done to me, I was at your beck and call still. But Melissa, who was my therapist, one thing she did teach me is that my mom is the reason for a lot of my fucked up relationships, man. And it didn't make sense but now it does as far as, wow, I wouldn't open up to women, you know what I mean, I guess I was scared of getting hurt, some shit like that, the way she put it. It didn't make sense till now but . . . . And I was still there, hold no grudges, nothing like that. I always had abandonment issues and shit like that and you [Mom] didn't give a fuck. You do the same shit again so it's cool, I won't. I was there for her. None of my family want shit to do with her none.

Family support for the men who were in recovery operated somewhat differently because the men living in recovery or sober houses were less financially dependent on family members. The organizations running these houses typically helped them complete the paperwork to qualify for food stamps and Social Security benefits, which the agency then took a share of to pay for food and rent. Ironically, these men were often the biggest earners in the sample, doing off-the-books trades work. Some of their family relationships had been strained or outright broken because of the lying and manipulation that so often goes along with addiction, but the men did not need to engage with their families of origin on a regular basis because they were living independently. Moreover, following twelve-step principles, these men were discouraged from forming romantic relationships during the first year of their sobriety.

So far, I have shown that men were often entangled financially with their families of origin, leading them to continue to engage emotionally with their damaging pasts. In the next section I examine their romantic relationships, with a particular focus on what they looked for in a partner and what they thought they could offer in such a partnership.

ROMANTIC RELATIONSHIPS

One-third (seventeen) of the Frankford men reported being in a serious long-term romantic relationship. Of those, only one-quarter (four) were legally married. This low rate of marriage is likely related to their marginal economic position, which decreases their marriageability.[6] Relatedly, it was common for the men to report that they did not feel like adults yet because they could not take care of themselves or others.

Views and Experiences of Marriage

In stark contrast to the chaotic, drama-filled romantic relationships I described among emerging adults (ages 17–23) in *Falling Back*, the romantic relationships described by members of this more mature sample were much more stable and more likely to be characterized by trust, support, and a genuine sense of partnership. Angel, a 33-year-old Latino man who had been married to his partner for five years, explained how being married was different from just being together:

> I was in a relationship—a real, live-in relationship before—and it is night and day. I have a commitment to my wife that I did not have to the previous young lady. And my ex was great, she was a dope girlfriend but she wasn't a wife. [In my marriage], I can't just leave, I have this commitment. I can't leave if we have a problem; we have to sit there and talk about it. If there's some sort of animosity we have to give each other room, but that room can't be outside, it has to be inside. Go and hang out in the living room, I'll sit in the kitchen, when we're ready to talk we'll talk, we'll hash it out, but that's how it's different. There's some serious strings attached to being married. And even though people like to think there is and people like to act like there is, there's really no strings attached when you're not married.

Kurt (31, biracial), also married, answered the same question by saying, "It's accepting problems and not using problems as demerits." As a follow-up, we asked if marriage was consistent with his definition of masculinity and adulthood. He said:

> Definitely more in tune to that. There's the urge of standard pride, conventional stability to have all of the wholesome things that you're supposed to have in life. You earn them honestly, you make a living to get them. 'Cause

what you want is happy, peaceful, and when you come to fight, you fight together, but not at each other. Our arguments are like an assignment 'cause when you are single, you only have each other to hurt. But if there's some hurt in a pact [partnership], the hurt brings everything down so there's only that to build up.

Kurt identified marriage as part of a "respectability package" that signaled stability and "wholesome things" to himself and to others.[7] Being "in a pact" like marriage meant that even in bad times, he was still growing and building a future. This conviction very likely helped him to manage the difficulties that he experienced living with Asperger's syndrome.[8] It is also worth considering that he considered resolving conflicts with his wife "an assignment," or a form of care work.

Similarly, Luke (32, White) discussed the work involved in maintaining a marriage:

You [gotta] keep that jawn [in this case, marriage] shining.[9] If you don't polish something it's going to get dull so like if you stop putting in work, like even the dumb shit, whatever something someone might consider trivial, doin' the dishes. Some of my bulls [male friends] be like, "well I don't wash dishes," like, if you live by yourself you have to wash dishes you fucking idiot, like what do you mean you don't wash dishes? I'm not saying you gotta be Fonzworth Bentley and do all the chores, but the fuck?[10] It's a whole situation—give and take.

Approximately half of the men reported that they anticipated being married in the future, suggesting that the institution of marriage is still relevant and meaningful to them. Many referred to very serious partners as fiancées, whether or not they were formally engaged. This may have been to signal to their partners and to outsiders (including competitors) that the relationship was more than just a fling. As a rule, marriage was considered a very serious commitment. Kareem (26, Black-Asian), who lived with his steady, long-term girlfriend, summed up this sentiment when he said, "You gotta be real ready, real committed." Similarly, Chase (27, White) told us: "I mean I think it can be a good thing like if the circumstances are right and both people are committed. Like I think it can be a beautiful thing, I'm not against it necessarily, you know, I don't know. It' something I've never seen work out. My folks aren't married, they actually never were, they were together for a while, a long time, but they were never married. I know as a kid I never saw good examples of marriage that worked out. It's kind of rare, but I think it does exist for some people." As this equivocal statement suggests, many men struggled to imagine a healthy marriage because their own parents had conflict-ridden relationships, and they had seen few models of working marriages as they grew up. Nick (33, White) was not in a romantic relationship. He was looking for someone who was a caring kind of person—genuinely caring, not just a front. He liked romance, which made him feel good. When asked, "Do you plan on getting married one day?" he responded, "Please no. Anyone might joke around like that after seeing what their parents went through and you don't want to follow in those footsteps. Nowadays most marriages do not last over the long haul; the statistics on tv show that they don't."

Isaac (37, biracial) told us that he and his long-term girlfriend regularly talked about marriage and had even considered buying her a ring. His reluctance to take that step reveals an internal struggle about the gravity and permanence of marriage:

I: What's the hesitation about actually getting [the ring]?

R: I don't know! I never trusted nobody enough. Once that ring is on that finger it's a wrap, like it's no room for error, no mistakes, no "oh I was drunk that night that's why this happened," none of them stories.

I: You're more accountable.

R: Yeah.

I: And you don't think you can hold yourself accountable?

R: Oh no no, I know I can! I don't know what's stopping me now though, honestly.

I: What are your general impressions of marriage?

R: They always been strong, I guess 'cause seeing my parents together the whole time. So that's why I always said I have to make sure everything is out of my system before I make that step [chuckles] cause once I make that commitment it's like I'm gonna go by the vows.

What Isaac didn't say here is telling. Earlier in the interview, he described experiencing serious downward mobility as a result of incarceration and a felony record. At the time we interviewed him he was selling plasma to survive. He may very well have known that he could not yet be a good financial partner to his girlfriend.

Economic (In)stability in Romantic Relationships

Romantic partners were a less common source of economic support than families of origin, but many men considered sharing resources with them more consistent with their definitions of adult masculinity. The financial arrangements in romantic relationships were typically more evenly matched in meeting economic exigencies, although a significant number of men we interviewed were wrestling with earning less than their partners or being unemployed while their partner was working.

It was common, although not universal, for men to talk about romantic partnership in terms of benefiting from shared financial risks and responsibilities. This is a departure from sociologist Jennifer Silva's findings, which emphasize more individualistic approaches to risk among working-class youth.[11] Members of her sample were likely to see the formation of romantic partnerships as a threat to stability, rather than a route to create it. I argue that this view is likely to shift as individuals age and they recognize that "going it alone" is neither emotionally satisfying nor a cost-efficient way to manage expenses in contemporary households.[12]

For example, Kurt analogized his marriage to property ownership: "I'm tired of test driving. I possibly want to own my own vehicle. 'Own' not by way of possession or control, but just how can we get the most value? There is nothing that is not mine that is not hers. It builds a conservative financial outlook." Similarly, Luke talked about having a team mentality: "She hasn't always had this sweet job at 7–11 but we were always going to make it regardless. Even if it's just treading water, like I refuse to drown, especially if she on my back."

Some noted that renting an apartment was nearly impossible on their own in today's housing and employment market. For example, Yusef, the 28-year-old Black desister featured in chapter three told us, "It takes two. I don't know one person who can just take care of the household, especially in this economy. If they do, they gotta be making a lot of money in order to survive."

Not everyone agreed that sharing risk was best. Many were either delaying marriage until their financial situations were better or viewed romantic partnerships as too economically risky.[13] Randall (27, White), for example, referred to marriage as "a headache." "You have to be committed and you have to split everything," which he worried would lead to arguments. He formed this impression by watching his own parents, although he said he would like to be married eventually. It is also likely that Randall, who had a history of incarceration and homelessness and was in recovery when we talked with him, was not a very attractive partner, leading him to reject an institution from which he had been excluded.

Some separated the contractual aspect of marriage from the emotional value of committed, intimate relationships. Alex (35, Latino), who told us that he didn't believe in marriage because it was "for White people," wondered why a "piece of paper" was needed to establish marriage. "If I want to leave, I have to get a whole divorce, and then I pay! No, no, that's stupidity." Later in our interview, Alex revealed some details that helped us understand his reticence to formalize a romantic relationship through an economic partnership. Although he spoke here in generalities, it appears that he had suffered a past indignity in a relationship with a woman who earned more than he did. After telling us that he didn't believe in female breadwinners, he added, "That's what's going on anyway." "Well now in society there actually is women making more than men now too, so it is what it is, you gotta adapt to the situation. But you'll never hear the end of the story with the woman making more, 'cause all they do is talk shit. 'I do this, I do that! You don't do anything.'"

This feeling of imbalance arose even when romantic partners were not yet working as an economic unit. For example, David (26, Black), who lived at home with his parents, reported feeling discontented with his intimate relationship because he wasn't working and couldn't contribute. "My pride is hurt because she's currently working and I'm unemployed. When we go out, she'll pay for everything, which makes me feel uncomfortable and emasculated. It's not about having more money. What bothers me is the discrepancy between having no money and having some money."

Most of the Frankford men agreed that they wanted to be economic partners with their spouses or romantic partners. Wesley (26, Black-Latino) summed this up with an apt analogy when we asked if it was okay for a romantic partner to be the breadwinner: "Let's both make some bread so we can make a whole sandwich!" A small number of men shared this sentiment, but most felt like Andre (32, Black), who told us, "A lot of people do that and it's a mistake. You won't want to have your significant other paying for everything. It's just a rule, you're a man, you have to be a man at the end of the day. Even though we love each other, if we're together and I'm down [unemployed] at the time, I wouldn't just sit there, I would be working on getting a job."

Nasir (34, Black), who was not at the time employed or in a romantic relationship, emphasized:

> That first thing there is bad to me—to have a woman taking care of you, unless it's Oprah, if it's Oprah, oh alright I'm gonna wash these dishes but if not, come on man. She could always be the breadwinner, but the *primary* breadwinner? No, she could even be the primary because . . . hell, I could be a bus driver, she could be a heart surgeon, but my thing is, I'm gonna have to be the best bus driver, I'm not just gonna be home doin' nothing. Now she can make more money than me, but don't be a bum just 'cause your wife [works], you know? Because why just sit on your butt when you could do something? Even if she got that money, you could get online and then come up with a business idea, something, just don't be a bum.

Here we hear echoes of the stigmatizing labels applied to men who don't work, who are often known as "bums." We also see men's struggle to affirm the dignity of work, even if their income is less than their partner's. It is interesting to note Nasir's belief that the gig economy ("get online") offered unlimited opportunities for entrepreneurship for those who were willing to put in the work. This belief that self-employment was the ideal situation for managing a low-paid and unstable labor market was pervasive.

Yusef told us that "a real man isn't going to let his woman do everything. . . .You have some men who's okay with that and you have some women who's okay with them not having a job or helping them. The woman I got, she's not tolerating it. I gotta have a job—at least I done did the steps to get my certification." The reader may remember that, in the opening to chapter 3, Yusef credited his mother, sisters, and girlfriend as the sources of informal social control that inspired his commitment to desistance from offending.

Later, I develop a case study of Marvin (24, Black), a stay-at-home father and primary caregiver for the household. Although only two of the men defined themselves this way, their stories are instructive for understanding the identity work needed to maintain a sense of masculine dignity while occupying a traditionally feminine domestic role. Grant (27, Black), the other stay-at-home father, described a loving partnership with his girlfriend and said that he made sure that his wife and daughter were "put together before I am. I can't have you going outside and representing me looking 'hit.' No, get your nails and your hair done, whatever y'all do, eyebrows, legs, I don't know anything about that. I'll pay for her to get everything done."[14] For him, the visible signs of being "pampered" were signals to outsiders of the financial sacrifices he made by running the home and were a source of masculine pride.

Frankford men are more likely than their younger (emerging adult) counterparts to have stable romantic partnerships; they value the institution of marriage, whether or not they can imagine themselves getting married one day, and the frequent imbalance of economic contributions to a romantic partnership creates challenges for their construction of adult masculine identity. Next I introduce Marvin, whose practice of caring masculinity had "the potential to change men and gender" but did not go unchallenged by his fiancée and male friends.[15]

CASE STUDY: UNPAID DOMESTIC WORK AND MASCULINITY

Marvin, a 24-year-old Black stay-at-home father and homemaker, shared an apartment with his fiancée and girlfriend of six years and their four-year-old daughter. Marvin moved to Frankford from North Philadelphia when he was 10 and lived in the Whitehall public housing project. Like Grant, he had cared for others his whole life, starting with babysitting jobs when he was 10 years old. "I was the same age as his [uncle's] oldest son, but I'm watching him. It was weird." Without a high school diploma, he had struggled to find adult employment at a living wage. "I tried to get a job at McDonald's and even they wouldn't hire me," he said, shaking his head. To contribute to the household, he did tattooing and haircutting, estimating that he brought in $400–$500 per month. He was actively searching for work, he said, and had started the process of qualifying to become a home health aide for his grandfather.

He had met his fiancée at age 18 and described the experience as "love at first sight." "She changed my life. Ever since I met her, I started slowing down with life, stopped partying all crazy, worrying about [other] females. She really opened my head up to the world and what being a real man means." Deseree, 25, worked full time as a dietician at a local university. Marvin oriented his day's activities around her work schedule. "I wish I had a job to wake up to," he said.

On a typical day, he woke up and cleaned the whole house, prepared meals, took his daughter to Head Start, did a tattoo or cut hair in his "man cave" in the basement, did online job searching, and cleaned again (he laughed and explained that he had OCD). "I like to take the stress off my lady's back so she doesn't have to do too much after coming home from work. I try to take care of everything at the house." "My mom taught me when I was younger—she raised three boys by herself—if you can't do nothing for your family, at least clean up, keep the household good, make sure you're still showing that you care about certain things . . . at least try."

Marvin and Deseree didn't plan to have a child together, but when their daughter "popped up," they assumed it was God's will and considered her a "miracle baby." He described his daughter as highly intelligent and their relationship as "great." "Fatherhood is a responsibility. It's a job. You gotta make sure you're there for everything; wouldn't want to miss a second. You gotta teach them, you gotta really push it in their head cause they can get brainwashed easily from the streets and TV, government, what have you. . . . Don't try to have too much of a friendly bond, but have it enough so they know they can come to you about anything." In fact, Marvin made regular bids to convince Deseree, his parents, and his male friends that care work was "a job," that cooking, cleaning, and childcare contributed to the household in the same way that Deseree's paycheck did. "Sometimes I want to forget about even looking for a job because I want to feel appreciated for who I am and not just the money," he told us. For decades, feminist activists and scholars have been making the same argument about the value and complexity of care work, which is typically done by women.[16] Making the case that he was working when he cared for the house and for their child, however, was complicated by traditional gender roles and masculine norms that view housework and child rearing as women's work. Although stay-at-home fatherhood is becoming more common in the wake of the Great Recession, stay-at-home dads must construct an alternative definition of masculinity or find themselves subject to ridicule and derision by others.[17] Marvin did both. When we asked him what makes a "real man," he said, "taking care of your family," and pointed to plenty of other fathers he knew who might have been working but weren't putting their "ladies" and children first.

He took a fair amount of heat from those in his social circle about not working outside the home. Men without jobs, he protested,

> get down talked a lot, especially if you have a female who's taking care of everything. That's the biggest problem with me. People feel as though if the lady has the job and the man is not working then he's really not doing anything with his life. But the thing is, it's not that he's not *doing* anything with his life, it's that he can't *get* anything with his life. . . . I try not to listen to it. But the judgement gets to me, 'cause it kind of hurts to hear somebody thinking that and it causes disruptions in relationships. The female may hear it and may start to believe it after so long with the man not being able to do something.

Marvin believed that it was acceptable for a woman to be the breadwinner in their relationship:

> The woman may not think it; she may come down on you like "you ain't doing nothing." But I was actually the one who sat back and let her get her life together, let her go to school and get a job first while I sat back and watched the child. I didn't put her in daycare or nothing; I stayed down and watched her every day. I view this as a sacrifice for my fiancée to better herself. I didn't want it to be "you ain't doing nothing with your life." It shouldn't be that. It should be seen as you're lucky to have a man who would take care of the child while you're doing what you're doing. A lot of men don't take care of their child at all and it's the single mother who has to take care of the child.

It seems clear that Marvin's efforts were not always appreciated by Deseree. Moreover, our interviewer had a conversation later with Marvin's former landlord, who had referred him for our study and to whom he still owed money (our gift card went to the landlord). He told her Marvin was "lazy and doesn't have a job and just lets his girlfriend pay for everything. All he does it sit around and play video games. He's lazy and has bad morals." From Marvin's perspective, however, he was staying home with the baby so that his fiancée could go to school and earn her degree to get full-time employment. Pained by these judgments, Marvin sometimes isolated himself, saying he "doesn't like to go outside." This, according to Scott Melzer, is a common strategy for men dealing with the stigma and shame of failing to live up to hegemonic norms of masculinity.[18]

FATHERHOOD

Half (twenty-three) of the men we interviewed were biological fathers, and a handful reported being social fathers to their partners' children.[19] Six were custodial fathers who lived, usually full-time, with their children. Of all the durable social ties discussed here, fatherhood was most often described by men in terms of warm, loving relationships that were affirming, and often "turning points" in their life trajectories. As we will see, fatherhood was a strong source of positive masculine, adult identities. Men measured their own success as fathers in terms of being more present than their own fathers had been or of providing better childhoods than their own.[20] Importantly, this was typically a low bar to surpass, and therefore fatherhood was a critical component of positive identity. As treated in depth in chapter 5, generativity, or giving back to the next generation, was a key tool to overcoming the stigma associated with poverty, unemployment, and scrutiny by agents of the CLS. The men found their relationships with children emotionally fulfilling and said that their children had taught them the meaning of unconditional love.

Grant, the other stay-at-home father, told us: "Fatherhood means everything to me, being able to support them financially, being able to be there. Sometimes it doesn't always have to be about material [things]; it's just about the time. 'Cause I know when I was a child that's all I ever wanted. I don't want your money." As a stay-at-home father, Grant was engaged in round-the-clock care work, which is traditionally carried out by women. He woke his kids up in the morning and fed them, before dropping them off and picking them up from school. This was familiar territory for him, since he had cared for his siblings as a child, starting at age five. His mother had worked two jobs and relied on him to be the adult in the household, leading to his frequently missing school. He took great pride in care work, which he recognized as labor because he actually did it on a daily basis. When we asked him about his favorite work experience, he said:

> My most positive work experience to date was being a father—full time. It's my favorite job. *I'm showing him* [the older son] *how to become a better man.* My kids are showing me how to present myself better. . . . [They] have put apps on my phone that include math quizzes and problems. They'll tell me things like I'm supposed to know it they'll say "Dad, don't you know that right there is a Dodge Millennium. It came out in 2012. The reason it came out is . . . ." They break it down to me; I just sits and listens. They're my best friends, they're my sons. *Sometimes I think they're the grown-ups.* They'll say "Dad, when you see someone you gotta shake their hand, you can't just say 'whatsup' and keep walking." They're just grown men trapped inside of a baby's body. They're my heart and my best friends.

To these men, being a father is a way of achieving and expressing masculinity and adulthood. Grant taught his sons how to be men, and in return, they taught him how to be an adult. Significantly, he mentioned fatherhood as a form of work, albeit as unusually fulfilling one. In this way, he turned full-time fatherhood into a caring, adult masculine identity. Like Marvin, he wanted his labor to be counted and appreciated as a real contribution to the family unit.

In a world where the Frankford men are so often held in low esteem and don't measure up to others' expectations, children are an important source of nonjudgmental interactions. For fathers such as Angel (33, Latino), who was racially profiled in school and on the street and told that he would never amount to anything, his son was a source of pride, including pride in his heritage: "Aw, man, yeah, he's my son [laughs]. . . . I read to him every night, we go to Amalgam and read comic books. I make sure that he's culturally aware of who he is. We went to his first Puerto Rican parade this year in Philly and he was decked out. He made me buy him a little Puerto Rico hat, a little fedora, he had the beads on, he had a little flag, he learned the chants."

Men also saw becoming a father as a "turning point" in their life trajectories, leading to a focus on others instead of the self, and to conformity, including desistance from crime.[21] Brady (33, White), a father of two, said: "The first time I felt like an adult was at 21 years old when I had my daughter. You never know when you're a real adult; I feel like a kid sometimes still. I feel like I could do more, be more responsible. Without my daughters I would probably be in a worse place, selling drugs maybe. My daughters made me grow up. A real man provides for his family, keeps a roof over their head, make sure the family has what they need." It is interesting to note that Brady's arrest record suggests that he was still selling drugs, albeit to support his kids. Critical criminologist Abbie Henson refers to this as "hurdling," or overcoming structural barriers to earnings and employment by turning to street crime.[22] Although a deficit perspective would focus on these men as "persisters" in crime, Henson's strengths-based lens focuses on the resilience of Black fathers who do what is necessary to support their families in the context of systemic exclusion and discrimination.

Fatherhood was also an avenue to hope for the future and redemption for past behavior or choices. Christian, a 26-year-old Black noncustodial father, told us: "I think I'm like my daughter's hero a little bit."

> I: How do you want her childhood to be different from yours?
>
> CHRISTIAN: I want her to be more active, I want her to be more involved in certain things so she doesn't feel uncomfortable to be involved when she gets older. . . . So being more active, whether it's cheerleading or like the peace rallies or just anything she may want to do that summer, whether it's karate or soccer, anything like that, just feeding her exploration that she wants to do. 'Cause I feel as though that makes people not want to dream anymore, I feel as though when they're told "you can't do that, you're never going to be that so you can't do this." So a lot of people are told this and they stop trying to achieve for things.

Although fatherhood was a positive source of masculinity and adulthood for many of the men we interviewed, the other side of the coin was the negative self-assessments held by men who were not meeting their own standards of good fatherhood. For these men, fatherhood became another source of shameful failure. Some men reported being without a roadmap because they had no positive examples of fathers in their lives. Dennis, a 33-year-old Latino man, had a daughter with cerebral palsy. He told us that he was closer to her than anyone else in his life, but he didn't really know what it meant to be a father:

> I don't know what fatherhood means to me. I don't know what fatherhood is. I don't have any examples of . . .or I guess I see fathers on TV. I see my

uncle's a father. I see my grandfather is [a] father, but I don't know, I guess . . . I don't know. I just know what I want to be and what I'm trying to be, which is obviously a mentor, a guide, which I guess, which would be the answer, which is a mentor, a guide and just there. Just what I didn't have, someone to actually help you when . . . and show you the right . . . show you the right path and the right things.

Vincent (30, Black) talked about how his homelessness and criminal activity affected his ability to be a good father. The interviewer asked, "Do your children know what you do?" He nodded. "What do you tell them?"

Your daddy a drug dealer, your daddy homeless sometimes, your daddy be selling women sometimes, your daddy be smoking weed all the time, your dad works sometimes, they know what its hitting for with me. Your dad a gangbanger, your dad will kill somebody, your dad has killed somebody, your dad did a lot of fucked up shit. . . . Aright, as long as you continue to love me I don't give a fuck, it is what it is. But it affects me because it breaks me down and makes me think like, damn, am I actually doing the right thing? Am I actually being somebody that's positive for them? Am I actually conducting myself like a father? What am I doing?

Vincent, like other men we interviewed, worried that he posed a risk to his family members, especially children. Investing in these relationships was emotionally risky for these men because the chances of not meeting others' expectations were real.

CONCLUSION

Durable social ties with families of origin, romantic partners, and children are critical sources of positive masculine identity and human dignity when those are denied in other aspects of daily life. The Frankford men, who were marginal to the labor market, were bonded to their families of origin and romantic partners through economic interdependence. Most recognized that economic survival was not possible if they went it alone, but also worried about bringing their families down, being a financial drain, or having a negative influence on their children. Their qualms about committing to these relationships were often grounded in what criminologists Paternoster and Bushway call the "feared self," anxiety about what they might become.[23] Many stigmatic labels and low expectations have been leveled at these men: unemployed "bums," recovering "addicts," criminals, and drains on society.

Men who recognize the limits of their economic contributions to family members often reinvent their definitions of masculinity and try to reorient others' expectations by adopting "caring masculinities."[24] Through the daily practice of caring for others and appeals for them to see their invisible labor, men challenge hegemonic gender norms and work to redefine them in terms of what they can realistically provide. This was more necessary for the men of color than the White men in the sample because they were more likely to be permanently excluded from the labor market or relegated to low-wage, unstable work. Moreover, the White men were more likely to have formal recovery supports. Some scholars, however, argue that Black men in particular draw upon cultural frames of interdependence and egalitarianism that go back generations and were even noted in W. E. B. DuBois's work.[25]

The COVID-19 pandemic has revived earlier concerns about the critical role of connectedness for individual and community-level health outcomes.[26] Former US surgeon general Vivek Murthy names loneliness as a serious public health problem that is a driving force behind "deaths of despair," or early deaths resulting from suicide, addiction and overdose, and alcoholic liver disease.[27] Millennials in particular have been identified as the "lonely generation" because of their unique experiences of isolation. One survey found that 22 percent of millennials reported having no friends.[28] Further, sociologists have found that this cohort views the formation of durable ties to be riskier than they are willing to tolerate.[29]

The advancement of neoliberal capitalism, including the shrinking of economic opportunities, disappearance of the publicly supported social safety net, and growth of the criminal legal apparatus, are critical mechanisms behind this isolationism. As noted in chapter 4, aggressive police presence paired with neighborhood gun violence drives men indoors and leads them to restrict their interactions and ties with others.[30] Prisons and jails separate family members, with significant negative effects on all parties, including a substantial marriage penalty for formerly incarcerated men.[31] In the absence of a social safety net, family and community members—mostly women, but also clergy—absorb the housing and other needs of men returning from incarceration.[32] In the book's conclusion, I take up some solutions, including reducing the footprint of the CLS by reframing public safety as stemming from communities rather than police and prisons and by creating social infrastructure designed to encourage community members to facilitate and support cohesion and solidarity.[33]

7 Meanings of Manhood and Adulthood

> There's a lot of adults who can go to work and provide but they're emotionally detached completely, they'll expect the wife—that's their job to cook dinner and clean the clothes and do the dishes and wait on them. . . . [What defines a real man is that he] goes to work every single day and then come home and listens to his wife and then helps do the dishes and clean up and then sits with his kids and does whatever they need. That's a real man, that's a hero.
>
> —Jason, 39, White, homeless (not employed or married)

This chapter examines subjective perceptions of manhood and adulthood. As critical components of identity, men's definitions of these constructs tell us something about how they view themselves and their current positions within their life histories and future trajectories. Because of their limited educational and economic achievement and the profound effects of the CLS on their lives, most of the Frankford men have encountered numerous barriers to reaching the visible, widely accepted markers of adulthood and manhood. Unlike their more privileged millennial counterparts who are granted the permission to muddle their way through their early twenties in a state of suspended or emerging adulthood, these more vulnerable men may never expect, or be expected, to have steady jobs, educational credentials, independent households, or marriages.[1] How then, do they formulate a social identity that reconciles their economically vulnerable positions vis-à-vis mature, masculine roles with the social expectations associated with their chronological stage in life? How do they frame the unique and positive qualities they can offer in the marketplace of durable ties discussed in chapter 6?

In addition to using masculinity and the related but distinct idea of adulthood as a lens to examine social identity formation, we draw upon men's narratives of masculinity construction to complement a wider picture of generational changes in "doing gender."[2] When we define gender scripts (e.g., the "working man," the "sensitive man," the "criminal black man") as cultural artifacts of a time period with a particular structural configuration, studying the work of being a "real man" today reveals seismic shifts in the availability of scripts that may be liberating or profoundly alienating for men (and for women). Conflicts over what constitutes masculine behavior highlight shifting cultural fault lines where the battle to define gender is currently playing out.

This chapter explores the following questions: (1) What are the narrative threads making up the Frankford men's masculinity claims? (2) Are there meaningful patterns or variations in how men define "a real man," and if so, what does that tell us about the structural viability of masculinity claims? The Frankford men viewed adulthood and masculinity as different, with adulthood coming naturally with age and masculinity as more elusive because it could not be achieved in the most socially conventional ways. Moreover, they often saw adulthood as defined by taking care of oneself, or not being dependent or a drain upon others, whereas masculinity was characterized as achieved through actions (not beliefs or mere claims) and an ability to care for others. In that way, adulthood was an inward-facing stage of life, whereas manhood was outward-facing. This points to another salient role of social ties and interactions, which are needed for men to have their gender performances validated by members of their social circles.[3]

The Frankford men described characteristics of a "real man," as distinct from a person who is merely male, and framed manhood in ways that were achievable, namely caring for or taking care of others.[4] Moreover, they often defined masculinity in terms of what men were *not* as they constructed gendered moral boundaries to demonstrate that they were virtuous and had avoided the worst predictions of absentee father, unemployed "bum," or violent "superpredator."

Millennials coined the term *adulting* to highlight the effortful nature of tasks and responsibilities associated with adulthood. Whereas members of earlier generations faced firmer normative expectations for the timing and ordering of key life events, such as the start of a career, marriage, and parenthood, today's young adults take longer to attain these milestones, if they do at all, and may even find some of them completely "irrelevant."[5] They may string these events together outside of what used to be the normative order—for example, having children before getting married—in case the other pieces never fall into place.[6] The drivers of this extension and reordering of adult roles are greater economic insecurity and risks that millennials must navigate in the postindustrial labor market and the expanding criminal legal apparatus.

Feminist theory provides a useful framework for understanding how men construct masculinities. Instead of conceiving of gender as an attribute that one possesses, contemporary scholarship points to its dynamic and active construction and has argued that it should be thought of as a set of practices that are performed within the boundaries of particular social relationships, for example in relation to male peers, romantic partners, or children.[7] In that regard, masculinity can be flexible and adaptive to changing circumstances but is also fragile because it requires constant effort to maintain. Men work to accomplish masculinity through "manhood acts," or attempts to present oneself in ways that comport with cultural expectations of men and which, although they may vary, are "all aimed at claiming privilege, eliciting deference, and resisting exploitation."[8]

Hegemonic masculinity, the most culturally valued form of masculinity, operates as an anchor point by defining a narrow ideal of a powerful, dominant man who controls his environment. Subordinated or marginalized masculinities are situated in relation to the hegemonic ideal, even though few men can attain it. Men with class or race privilege may practice *hybrid masculinities*, or selective incorporation of identity elements from marginalized groups such as Black men, gay men, or even women. When middle-class men, for example, buy expensive grooming products or get manicures, others may see them as practicing a progressive form of masculinity. The masculinities practiced by working-class or Black men, by contrast, are often positioned as retrograde. Nevertheless, most research suggests that rather than transforming the existing gender (racial and cis-heteronormative) order, these manhood acts obscure them by creating symbolic distance from the hegemonic or toxic archetype.[9] Men who are marginalized by social class or race likely need to fight harder to get alternative definitions of masculinity validated by others.

A lesser emphasized matter in the gender literature is the age-grading of masculinities, with boys' concerns subordinated to and trivialized by those of grown men (sometimes referred to as "grown ass men" for emphasis).[10] As I discussed in the chapter on desistance from crime, the boundaries between childish and adult activities were very often emphasized in discursive constructions of masculine narratives. So, while adulthood and manhood were viewed as distinct, the spectrum of definitions of manhood also ranged from juvenile to adult.[11]

It is important to acknowledge that these men were doing gender in their interviews, and their performances were likely not always consistent with their actions and interactions with others. We did hear, for example, of gender policing by the Frankford men's male peers that clearly drew on patriarchal tropes likening weak men to gay men or women (e.g., "pussies"). As gender scholars have argued, masculinity, particularly hegemonic masculinity, is generally performed for other men.[12] That most of these interviews were conducted by women requires us to imagine that the Frankford men were presenting a potentially different side of themselves than they would have in their male peer group. Nevertheless, even if we understand these claims as a performance, they reveal what men consider idealized masculine identities. Next, I examine the Frankford men's masculine narratives and how they viewed adulthood and masculinity as related or distinct.

DEFINING AND CONSTRUCTING
MASCULINE ADULT IDENTITIES

In trying to tap into the process of identity construction and subjective perceptions of adulthood and masculinity, we asked the Frankford men to tell us how old they were when they first felt like an adult and how they knew that someone was a real adult. Then we asked how they identified "real men," whether this was the same as or different from being a real adult, and whether and why they felt like men.[13]

The Frankford men viewed the achievement of adulthood and masculinity as separate processes, whereby the former happens more or less naturally with age and the latter involves more effort and may ultimately be elusive. In short, they may have felt like adults for many years but reported that they had only recently begun to—or did not yet—feel like "a real man." This distinction between adulthood and manhood was especially marked for those who reported precocious adulthood, or the taking on of adult roles during their teen years. Moreover, they tended to hold the view that once adulthood had been attained, it was a permanent state, while masculinity was something that needed to be accomplished with consistency and was a status that could be lost.[14] Manhood, they explained, is effortful, moral, and emotional, requiring daily enactment. Moreover, masculinity is very often defined as doing for or caring for others, whereby adulthood is more about taking care of oneself.[15]

Hector, a 34-year-old White Latino man who was both returning from incarceration and in substance abuse recovery, provided a distinction between adulthood and masculinity that was shared by many others. "I felt like an adult very early," at age 16. "When I moved into my own place I felt like an adult." We asked, "What makes someone a real adult?" Hector responded, "Being responsible and working and paying their own bills and having their own place." When we asked, "What about a real man?" he replied: "Somebody who takes care of their family and is there for his family." Hector defined adulthood as independence and financial self-sufficiency, not relying on family members or romantic partners. In contrast, a real man takes care of others as well as himself. Interestingly, Hector did not have children of his own, but he was in a long-term relationship with his girlfriend, whom he treated very lovingly on the phone during a break in his interview. His definition of family was based on his family of origin, his romantic partner, and looking forward to having children as part of how he viewed his potential for future success.

Grant, a Black stay-at-home dad, made a similar distinction:

There's a lot different between a real man and a real adult. A real man knows his place and knows his responsibilities. Being a real adult doesn't make you a man. You're a real adult when it starts hitting you that you have to pay rent and bills and electric and gas and all that and you can't call out for help and you have to spend that bread [money] and you have responsibilities. *You can't be a grown-ass man if you live with your mom and don't pay rent or bills.* When you got your own [children] and responsibilities that's when you're grown. [But] you're a real man when you stop putting yourself first and start focusing on everything else.

Nasir, a 34-year-old Black father, agreed: "A real man is a different type of thing 'cause everybody is an adult, you're really an adult when you hit a certain age, but a man, you got 40 year-old boys." Someone becomes a real man "when he's taking care of others, I ain't just going to say his family, but when he actually providing for others." Nasir took great pride in spending time with and providing for his children, such as watching movies with his son or buying his daughter a school uniform.

Alex, a 35-year-old Latino man who had left his criminal career behind when he formed a family but was also prepared to commit violence to protect them, pointed out that manhood entails action: "Anybody can say they're a man but what are you doing to be a man? . . . Everybody say they're a father, [but] no, you're a father every day, not just one day, no, you don't get to pick and choose when you're a father." He maintained that fatherhood was a primary means of defining manhood, but also argued that being a "real man" was a status that was earned every day by actually "doing" fatherhood and thereby masculinity. Here, Alex constructed a moral boundary around consistency of fathering activities and indirectly called out men whose fathering was merely a posture they put on for show.

As scholars of gender commonly argue, masculinity is often accomplished through boundary construction.[16] That is, manhood is often as much about what men *are not* doing as what they *are* doing, and very often men's own fathers are the negative reference point used to construct their own masculinity. For example, Anthony, a 26-year-old White man, told us: "A real man doesn't hit a woman and puts food on the table and has a kid and doesn't leave the child or wife and plays with his family. . . . A person who isn't a real man is someone who runs out on their family." Here, he was referring to his own father's absence during his childhood, leaving him to be raised in a household filled with women. Fathers were absent for a host of reasons, including infidelity, substance abuse, death, or incarceration, leaving the Frankford men with some lessons in the kind of fathers and men they wished to avoid becoming.

Several of the men commented that men's roles were changing and that the hegemonic, hypermasculine version of masculinity was outmoded. This was most visible in their reactions to the masculinity checklist we presented during the interview, which contained several stereotypical definitions of manhood.[17] Many objected to the checklist and commented that the items were silly, particularly "having many sexual partners" or "being successful with women" (which is also heteronormative). Importantly, Black and Latino men, who are stereotyped in this way, were more likely than the White men we interviewed to object more vociferously to these items.

Miles, a 33-year-old Black college graduate, defined a real man as "someone who's there for the people that he loves, he cares about." He suggested that this item be added to the masculinity checklist. Yusef, the grill chef who credited the women in his life for his desistance, said, "A real man will never see his family go starving." His emphasis on "providing for" was distinct from caring for or "being there."[18] Although most of the Frankford men described masculinity as achieved through these softer or more affective means, some relied on the more traditional masculine ideals of financially providing for others.

Similarly, many were skeptical of hypothetical men who defined themselves as a "real man," pointing out the problems with what is popularly known as toxic masculinity.[19] They referenced hypermasculine men they knew who, in their opinion, were not real men because they weren't taking care of their responsibilities as engaged fathers and performing other types of caretaking. Some told us that when a man says he's a "real man," it's often a pose to obscure the fact that his actions are inconsistent with the more effortful vision of masculinity.

Malcom, a Black 31-year-old AIDS outreach worker, demonstrated this distrust toward anyone who presented himself as a "real man." "I would say a real man is different from being an adult. Because a real man, even though they say they are a real man, they are still doing little boy stuff. So, you think if you're calling yourself a real man you aren't doing the stuff you need to? Right." Interestingly, Malcolm was one of the few respondents who saw adulthood in more active and challenging terms than manhood: "Taking care of responsibilities. Paying bills on time or taking care of your family and making sure their needs are met before yours." As a gay man, however, he had likely experienced the problematic application of the "real man" label and saw the disjuncture between the facade of manhood and the enactment of adult roles and responsibilities.

Many others, however, seemed to welcome the freedom offered by alternative definitions of masculinity that are not as constricting as those used in the past. David, the 26-year-old pastor's son, believed that there are more definitions of being a man today than there used to be: "Being a man used to be having a chin up, 'don't cry,' but it's been stripped down now to being honorable, honest, and strong, not with your chest out, but being there for the people you care about and love. Being a man is being a present father. There are just a few common things to be a man—it's not about how you dress or look anymore, it's more about character now." David's notion of masculinity was likely shaped by his history of being perceived by others as effeminate or gay (although he did not identify as such) and as a nerdy "weakling" who was interested in becoming a graphic artist. As he got older, he found a small group of friends who shared his interests in comic books and other creative pursuits.

Angel, the 33-year-old Latino family man who reported experiencing extensive racial harassment in school, emphasized the affective aspect of masculinity. He defined a real man as "someone who takes responsibility for the things he has done, takes responsibility for his immediate family as far as his children and his wife. Someone who is willing to be vulnerable and willing to be humble enough to accept when he's wrong and not be afraid to ask for help, cause a lot of times men are like 'I'm a man I don't need anybody's help'. *Men need help and we need to be able to express that.*" Angel had been in a well-known gang during his teen years and was likely referencing both some of the harmful actions he had engaged in as part of that group, as well as the masculine norms generated in and enforced by the gang.[20]

When I did a follow-up interview with Angel during the pandemic lockdown, I asked again about his ideas of masculinity. He responded:

If you had asked me that question ten years ago, I would have given you a very maschista type of answer.[21] I think it's maturity. . . . Because when you're younger, you look up to the men that you know and you're like that's what you're supposed to be. No matter how bad at being a man they were. *Those men might have thought being a man meant being in charge of everything. And that's not it.* As I get older, I no longer see being dependent on my wife for certain things as wrong, because she's stronger than I am in certain ways, and we complement each other in those ways.

Declan (33, White) also emphasized "the emotional support you can provide to people. I don't have a job or anything [laughs], but I can give good emotional support to someone." He suggested that be added to the masculinity checklist. Since Declan had a traumatic brain injury and was consequently unable to work, he implied that manhood should be defined in ways that are achievable, given the particular "masculinity challenges" a person encounters.[22] He had little to offer in the romantic marketplace because he could not be a provider, but he was a good listener.

Nick, a 33-year-old White man living with addiction, told us: "There are so many different versions of 'a real man.' For me, a real man is an honest person who does what he's supposed to do and takes care of his own responsibilities. . . . Once you meet a certain age, you're always going to be a real adult, but *being an actual real adult man is when there's details in it,*" when it is demonstrated in action. "What you do in your daily life, things you say, what you represent, your beliefs, how you speak. I believe" a real man is "an honest person and a responsible person and takes care of himself."

So far, I have established that (1) men define masculinity and adulthood as different from one another; (2) most view masculinity as more effortful to achieve because it requires daily enactment of masculine roles and duties; and (3) the marginalized men we interviewed have found some freedom in adopting divergent definitions of masculinity, such as expressing their emotions or providing affective support for loved ones. Another thread from these definitions of manhood and adulthood involves the outward-facing nature of masculinity and the inward-facing nature of adulthood. In short, although there was variation, most of the Frankford men told us that adulthood was about taking care of oneself and manhood was about taking care of others. This was typically described as a progression in which adulthood came first and achieving the status of a "real man" came second, if it happened at all. It is important to note how common it is for these marginalized men to emphasize relational definitions of masculinity. This is likely related to their inability to achieve the more attainment-based definitions, such as having a good job.

BOUNDARY CONSTRUCTION IN MASCULINITY ACHIEVEMENT

Identity is very often cemented by drawing boundaries around those who are not successfully achieving a valued status, such as manhood. Sometimes men used themselves as negative examples, as did Cam (23, Black-Latino), who was a full-time drug seller and lived with his mother: "I don't feel like an adult right now. I'm not in the place I should be as a man right now. I should have my own spot, with my daughter, working full time, being a man. When I was 16, I was there, I was ahead of the game, I had a lot, but I messed up." Because Cam's sense of manhood was so precarious, he found himself needing to address masculinity challenges on a regular basis, which he did through physical violence. This brutal form of masculinity was also likely necessary to avoid appearing weak, which probably reduced his own chances of victimization.[23]

TJ, a 28-year-old White home health-care aide, pointed out that his roommates in a recovery house were not real men: 'Society tells you it's to be tough, pay the bills, etc. A real man to me is to help other people. There is a difference between being a real man and a real adult. I live with five other guys in a recovery house who are adults but not real men. They don't contribute, they're selfish. A real man is supportive and helpful." TJ told us that he had only felt like a real man within the last two months because he had started to help others through volunteer work and was "at least trying to be a real man now." Generative activities were a very common way that men accomplished a positive, masculine identity whether or not they were meeting the ideal of financial support.

Andre, a 32-year-old Black father, offered definitions of a real adult and a real man that he wasn't currently meeting: "You know someone's a real adult through pay stubs, wallets, and IDs. A real man is a working man, a steady job. There's no difference between being a real man and a real adult; they go hand in hand." This was a very different definition from that shared by most men in the sample, who instead of focusing on objective markers of manhood typically used more relational or affective definitions, which they were also more likely to be able to meet. Andre had not resolved this disjuncture and appeared quite sad as he discussed the moment when he was on the cusp of a big change in his life. "Back in 2011, I got $1,700 from taxes and I *thought I was the man.* I was going to change this, that, and a third, but I got locked up again and I had to pay the lawyer with all that money. You live and learn." Without a high school diploma, Andre was relegated to the secondary labor market. He also continued to have contact with the CLS; his last arrest, at age 33, was for retail theft, but he had also spent time incarcerated for selling weed and loose cigarettes.

Marvin, a 24-year-old stay-at-home father, created boundaries around active fatherhood, pointing out that some men who had children with different women take care of their younger, but not older, children. "You can be a real adult and not be a real man. You can look after everyone else's kids and you have your own child but you're not looking after your kid. . . . I know a couple of people like that who do not worry about their first children but worry about the next child. That's an adult, but you're not a man."[24] This pattern of taking responsibility for more recent children but not ones with earlier partners is analyzed by Kathryn Edin and Timothy Nelson in *Doing the Best I Can.* They argue that economically marginalized men, contrary to the "deadbeat dad" stereotype, earnestly want to be involved in their children's lives but face numerous financial and policy hurdles to doing so.

Men who grew up during the "superpredator" scare are encouraged through their interactions in the labor market and with the CLS to define themselves as a source of risk. The Frankford men distanced themselves from stigmatic, risky archetypes by claiming to be productive contributors to households or communities or morally good. They did this by constructing boundaries against unemployed "bums" and violent men, articulating cultural prescriptions and proscriptions about what adult men should be doing with their time. The first was used by marginally employed men of all races, but the second was only used by Black men, since the superpredator image specifically targeted this group.

Several men we interviewed articulated the gendered stigma of being unemployed. For example, Wesley, the 26-year-old veteran, who defined himself as unemployed even though his odd jobs made a substantial contribution to his household, told us that a man without a job was viewed as a "nobody" in his community. "In neighborhoods like this people tend to hold their heads high when they have a job; people respect individuals who work. People want to migrate towards you and help you when you have a job." This comment suggests that work creates social capital, just as social capital enables work.[25] Wesley was a military veteran, making his current economic situation a significant departure from the earnings and esteem he was used to.

Tucker, a 35-year-old Black transplant from the South, reported: "A lot of people don't care for men that don't got jobs. You ask some guy for a quarter, and they'll tell you, 'No, get a job.' So they don't view people without jobs as decent people, even though some of them got disability or whatnot." Tucker, who reported having been diagnosed with bipolar disorder and schizophrenia, had been labeled throughout his life as having an intellectual disability. Although he had held a series of low-wage jobs in the past, he was the victim of chronic bullying, humiliation, manipulation, and violence by others at work, at school, and in his neighborhood. His ability to hold down a job was severely constrained, but he still felt the shame of being jobless.

The most common term that men used when we asked them how society viewed men without jobs was *bums*. Andre, who did not meet his own definitions of adulthood or manhood, told us: "Society views men without jobs as bums, deadbeats—that's what they get labeled as. I view men without jobs as still a man. I just feel as though they're in a rough patch, cause everyone has a rough patch. It's not guaranteed they're going to be that way forever. They could be bums right now but then next week they have got 3–4 jobs and you don't got no job." Andre was among many men of color in this study who were careful to avoid stigmatizing others because they had been the subject of such labeling in the past. Unemployed men may appear to others as bums, but that is a temporary rather than a permanent status.

Men without jobs were viewed as particularly problematic when they relied on women for financial support, whether as romantic partners or family members. Nasir, the 34-year-old Black former boxer, articulated this common attitude:

> You gotta consider where I come from and my background. I respect men with jobs, men that take care of their kids and men that don't sell drugs, never sold drugs. And then there's guy that sold drugs and they do the right thing with that money. They'll put their kids through school—I respect them, I commend them. But now the ones that 'aw they're making the money' they trick the girls, they want to go to the club and throw off the ones [dollar bills] for everybody to see so they could say "that's the guy that did this! I want to deal with him." I look down on that. If you don't got no job, you're a grown man and you got kids but you get high or you're always in this girl's face, you got kids and you're broke, you don't got no money but you're always in her face and you're driving her car—I look down on that.

In this view, the moral choice is to take care of your children and not to be a drain on "your girl," even if that means selling drugs because legal jobs are so difficult to attain. In the hierarchy of options, selling drugs is not as valued as legal employment, but it is better than being a burden to others.

Given the profound barriers to stable employment, the general consensus was that searching for work was enough to maintain some sense of masculine dignity. Colin, a 28-year-old White man with a GED and untreated mental health problems, reported: "I know how it is to be without a job, if you're just laying in the house all day not even trying to do work then I see you as a piece of shit, but as long as you're out there trying, going on the internet, going to the wall filling out applications, pressuring, calling jobs, then you're trying. But if you're not trying then you're a piece of shit."

Jason, a 39-year-old White homeless man with a GED and felony record, told us that his opinion of jobless men in the community depended on the circumstances. "There's people I know that have no interest in working, they don't even try and I know that they're looked down upon. They just sit around and don't do anything. And there's other people that are out there really trying to get their recovery, to get employment, even if they don't have a job, you can tell the effort went into it."

Receiving public assistance also carries a substantial stigma. Malcolm, a 31-year-old Black man with a high school degree, clean record, and a full-time job, had been able to get off Social Security benefits. "I wasn't working before due to my disability. But I didn't let that stop me. And now I try to tell people, don't let a disability stop you. . . . Nowadays they want you to go get tested for that so they can get that extra check instead of going out and working for it. . . . Once upon a time, I was on SSI. Now I get the amount I get now" through work, and "I don't need SSI no more. So, it's like use the system to help you get ahead but don't sit there and fraud the system knowing you're capable of going to work."

Men who were unemployed or underemployed reported volunteering to stay busy while they looked for work. For example, Wesley, the veteran who said that an unemployed man was seen as a "nobody," kept himself and his family on a regimented schedule, which he believed was necessary to be a productive citizen. His daily routine began at 6:00 a.m., when he fed his kids breakfast and got them out the door to school. Then he reported to a nearby church's food pantry, where he stocked shelves and gave out groceries. He spent his afternoons at the Community Development Corporation, using their computers to search for work. He and his wife had a family dinner every night. This routine enabled him to be viewed and to view himself as a productive citizen and thereby a man, despite being unemployed.

The Frankford men were motivated by the expectations of their romantic partners and family members and by society to work in order to be considered adult men. To be unemployed is to be a bum or a freeloader, draining resources from these men's own families and from taxpayers. Despite the numerous personal and structural obstacles they faced in finding employment, looking for work and staying busy while giving back to their community was sufficient to maintain a sense of masculine dignity and purpose, distinguishing them from bums or men who are a drain on romantic partners or family members.

MANHOOD AND MORALITY

The final element of masculinity construction apparent in the narratives shared by the Frankford men involves a moral component. A real man is a good man, who is honest, loyal, and chooses to travel the right path to support himself and his loved ones by avoiding criminal offending. A consensus emerged among many of the men we interviewed that, as 26-year-old Black IT professional Christian told us, "You can be a bad man and still be a man, but you can be a good man too." In making moral distinctions between good and bad men, they were pointing out that constructing a version of masculinity based on engaging in crime is the easy way out, but being a "good man" is the real challenge and something to be valued. Evaluations of good men were not just based on avoiding crime or system involvement, however; they were also based on definitions of good fatherhood and good partnering, the outward-facing forms of caring about and caring for others.

Kareem, the 26-year-old Black and Korean community mentor, defined manhood as "having and taking care of your responsibilities, spending time with and taking care of family, being loyal, and having good morals." As noted previously, Kareem had taken on the responsibility of caring for his aging father, who was in an assisted living facility, and his mother, who had recently attempted suicide after bankrupting the family with her gambling. He also constructed masculinity through his generative (volunteer and paid) work with male youth in the community, so being a moral role model was central to his sense of self.

Jelani, a 33-year-old custodial father, claimed, "A real man is someone who takes care of their children, believing in God and putting God first before everything, and working. You can be an adult and doing things wrong, but a man does the right things." It is interesting to consider that being self-sufficient through drug sales or other forms of financial crimes is enough to achieve adulthood but not to be considered a man.

Angel, the former gang member, talked about teaching his son his moral values and religious faith. "Fatherhood means that I provide for my son, that I make sure he has an example to look up to. That he learns how to treat women from me, he learns what a marriage is supposed to look like from my wife and I, and as a father he knows most importantly God relates to him. So when he sees me and he sees the unconditional love that I have for him, when we talk about God he also knows that that's how God loves him—even more than that." Chase, who had moved to Frankford for recovery, said: "I don't necessarily think to be a real man you have to have the stereotype thing. . . . You don't have to have a bunch of different sexual partners at the same time. . . . I don't think [that] defines a real man. I think it's more along the lines of what being an adult is: being responsible, being honest, shit like that. Being a man of your word." Christian explained:

I think it's how you truly hold your values and morals . . . and stay true to them, so I think that's the value of a man. . . . 'Cause to be a real adult I think you're adding some type of value to society and for being a real man it's more so the impactfulness to your family, to the people who are around you to see the characteristics of you as a person, so I think that's more important to them to see you be a real man. But as an adult it's more important to society.

Note that Christian pointed to his family as an audience for his performance of masculinity. Gender is performed and most likely to be incorporated into a man's identity when he receives reflected appraisals by others that his performance of manhood is authentic and believable.[26]

IMPLICATIONS

For economically and socially marginalized men, manhood is a minefield. The Frankford men were conscious of and did their best to distance themselves from the numerous negative images of men who are deadbeat dads, unemployed bums, leeches, or immoral, violent offenders. With limited ability to provide for their loved ones financially, they constructed definitions of masculinity that they could attain, namely caring for and caring about others. Moreover, they called attention to the effort and consistency needed to do gender in this way, in the same fashion that feminist scholars have historically done to highlight the invisible nature of care work.

At the time of this writing, the United States is awash in mass shootings, largely by men who are acting out their rage and disillusionment at not being able to meet hegemonic definitions of masculinity. In light of this, it seems important to discuss *what we didn't hear* in our interviews. Compensatory hypermasculinity, as described in ethnographic studies of Black and Puerto Rican men in their twenties, was rare, although participant observation methods may have found this.[27] Similarly, there was little evidence of Black men's wrestling with gender norms shaped by respectability politics, as sociologist Saida Grundy found in the class privileged men who attended Morehouse College.[28] Some men were in such desperate straits that housing or active substance use was their only focus. Most of the men we interviewed, however, were creatively constructing definitions of masculinity by working to contribute to society rather than take from it. Their status as men was precarious, and sometimes their failures caused them great pain.[29]

It is clear, though, that the men who were successfully meeting their own and others' definitions of manhood were those with close social ties. Masculinity is accomplished through social interaction, and men seek out audiences to whom they can perform this role credibly, namely children, romantic partners, and to a lesser extent, members of their family of origin. These are the same connections that some men work to avoid because they bring the risk of drama or attention by the police. But these men have much to offer in their capacity for caring, and their community is in dire need of people who care. Tapping these men as community leaders or credible messengers could provide them with a platform for expressing a caring masculinity and build collective efficacy designed to make Frankford stronger and safer.

Conclusion

NEW FRAMES FOR CREATING SOLIDARITY AND JUSTICE

> Some of the old head ladies are solid here [in Frankford].
> I have a thousand grandmas, a thousand aunties,
> a thousand uncles.
>
> —Grant, 27, Black, stay-at-home father

This book set out to understand the lives of marginalized millennial men. The Frankford men found themselves in a place and time in which the CLS was expanding and economic opportunities were contracting. The structures created by the interlocking institutions of racial capitalism and the surveillance and control apparatus from police to prisons framed these men's choices, trajectories, social relations, and dreams. They grappled with the leftover cultural baggage from earlier generations, navigating traditional hegemonic constructions of masculinity while redefining their pursuit of adult manhood in more expansive, care-centered, and community-oriented ways.

Most were managing one or multiple forms of stigma, such as racial-criminal stigma, felony histories, addiction, disabilities, chronic health problems, and the cumulative effects of years of grinding poverty. Some carried substantial trauma from witnessing and being victims of violence, food or housing insecurity, spells of incarceration, and loss of family members and loved ones. They shouldered financial and social debts that limited their pathways to stability. Their precarious positions in the labor market and their vulnerability to the vagaries of the legal system pushed many of them underground, striving to construct dignity and durable social ties in relative obscurity, remaining invisible in public but yearning to be seen, recognized, and remembered as good people for their compassion and generosity.[1]

Despite the dominant neoliberal framework of "atomistic individualism" in the contemporary United States, these men need and desire to form meaningful social and civic connections.[2] Although a handful of the most vulnerable men are going it alone, the vast majority are striving to build durable social ties but lack the weaker ties or expansive social networks that provide social capital.[3] The forms of agency delineated in their narratives were very often collectively based, such as resisting categorical forms of stigma directed at people of color or their neighborhood, help-seeking, and generativity.[4] This finding departs from the typical scholarly treatment of human agency, which incorrectly characterizes it as a personality trait rather than a dynamic social or interactional accomplishment.[5]

The narratives of the Frankford men both support and complicate existing developmental paradigms. For example, although almost one-quarter of the men were never involved in criminal activity or the CLS, the men's accounts of desistance are consistent with a maturation process in which criminal offending is incompatible with the adult masculine expectations that significant others held for them.[6] Becoming an adult means considering the impact of our actions on aging parents, romantic partners, and children. Desistance is normative because it occurs as individuals begin to see themselves as intertwined with others' lives as well as societal expectations for adult men.

In terms of psychosocial development, the Frankford men, who were roughly ages 25 to 34 when we interviewed them, were firmly within the stage of working out the conflict between intimacy and isolation.[7] Because of their marginalized economic positions and their vulnerability to getting caught up in the CLS, isolation seemed to provide some protection against the risks and unpredictability of creating social ties with others. Yet the men found profound meaning in the intimate relationships they had with their own children, their families of origin, and to a lesser extent their romantic partners. If there was any consensus about what the American Dream meant, it was relational stability, as much as, if not more than, economic stability.

The focus of so many men of color on generativity is earlier than Erikson would predict, as his model identifies this stage with ages 40 to 65.[8] Perhaps during the postwar period when he developed this theoretical model, he pictured grandparents who were volunteering in their communities or providing childcare to their grandchildren in order to stave off the sense of stagnation that might accompany this stage of life. In our contemporary economic-political configuration, generativity is expressed earlier than Erikson posited *and* before some of the other stages have been resolved. As one example, our analysis of durable ties demonstrates that many of the Frankford men are still working to resolve issues of trust versus mistrust regarding their parents and guardians. It seems clear that, departing from Erikson's linear model of human development, these men are working to resolve multiple dilemmas simultaneously. How they cope with one sometimes impinges on how well they can manage another, both for better and for worse.

In addition, I conclude that generativity is a proactive way of addressing stigma, particularly racial-criminal stigma. These men's narratives are replete with examples of giving back to their families and communities as they work to craft counternarratives that value Black and Brown men and to avoid becoming "a statistic."[9] They do this to reconstruct a spoiled identity and as a larger project of racial uplift.[10]

As this book was being written, the material and social conditions for the "unluckiest generation" worsened yet again as COVID-19 pushed them into their second economic recession and laid bare many of the unsustainable conditions of racial capitalism. The global health pandemic shifted work practices, creating a gap between "essential" workers who had to interact with the public and higher-status employees who could work from their home offices, and had devastating effects on women's economic progress as they assumed the heaviest burdens of childcare during school closures.[11] These changes, which are unlikely to be quickly reversed, will alter some men's positions vis-à-vis the women in their lives and challenge earlier predictions of the coming "end of men."[12] The current labor shortage and increased union organizing (e.g., the Teamsters effort to unionize Amazon employees) may yield much-needed and lasting wage increases and better working conditions. President Joe Biden's "Build Back Better" platform, if successfully realized, could grow new jobs in the green energy sector and infrastructure, which are likely be held largely by men, and in childcare and home health care, which are likely to be held mainly by women, as well as shoring up the safety net for families.

The global racial justice movement that developed in the wake of the murder of George Floyd in 2020 by police officer Derek Chauvin set the stage for a burst of public anger and organizing to address the seemingly unchecked power of the CLS. Widespread protests throughout the country, as well as internationally, opened policy conversations that would have been unthinkable a decade ago. Criminologists Jennifer Cobbina-Dungy and Delores Jones-Brown argue, "Because the conduct involved [in this case] was so inhumane, it is possible that the horrific videotaped death of George Floyd marked a tipping point in public tolerance of excessive police behavior beyond that invoked by previous cases."[13]

For a short time after George Floyd's murder, mainstream media covered protesters calling for alternative forms of public safety and the shifting of funds from the police to mental health and social services. These calls have been buttressed by heavy-handed and militaristic responses by the police to protests, including but not limited to the teargassing of peaceful protesters in Minneapolis, Portland, Washington, D.C., and Philadelphia and the refusal of police in New York to allow people whom they ordered to disperse to do so, surrounding and arresting protestors and bystanders instead. Continued coverage of Black people dying at the hands of police, such as Breonna Taylor, who was killed in Louisville, Kentucky, as a no-knock warrant was served on the wrong house, and Rayshard Brooks, who was killed by police after a Wendy's employee called 911 to report that he was sleeping in his car, have resulted in swift policy responses. Breanna's Law, passed in June 2020, ended the use of no-knock warrants in Kentucky, and Garrett Rolfe, the officer responsible for Brooks's death, was fired and charged with felony murder within a week. Derek Chauvin was found guilty on two counts of murder and one of manslaughter and sentenced to twenty-two and a half years in prison, the longest term an officer had ever received in Minnesota and one of the longest an American officer had received after killing a Black person.[14]

Despite these steps toward accountability and reconsideration of the appropriate role (if any) of police in contemporary society, both racism and systemic resistance to change are durable forces. Racism is a shapeshifter, as Michelle Alexander so poignantly describes in *The New Jim Crow*, and White supremacy paves the way for the creation of new configurations that disguise the permanence of systemic racism.[15] The current backlash, with its political bans on teaching CRT, is but one of many examples of White Americans' refusal to reckon with the legacy of slavery and the continued maintenance of racial inequality through the stratified labor market, mass incarceration, residential segregation, and voting restrictions.[16]

As legal scholar Jonathan Simon has convincingly argued, despite reforms, agents of the CLS inevitably adapt their activities in ways that maintain its core functions: to socialize the poor to frame their failings in terms of "personal responsibility," reproduce racial caste, and inhibit collective solutions to social problems.[17] Every aspect of this system, which now forms a massive apparatus, strains and breaks the social ties that are essential for healthy human development, families, and communities. This system weakens our fundamental institutions and jeopardizes public safety. Yet as gun violence has recently reached crisis levels, there is a very real risk that fear of crime will push us back to a reliance on regressive policies, as suggested by the 2022 recall of progressive prosecutor Chesea Boudin in San Francisco and the ironic but predictable rise in most police budgets since the summer of "reckoning" in 2020. It is possible that a new generation of "superpredators" will be imagined and controlled, to the great benefit of racial capitalism and its shareholders—as the recent boom in sales of guns and body armor suggests. There is no way to avoid this destructive process without substantially reducing the footprint of the criminal legal apparatus. But the reader should not feel disheartened, as the abolition movement is quietly gaining traction among today's college-age young people, if my students are any indication. They have been ignited by George Floyd's death and will not go back.

The remainder of this conclusion considers the implications of the book's findings. Like Susan Starr Sered and Maureen Norton-Hawk's marginalized women described in heartrending detail in *Can't Catch a Break*, the Frankford men are "canaries in the coal mine," already experiencing and expressing the vulnerability that will engulf more and more people if massive economic and social restructuring and reimagining of the common good does not take hold in the United States.[18] The most significant steps we can take in the public policy sphere are those that strengthen and empower communities to reconceive public safety and create so-cial infrastructure supporting human connections and collective action. Finally, I turn to my own academic community and discuss how the prac-tice of positivistic research has caused harm by legitimating police as the most effective solution to crime and through its misguided commitment to "objectivity" rather than a critical perspective grounded in experiences and voices of the vulnerable, who warn us of the dangers that face us all.[19]

REDUCING THE FOOTPRINT
OF THE CRIMINAL LEGAL SYSTEM

At present, we leave ensuring public safety to the CLS, which is consti-tuted by the "three Cs": cops, courts, and corrections. Despite being a mas-sive drain on city and state budgets, this system is an undisputed failure in producing public safety and has actually made our society far less safe. Police spend just 4 percent of their time addressing violent street crime, yet despite decades of declining crime rates in the United States, make ten million arrests annually, which translates to one arrest every three seconds.[20] As part of "proactive policing," officers have spent the last sev-eral decades focused on minor quality-of-life offenses such as turnstile jumping or loitering. In fact, 80 percent of the cases processed through the CLS are misdemeanors.[21] Stop, question, and frisk continues today in Philadelphia and other cities, even though in New York City it was halted when the court found that the policy is racially biased.

These practices targeting impoverished Black and Brown communi-ties have created trauma, fear, and legitimate mistrust of the police. Men of color in Frankford reported that the police are a constant presence in their community and that their direct and observed experiences of police contact, which include degrading treatment, physical brutality, and false charges, led them to avoid leaving the house and minimize their social contacts to reduce their risk of having an unpredictable and possibly fatal encounter with the police. One recent national survey found that 42 per-cent of Black and 11 percent of White respondents are "very afraid" of being killed by police in the next five years.[22] Black participants in this study were more afraid of being questioned by the police than they were of being the victim of a serious crime. In fact, 45 percent of the Black respondents and 18 percent of their White counterparts reported that they would prefer to be the victim of a robbery or burglary than simply to be questioned by the police. They fear for their loved ones as well; Black parents' response is embodied in "the talk" that Ta-Nahisi Coates so eloquently describes in *Between the World and Me*.[23]

Although in public discussions most Americans still regard the police as synonymous with increased safety, the facts disprove this assumption. Let us look at homicides, the crimes that most people agree should be their greatest focus. Nationwide less than half of homicides are followed by an arrest of a suspected perpetrator.[24] In Philadelphia, the clearance rate is even lower than the national average and declining as gun violence has surged during the pandemic.[25] Philadelphia police now solve just 37 percent of murders and a paltry 19 percent of nonfatal shootings.[26] At the same time, proposed spending for the Philadelphia police in fiscal year 2021 was $727 million, making it the largest category in the city's budget. Imagine what that sum could do for community centers, affordable housing, mental health and substance abuse services, libraries, and more, all of which have been starved during and since the pandemic.

The men in this book, like most readers, have never lived during a period when the CLS was not growing rapidly, which can limit our imaginations about alternatives and make calls for defunding or abolishing the police seem terrifying even to those who are afraid of them. In their seminal article on Philadelphia youth, "We Never Call the Cops and Here Is Why," the late Patrick Carr and colleagues found that it was common for teens of color to have negative experiences with the police and to report not calling them if they were the victims of a crime.[27] Yet startlingly, when they were asked to make recommendations for improving public safety in their communities, their most common response was to increase police presence. Similarly, sociologist Michaela Soyer's study of formerly incarcerated youth found that their correctional "treatment" led them to believe they lacked self-control and therefore to welcome restrictive measures such as ankle monitors.[28]

Although the slogan "defund the police" is new, the idea has been promoted by public policy experts for almost two decades as "justice reinvestment."[29] This proposal came in response to mass incarceration, not policing, although the two are obviously related. The concept underlying both movements is to redirect spending on the criminal legal apparatus to community-based, preventative services that reduce harm and improve the quality of life for everyone. Public safety could be enhanced by reducing the size and cost of the correctional system *and* reallocating a portion of correctional spending toward "rebuilding human resources." Under this model, locally directed investments in jobs, housing, health care, and other social services would improve or restore communities, which would have the downstream effect of reducing crime rates. Justice reinvestment is worth studying, since it successfully changed the narrative about incarceration, which led to shifts in budget priorities and reductions in prison populations. Justice reinvestment highlights that it is possible to reallocate funds and even the responsibility of police departments.

One example of such an effort is Advance Peace, an initiative founded in Richmond, California, that offered material assistance to men who were most involved in cyclical and retaliatory gun violence. In addition to cash incentives to avoid violent situations, this program provided case managers who invested in the health and well-being of their clients, connected them to social services, and helped them solve small but important problems such as getting a driver's license. Outcome evaluations of Advance Peace in Richmond, Stockton, and Sacramento, California, show positive results.[30] In addition to producing significant overall reductions in shootings involving death or injury, the initiative has proven that this support can help those most at risk for perpetrating violence meet their personal educational or employment-related milestones.

Another intervention that targets those most likely to be involved in serious violence is Chicago's Rapid Employment and Development Initiative (READI). This program directly addresses criminogenic conditions such as poverty and trauma by providing cognitive behavioral therapy, employment opportunities, and support services.[31] An early outcomes evaluation of READI found participants were significantly less likely to be involved in the most serious and costly forms of violence (e.g., shootings and homicides) twenty months after the intervention began. Moreover, the cost savings derived from lower violence was $184,000 per participant, which researchers estimate is a 3:1 benefit cost ratio for the intervention.[32]

Critical scholars and prison abolitionists argue that the failure of the CLS to achieve public safety is "not a bug, but a feature." If it actually produced public safety, it would put itself out of business. Given how heavily both urban and rural communities and private industry rely on surveillance and incarceration, there is little incentive for those who work in the system to do so. Adopting community solutions to social problems requires embracing an entirely new framework whose conception of "public" is inclusive (eliminating the false dichotomy of "good guys" and "bad guys") and whose notions of "safety" include protecting people from the harms caused by the CLS. We can, and must, shed the individualistic frame that prevents us from collective action.

COMMUNITY SOLUTIONS

Shrinking our CLS and shifting the responsibility for public safety to communities rests on a long-standing and evidence-based premise of crime control: that safety is produced in spaces where residents build social ties and are willing to look out for one another.[33] This is known as collective efficacy, or shared responsibility for safety.[34] According to this framework, informal social control built upon relationships between people is always more effective than formal social control (e.g., police) because it is preventative rather than punitive. Significantly, it is hard to imagine serious harms that would come from social cohesion, whereas the CLS poses numerous harms ranging from constant harassment to long incarceration or instantaneous death. These two frameworks work in opposition, since the CLS is a wholly disintegrative institution, weakening already vulnerable individuals, families, and communities. Cohesive communities, however, generate social capital, shared information, and resources that can be traded in the economic marketplace for greater opportunities.

Some observers have decried the diminishing opportunities for social cohesion.[35] The leaders of the Frankford Civic Association would likely agree, as this was the subject of much conversation over the years. The group's board members, all senior citizens, worried about younger generations' lack of interest in addressing community concerns. But our interviews with the Frankford men suggested that they saw few local institutions with which to engage. While we were conducting our field research, many local nonprofit social agencies closed, including the YMCA, the Salvation Army, the Frankford Arsenal, and the Frankford Group Ministry, which served youth. Moreover, the constant presence of the police drove the men indoors in order to avoid the unpredictable drama that could result from something as simple as walking to the store or shaking someone's hand.

Despite these fears, the Frankford men expressed a desire to give back to the community and to be connected to others through generative activities. Many had dreams of being employed in caring or helping professions, and a few had managed to do so. They were concerned with being remembered as good and generous people and very often served as informal mentors to youth. Angel, the former gang member turned loving father, reported, "My ideal job is so different. It would be helping people, possibly community development, working hands-on . . . to better the neighborhood. My ultimate goal is to become a pastor and to help the community that way. It doesn't pay as much as people think it does but the reward ain't the money. It's a lot of joy in seeing people change." Mateo, the homeless man who did street recovery, said, "What do I want to be remembered for? My philanthropy. More than anything, just that. Not from a self-ego or whatever the case may be but just to let my people know there's hope. I'm a living testament, so just to let them know there's hope. If I can do it y'all guys can do it."

These men are largely untapped resources because they are assumed to be unskilled or even dangerous and because they are so busy keeping themselves under the radar. What if their expertise and value were acknowledged and they were formally connected to their community as credible messengers? This model involves employing persons in helping professions who have shared experiences and struggled to overcome them. These local experts have been used as violence interrupters, probation officers, and mentors for system-involved youth. Philadelphia is home to many of these publicly known role models, including John Pace, Andre Simms, and Tyrique Glasgow, who was nominated for CNN's Hero of the Year Award for 2022.

Although this notion is relatively new, early studies have shown that credible messengers are effective in building rapport and reducing recidivism among youth in the Arches program in New York City.[36] Building and funding programs could strengthen communities by offering alternatives to relying on police for public safety, creating jobs for individuals who want to work, both to make ends meet and to help others, but are too often barred from employment by their past histories. Sadly, we have an ample pool (approximately 600,000 each year) of motivated individuals who are returning from prison from whom credible messengers could be drawn. It is worth noting, however, that credible messengers are generally compensated at a fraction of a police officer's salary. Instead of hiring more Black officers, which has questionable benefits for reducing problematic police behavior, these funds should be redirected to hiring Black and Brown individuals from the community to serve as teachers, school counselors, mental health clinicians, violence interrupters, housing developers, drug treatment specialists, and social workers. Making large investments in marginalized communities can play a potent role in crime reduction and prevention and ultimately reduce our need to rely heavily on law enforcement in the first place.

Nonprofit community organizations are critical not only because they bring residents together but also because of the resources and opportunities for social contact they provide. Several of the Frankford men discussed the importance of nonprofits in providing training and credentials they needed to navigate the job market, financial assistance for college courses, substance abuse recovery services, and basic needs like shelter and food. Nonprofits can help to fill the gaps created by individuals' lack of durable social ties that serve as safety nets and by families' lack of financial reserves. Importantly, these organizations have a direct impact on violence. Patrick Sharkey and colleagues found they accounted for a substantial amount of the decline in crime between the 1990s and 2010s.[37]

The collective efficacy required to generate public safety is possible by building what sociologist Eric Klinenberg calls *social infrastructure*, elements of the environment that encourage people to gather together and form social ties.[38] Public libraries, once referred to as "palaces for the people," are a prime example of social infrastructure because they bring together users of all ages and walks of life in activities that go far beyond reading. Parks; gardens; community centers; churches; and even private "third spaces" like coffee houses, bookshops, beauty shops, and barber shops provide the space for residents to congregate and get to know each other.

Public spaces, especially outdoor amenities like playgrounds, parks, and swimming pools, have become more vital during the COVID-19 pandemic. For example, the Philadelphia Parks and Recreation Department reports a 50 percent increase in use of parks, forests, and trails in 2020.[39] Yet the shutdown revealed stark inequities in access to these spaces across neighborhoods, which has been made even worse by the budget crisis brought on by the pandemic. In 2021, during a summer of numerous heat waves, more than 30 percent of the city's pools remained closed due to lack of staffing, and almost three-quarters of those were in communities with median household incomes below $40,000.[40]

Improving the physical environment is one of eight recommendations made in a recent report outlining evidence-based strategies for violence reduction that do not rely on police.[41] Although "broken windows theory" has been embraced by law enforcement agencies for decades, jurisdictions were slower to support actually fixing broken windows. Nevertheless, addressing dilapidated houses and weed-choked empty lots, planting trees, and opening community gardens are examples of improvements that have been shown in multiple studies to reduce violence and provide substantial health benefits to residents. Studies conducted at the University of Pennsylvania, for example, have found that urban residents have lowered heart rates as they move into greener spaces.[42] These programs are most effective when they employ neighborhood residents in performing the work and operating the projects.

One persuasive idea is community justice, advanced by justice policy expert Todd Clear and colleagues.[43] Community justice is a mix of strategies tailored to each particular community's unique features that can increase public safety in "high-impact locations," or "places where both crime and criminal justice responses to crime exist in concentrated levels."[44] By drawing on the resources of private and nonprofit organizations, communities can reduce their reliance on police and reinvest savings in activities that enhance the ability of community members to create their own safe spaces. Key to the success of community justice is partnerships between local businesses, residents, and social service agencies.

Investment in these community-strengthening approaches is easily possible by reallocating a portion of the $255 billion annually spent by local and state governments on law enforcement, courts, and corrections.[45] When we consider that the United States has systematically defunded the educational system and the social safety net for decades, the idea of defunding the police seems not merely reasonable, but essential.[46]

THE POTENTIAL OF A NEW FRAME

Shifting resources and responsibilities away from the CLS cannot be done piecemeal; it requires a new framework for how we think about a wide set of social problems and their solutions. Generating the buy-in needed for a whole new way of acting is a challenge, but adoption of a new frame opens opportunities to achieve numerous integrative goals, including but not limited to public safety. Many alternate frames exist, some of which I highlight here.

Clear's vision extends from community to *social* justice: "Criminal justice is a type of 'negative' justice. It is concerned with the way a society allocates undesirable experiences to its members. . . . By contrast, social justice is concerned with the distribution of 'good' things within a society: opportunities for advancement, personal wealth, and other assets such as health care, housing, and basic goods of life. In a socially just society these benefits are provided by a fair set of rules and are applied to everyone equally."[47] In his concern with criminal justice as a negative justice, Clear highlights a deficits perspective that frames groups of people (most often children) as "at risk" of negative outcomes such as arrest and incarceration, teen pregnancy, and dropping out of school.[48] Numerous scholars have worked to replace the deficit framework with a strengths-based perspective, identifying the assets and resiliency possessed by individuals growing up in challenging circumstances.[49] Sociologist Victor Rios successfully lobbied the California Department of Education to change its language from "at risk" to "at promise" when referencing schoolchildren.

Sered and Norton-Hawk advocate that the United States adopt the international community's model of human rights, which "spell[s] out the responsibility of the state to respect, protect, and fulfill human rights . . .

[and guarantee that] by virtue of being human, each of us is born with and possesses the right to basic minimum standards of food, housing, health care, and safety; the right to make free and informed choices in all spheres of life—including sexuality, reproduction, marriage, family formation, and the timing and spacing of children; the right to have access to the information, means, and security needed to exercise voluntary choice; and the right to liberty and freedom of expression."[50]

This framework is detailed in the United Nations 1948 Universal Declaration of Human Rights. As the American Civil Liberties Union emphasizes, however, the United States has been slow to adopt these principles and has ratified or agreed to fewer human rights treaties than any other member of the G20.[51] We have only to look around at the atrocities of recent years, including the caging of children on the US border with Mexico, the separation of families seeking asylum, the continued sentencing of children to life without parole, and incarcerated persons dying of heat exposure and COVID-19 in prisons to see proof of our country's lack of commitment to basic human rights.

Another framework is inclusive feminism, outlined in an easy-to-read fashion in Mikki Kendall's *Hood Feminism*.[52] The inclusive and intersectional form of feminism led by women of color expands the ways feminist issues are framed. Rather than focusing on narrow definitions of "women's issues," such as sex discrimination in women's employment and earnings, it encompasses a living wage, food security, and access to quality education and medical care.[53] This expansive collective vision centers on meeting basic human needs, including those of men in marginalized communities.

Health justice and public health approaches to issues that are addressed poorly, if at all, within the CLS offer another set of alternative frameworks. Encompassing both physical and mental well-being, the health justice movement seeks to eliminate disparities in access to health care and enable people to control their own bodies through community-driven, collaborative approaches. Collectives like the Health Justice Commons employ intersectional and trauma-informed lenses to "catalyze the creation of healthcare systems outside of the Medical Industrial Complex which honor the sacredness of Life and place people and the planet above profit."[54] As police officers have increasingly become first responders to drug overdoses and behavioral health crises, they have done irreparable harm. In the wake of fatal police shootings of people suffering from acute psychological problems whose loved ones called for an ambulance to take them to a hospital, some jurisdictions have moved to a crisis intervention model, whereby unarmed teams of experts take the lead in getting people the help they need. Reducing the responsibilities of the police may also free up their time to solve serious crime, a role that even the most strident critics of policing would support.

The critical point of these alternate frameworks is that they protect public safety more effectively than any criminal legal intervention, operate from a preventative stance that is not coercive and carries little risk of harm, and redefine justice in far broader terms than crime. As worrying as the current crisis of gun violence is, we are also facing imminent crises in affordable housing, school funding and college debt, working conditions, food availability and safety, infrastructure, and climate change. Racism has been named as a public health crisis in a growing number of jurisdictions.[55] To address these interlocking and cumulative crises, we urgently need a new frame of reference to understand their causes and solutions.

HOW CAN RESEARCH IN CRIMINAL JUSTICE SUPPORT THIS PROJECT?

Critical criminologists have argued that the field of criminology and criminal justice is complicit in reproducing and sustaining the unjust nature of the system through research.[56] It does this, in part, by creating hierarchies of knowledge production in which scholars' activism and advocacy are dismissed as unscientific "me-search" or as lacking in objectivity.[57] The positivist theoretical framework, which seeks to distinguish offenders from nonoffenders instead of focusing on the social construction of the law, and the positivist epistemological approach, which insists on value neutrality, are both structural impediments to imagining a society in which social rather than legal solutions create and sustain healthy individuals, families, and communities. It is also, not coincidentally, a way of Whitestreaming the field by marginalizing the kinds of knowledge produced by scholars of color, whose communities are so deeply affected by the CLS that it would be impossible to be unbiased or impartial about it.[58]

In a classic treatise, sociologist Howard Becker argued that value neutrality is a false premise and the real question for researchers is "Whose side are we on?"[59] Studying a particular group, such as system-involved individuals, often results in charges of bias. Accusers believe that our sympathies have been aligned with oppressed groups and that we have not given equal attention to the perspectives of those in power, such as police officers or correctional administrators, since the hierarchy of credibility suggests that they know more than members of subordinate groups. But once we have accepted this hierarchy and the "truths" of the powerful as *more* truthful than those of their counterparts, we have taken the side of the superordinate group. It is actually *more* value neutral to assume that the narratives of the powerless are equally true. Thus, feminist epistemologists argue that "strong objectivity" requires reflexivity, or the acknowledgment of how researchers' standpoints necessarily lead us to take a side.[60] Howard Becker's treatise debunks the idea that it is possible to be value-neutral but leaves the issue of which side to choose as a philosophical issue to be determined by the researcher. Critical criminologists, feminists, and antiracist researchers take the stance that, in Desmond Tutu's words, "If you are neutral in situations of injustice, you have chosen the side of the oppressor."[61]

In fact, the field of criminal justice (as distinct from criminology) has a history of taking the side of the powerful, in part because of the field's grounding in police studies. It formed in the late twentieth century when the federal Law Enforcement Assistance Agency funded university programs to examine the operation of the CLS with an eye toward improving its practices.[62] Early criminal justice departments, and many still today, emphasize police studies and attract substantial numbers of students seeking careers in law enforcement. As critical criminologist Sebastian León notes, Derek Chauvin was a criminal justice major.[63] Many policing scholars are apologists who frame police violence as episodic instead of systemic, the result of a few "bad apples," and as exaggerated by contemporary "social justice warriors." They design seemingly value-neutral studies wherein both the treatment and control conditions are police-driven, leading them to the necessary conclusion that policing is "evidence-based."

One common "value-neutral" practice in social research is the agnostic framing device in research of the effects of racism on decisions made in the CLS. These studies typically begin with a discussion of the differential involvement versus differential treatment theses, which hypothesize that people of color are overrepresented in the CLS because they commit more crime or, by contrast, are victims of discrimination by it. This amounts to the academic version of bothsideism, wherein either the former or the latter is equally probable to be true. In other words, researchers often use the "penology of racial innocence," a framework by which the CLS is considered innocent of systemic racism until proven guilty by employing narrow definitions of racism.[64]

In fact, there is overwhelming evidence that the CLS is an inherently racist institution, from the formation of American police forces designed to protect property and suppress racial uprisings through Black codes that delineated unlawful behavior exclusively for Black people to the contemporary prison farms such as Angola and Parchman, where mostly Black people pick cotton for pennies per hour.[65] Ample evidence exists of racial bias in lawmaking, law enforcement, sentencing, and the use of punitive versus treatment-oriented responses. Moreover, this supposed "social fact" neglects corporate and governmental crimes, which cost more money and lives than all the street crimes combined.[66] As Khalil Gibran Muhammad has convincingly documented, the use of crime statistics to construct the essentially criminal nature of Blackness began in the 1890s, shortly after Black people became citizens and were eligible for prosecution in court.[67] "From the beginning, the collection and dissemination of racial crime data was a eugenics project, reflecting the supremacist beliefs of those who created them. It was an intentional way of sorting humanity . . . by a convenient tool that simplified reality, justified racism, and redistributed political economic power from Black to White."[68] Even today, racially biased rates of arrest and incarceration are taken as "objective" evidence that people of color are more prone to crime than White people, which in turn justifies racially biased policing and sentencing.

Another supposedly value-neutral discourse involves framing Black fear of the police as irrational because only a very small proportion of police contacts end in death, or, still worse, that unarmed Black men are comparatively less likely to be shot by police when we consider their rates of violent crime.[69] In addition to minimizing the human impact of state violence, this stance ignores the heightened risk among Black men, for whom police violence is a leading cause of death and whose risk of dying at the hands of police is one in one thousand.[70] These grim statistics do not capture the nonlethal violence that is grossly undercounted and underreported in police incident databases but is documented in interviews with the Frankford men, as well as countless studies of experiences with the police among people of color.[71] Using life tables to estimate race- and sex-specific life expectancies, Elizabeth Wrigley-Field finds that 5,696 collective years of life are taken from every 100,000 Black men by police encounters in the United States.[72] When academics dismiss fear of the police from the safety of their own largely White, middle-class campuses and communities, they deny the humanity of people who bear the brunt of the trauma, injury, and death resulting from police actions.

What are the practical effects of this "value-free" research program? In our insistence that only "evidence-based" solutions to problems of crime and violence are worth funding and enacting, criminologists limit the range of options for solutions that draw primarily on social institutions beyond the CLS. The claim that randomized controlled trials (RCT) are the "gold standard" of knowledge production inhibits criminology from studying community-based interventions because they do not fit neatly into the parameters of an experimental research design.[73] Community-based social justice initiatives are often multisystemic, which makes them less well suited for conventional experimental designs. Moreover, it is likely that what works in one community may not work in another. Rather than seeking to control the conditions that criminologists study to isolate their independent effects, community-focused research insists upon historical and social context.

Thus, a self-perpetuating cycle is instituted, in which funders solicit proposals for RCT research designs or CLS interventions, or both. This creates a pipeline of evaluations of interventions whose target is individual behavior modification, such as cognitive behavioral therapy, or are initiated by police.[74] Meanwhile, community-based efforts are dismissed as risky because they are untested.[75] As policy expert John Roman has pointed out, one of the most important but rarely considered aspects of preventive interventions is that they are unlikely to do any harm, particularly when compared to police-led practices.[76] Moreover, evaluators rarely measure the harm of interventions; at best, they typically learn about the harmful effects of interventions when their primary dependent variable (e.g., recidivism) moves in a different direction than hypothesized. One of the key steps in moving forward is for researchers to acknowledge the possibility of harm and build it into their research designs. This may involve going beyond the targets of the intervention and collecting data from families or communities that are disproportionately impacted by CLS interventions.

At present, most research in criminology and criminal justice both reflects and reproduces a lack of comprehension of the meanings of justice. Science alone cannot address the myriad crises the United States and the world will face in the coming years. We must, as abolitionists have argued for decades, employ our imaginations to reframe "justice" as something for and by the people that is achieved collectively, not individually.[77] Just as I have recommended that policy makers embrace new frameworks that are community-driven and oriented toward social justice, human rights, health justice, inclusive feminisms, and racial equity, researchers must do the same. To continue with positivistic, agnostic research questions, designs, and analyses is to perpetuate the inequities, misery, and destruction produced by the system we study.

This idea is the genesis of the Square One Project, which brings together researchers, policy makers, and practitioners to imagine "a future for justice and public safety that starts from scratch—from square one—instead of tinkering at the edges or cherry-picking cordoned-off areas for reform. To do so, we need to get to the root of the problem: decades of neglect around communities with chronic poverty and the twin crises of ingrained racism."[78] Square One, along with the initiative for a Justice Society, has developed a higher education curriculum, the Racial Justice and Abolition Democracy Project, which integrates education and justice as the "twin pillars of democracy" and brings together disciplines within the humanities and social sciences to produce public knowledge about social justice.

What other changes can we as researchers make to support social justice? One starting point is to commit to teaching students that positivism is but one of many epistemologies from which they can choose. Critical, feminist, constructivist, and liberatory epistemologies challenge the idea that researchers can be or should even desire to be "value free" when studying social institutions. These approaches have been so marginalized in our field that students must train in other disciplines such as sociology or in Europe, where positivism is considered a relic of a bygone era. One needs only to compare studies published in *The British Journal of Sociology* or *Punishment & Society* to see that the hegemonic embrace of positivism is a uniquely American phenomenon. In these outlets, we are exposed to in-depth case studies; narrative analyses; all forms of qualitative research; and scholarly products that draw on literary, photographic, or musical techniques to advance understanding of the human experiences within the CLS.[79]

Although there are signs that this situation may be slowly changing, the hegemony of positivism in the United States has led to the devaluation of qualitative methods as unscientific, biased, and limited in generalizability when compared to large-scale quantitative studies. The White masculinist arms race of increasing statistical sophistication or "big data" has not led to a proportionate increase in our understanding of criminal behavior or the effects of the CLS on individuals.[80] Valuing qualitative or human-centered research would entail requiring graduate courses in qualitative research methods, widening the scope of top-rated journals, drawing upon qualitative-qualified reviewers for paper submissions, and relaxing word counts so that qualitative researchers are not forced to strip their analyses of the contextual data that is uniquely essential to this type of work. It would involve reconsidering contemporary institutional reward structures and markers of productivity, which currently favor the quantity of publications over quality. Above all, federal agencies such as the Department of Justice must commit to funding qualitative research.

Our commitment to positivism has built-in systemic disadvantages for women and scholars of color, who disproportionately produce qualitative research and embrace emancipatory aims. Devaluing these methods and ideals is a seemingly gender- and race-neutral strategy for excluding and marginalizing these groups. When departments use merit, tenure, and promotion standards that only count publications in the top-ranked journals, it is a way of weeding out qualitative scholars. Let's compare the ranking and 2020 impact factor for the *Journal of Quantitative Criminology*, our tenth-ranked journal with an impact factor of 4.239, to that of the *Journal of Qualitative Criminology and Criminal Justice*, which, because of its fairly recent debut, is unranked and has no impact factor at all. The flagship journal of the American Society of Criminology, *Criminology* (impact factor 6.692), has recently begun to publish more qualitative articles because the coeditor, Jody Miller, has made it her mission to increase representation, which she does by drawing on reviewers who have been trained to assess qualitative research. *Crime and Delinquency* recently announced two special calls for qualitative submissions after a rejection letter was posted on Twitter in 2020 and readers expressed outrage that qualitative research would immediately be rejected because it was not within the journal's scope.

The language we use as researchers-writers can either exacerbate inequalities or alternately, portray those who are the subjects of our research with dignity, humanity, and agency. Many have called for "person first" language in writing and pedagogy, including eliminating terms such as *felon* or *inmate* and replacing them with *incarcerated persons* or *system-impacted individuals*.[81] Jason Williams and colleagues advocate referring to study participants as "narrators, as we believe this term humanizes our study participants as the true storytellers and facilitators of knowledge regarding their lived experience."[82] Others have noted that researchers commonly refer to "race effects" instead, naming racism as the system that produces whatever racial differences we report in our research.[83]

A social justice vision for research would need to reckon with higher education's relationship to communities by dismantling hierarchies of credibility that dismiss lived experience as a valued form of knowledge and by working in partnership with community members.[84] Community participatory research relies on the expertise of the people who are most impacted by social issues to generate research questions and designs that are useful to achieving their goals.[85] Citizen scientists can be trained to collect and analyze data or operate as a steering committee to vet analyses conducted by university researchers. Another way of avoiding the "extractive transactional" power relations historically characterizing research conducted in marginalized communities is community research review boards. These bodies are comprised of community members who use their own yardsticks to assess risks and benefits of proposed research and set guidelines around ethical data collection practices, transparency of research procedures and written findings, authorship, and data ownership.[86]

THE IMPORTANCE OF CONNECTION AND SOLIDARITY

This is a book about men, but their stories are interconnected with those of women and children. The adult women in these men's lives are engaged in the heavy lifting of being the sole or primary contributors to the household finances and providing emotional support for their sons, nephews, or intimate partners who are precariously positioned in the labor market. They run de facto prison reentry, housing, and food programs, all with little recognition and no funding. They set expectations for their relationships with men that encourage maturity, stability, and care. Children similarly play a key role in socialization for their fathers and a sadly lacking source of unconditional love.

We've seen the consequences of American individualism and isolation as "deaths of despair" are rising and White nationalist groups present a growing threat to democracy and safety. We know the history of policy makers and union busters who have used (often racist) wedge issues to prevent class-based coalitions from taking hold.[87] With this in mind, and with the growing threat of climate change and the rise of authoritarianism on the horizon, it is imperative for Americans and global citizens to come together and build community in big and small ways. Solidarity is the key to public safety and to countering the destructive effects of racial capitalism, including its big earner, the CLS. Solidarity is responsible for bringing up wages, holding the police to account for their treatment of the public, and demanding housing as a human right. These systems can only survive through continued growth, which relies on our being suspicious of and hostile to one another. Human connection between individuals and groups is thereby an important act of resistance.

Methodological Appendix

Since this book was written with a broad audience in mind, this appendix explains my methods of data collection and analysis in detail and contains tables 1 and 2, referenced in the chapters.

Analysis of interview data began with constructing detailed biographies that contained interview excerpts and summary details for a standardized set of characteristics, such as family of origin, connections to the neighborhood, and social ties. Each piece of data remained contextualized within the individual's life story, rather than being parsed out into disparate categories, as qualitative software does. Instead of simply reporting how many fathers did not have regular contact with their children, for example, this method highlighted how this fact might be linked with being homeless or in recovery. I also constructed a master Excel database that coded approximately fifty key participant characteristics, such as being currently employed, being married, and having a history of incarceration, which enabled me to do counts and make comparisons. At some points, I did cross-tabulations using Statistical Package for the Social Sciences (SPSS), for example, to look at definitions of masculinity by race (no meaningful differences). Analytical memos were developed to integrate findings from extant literature with those from the study, allowing for the testing of tenable propositions.[1] This process, consistent with grounded theory, allowed the data to reveal themes and relationships over time and enabled data collection and analysis to operate in an iterative fashion.[2]

One note of caution involves the comparisons made of men in different racial categories. Approximately half of the White men in the study (nine of seventeen) were in recovery from substance abuse. Conclusions drawn about White men's experiences and perceptions cannot be separated from their membership in the recovery community, which is geographically concentrated in Frankford and involves economic assistance and social supports that likely made their experience unique. That said, these men commonly had legal system contact and many were on probation or parole, so their strategies for managing the shifting masculine adult ground are likely framed by both White privilege and personal experiences in the system.

DEFINING AND MEASURING DESISTANCE

Respondents were asked to self-report their recent and past involvement in a wide variety of illegal activities, ranging from graffiti and retail theft to more serious offenses such as shooting at someone or beating someone seriously enough for them to need medical attention. They also described their contact with police, whether or not it resulted in arrest, and their deeper involvement with the system, such as being on probation or parole and spells of incarceration. Why would we expect men to truthfully admit to committing crimes, especially those that might have gone undetected and unpunished? This is a fair question for studies that involve a single in-depth interview. My research team and I worked hard to develop rapport during interviews, cultivating a nonjudgmental stance toward the information these men shared with us. We waited to ask sensitive questions related to offending and legal system involvement until late in the interview, generally after the ninety-minute mark, when these men had already recounted their life histories. While concealing sensitive information is to be expected in interviews, we heard a lot of admissions to criminal involvement. We were able to confirm self-reported criminal activity and prior incarceration using the Pennsylvania court system's online database, which makes criminal and civil offenses visible to the public. Sometimes we uncovered apparent deceit in a man's claim to have desisted from offending when we conducted a record check. Far more often, we found official reports to be in line with self-reported criminal or system involvement and, even more telling, many instances where respondents admitted to criminal activity for which no official record existed.

It is important to avoid conflating offending and system contact.[3] Prior research has established that the loose connection between criminal activity and official sanctions works in two directions: most crimes do not result in arrest or formal processing, and, particularly for young men of color in highly surveilled communities, official system contact does not require commission of a crime.[4] Relying exclusively on administrative records leads to a systematic overestimate of persistent involvement in crime among those who experience the greatest degree of scrutiny by the police and agents of community supervision. For that reason, I do my best to distinguish between self-reports and official measures.[5] My measure of official offending has the benefit of recording contact that occurred in the months or years since the interviews occurred. The behavioral or self-report measure reflects behavior up to and including the time of the interview.

This method of triangulation in using court records has some important limitations. It is largely limited to contacts that occurred in the Philadelphia metropolitan area, since the search engine required us to specify a county. Thus, it might miss any prior or subsequent points of contact occurring elsewhere. To address this limitation, our team did a second round of record checks, searching specifically within New Jersey, Delaware, and Maryland. We also conducted Google searches of respondents' names, which sometimes turned up news coverage of arrests or police blotter information reported on social media. Where reports of activity in other Pennsylvania jurisdictions were found using this method or where interviewees reported living in other counties, we then conducted a special courts database search there. We searched news reports for deaths, although we did not become aware of any using this method.

I used a combination of self-reported involvement in criminal offending and official records to sort men into categories of desisting or persisting over time. I coded their system involvement separately. As countless other life course criminologists before me have done, I emphasize that these classifications are difficult to make.[6] Some men self-reported criminal involvement or even system involvement that was not reflected in their official records, while others had records of contact but claimed to be uninvolved in criminal activity. Others were incarcerated during the follow-up period, eliminating the opportunity that they would be involved in new street crime, and thus could hardly be considered "desisting." Finally, several men had continued system contact for low-level offending such as misdemeanors or civil offenses, which must be distinguished from those whose later offenses were more serious. I did not consider civil offenses as evidence of persisting, since citations for disorderly conduct or loitering reflect police discretion and jurisdictional priorities enacted in "broken windows policing" rather than criminal offending.

In general, I have categorized men into three behavioral offending trajectories: no history of criminal activity, desisting, or persisting. The first category includes only those who reported no more than minor involvement in teenage lawbreaking in their life history interviews and for whom we could find no arrest record. Desisting men were those who reported prior engagement in offending, but either they told us it had been over three years since their last offense or their record check confirmed that more than three years had passed since their last arrest. Persisting men either reported ongoing offending or had been arrested during the three years prior to our record check. The result of this attempt to apply a meaningful label that accounts for all these complexities should be considered a rough (and sometimes arbitrary) estimate of offending trajectories. The differences between these three groups should not be reified or treated as objective facts rather than potentially useful distinctions.

Men were classified as persisting if their official records showed a felony arrest in the three years prior to the record check. Where they self-reported desistance but were arrested, I looked carefully at whether the new charges were consistent with their prior record and, where possible, continued to follow open cases to see their resolution. They were not counted as new arrests if those arrests resulted in dropped charges due to lack of prosecution or evidence. A conflict between official desistance and self-reported desistance could occur because the respondents were in fact desisting at the time of the interview but later engaged in offending or were targeted by law enforcement and charged with criminal behavior but were actually innocent. Although some claims to desistance made during the interview were likely duplicitous, we could often flag this early because respondents were evasive throughout the interview or, after the recorder was turned off, implied that they had told less than the full truth. In many other cases, their desistance claims appeared to express a sincere desire to avoid criminal offending, while their behavior reflects the economic pressure they were under to make ends meet while occupying society's margins.

Table 1   Frankford, Philadelphia: Crime and Demographic Comparisons, 2017

	Frankford	*Philadelphia*	*United States*
Violent crime rate 2017 (per 100,000)	17.31[a]	9.48[b]	3.83[b]
Black	41.5%	42.9%	12.6%
Hispanic of any race	38.1%	13.8%	17.3%
Below poverty	33.9%	25.9%	15.1%
Unemployment	19.3%	12.5%	7.4%
Median income	$30,276	$39,770	$55,322
Less than HS education	17.4%	17.4%	13.0%
Renters	49.0%	47.6%	34.9%

SOURCE: All data except where specifically noted is from US Census Bureau, "American Community Survey, 5-Year Estimates, Table DP05 (ACS Demographic and Housing Estimate)," 2017.

[a] From "DataHub Philly, 2017," *Philadelphia Inquirer*, accessed November 12, 2018.

[b] Compiled from Federal Bureau of Investigation *Uniform Crime Report*, 2017.

Table 2 Frankford Men's Study Sample Characteristics

	Demographics			Offending/System Contact				Social Ties	
Pseudonym	*Age*	*Race/Ethnicity*	*Educational Level*	*Offending History*	*Criminal Record*	*In Recovery*	*Employed*	*Stable Romantic Relationship*	*Father*
Kareem	26	Black/Asian	Some college	•	•		•	•	
Cory	29	Black	HS	•	•			•	
Wesley	26	Black/Latino	AA				OTB	•	•c
Anthony	25	White	GED	•			•		•
Cam	23	Black/Latino	Some college	•	•				
Nelson	26	Black	HS	•					
Marcus	26	White/Asian	HS	•	•				
David	26	Black	HS	•	•	•		•	
Randall	27	White	HS	•	•		OTB	•	
Tim	30	White	<HS	•	•	•	OTB		•
Lewis	30	Black	Some college	•	•		•		•
TJ	28	White	HS	•		•	•		
Stallworth	28	Black	Some college	•	•	•			
Bryan	31	Black	HS	•	•				
Colin	28	White	GED	•	•		OTB		•c
Brady	33	White	HS	•	•		•		•
Paul	30	White	<HS	•					
Andre	32	Black	<HS	•	•			•	•
Yusef	28	Black	Some college	•	•			•	
Nick	33	White	HS	•	•				
Marvin	24	Black	<HS	•	•		•		•
Roderick	28	Black-Latino	HS	•			•		
Grant	27	Black	<HS	•			•	•M	•c
Jelani	33	Black-Latino	GED	•	•	•	•		•c

•M = married; •c = custodial father

AA = associate of arts degree; BA = bachelor of arts degree; GED = general equivalency diploma; HS = high school diploma; OTB = Off-the-books work

Table 2 (Continued)

| | Demographics | | | Justice Involvement | | | | | Stable Romantic | |
Pseudonym	Age	Race/Ethnicity	Educational Level	Offending History	Criminal Record	In Recovery	Employed		Relationship	Father
Keith	27	Black	GED	•	•		•			•
Vincent	30	Black	GED	•	•					•
Luke	32	White	GED	•	•				•M	•
Oren	31	White	GED	•			•			•
Nasir	34	Black	GED	•						•
Christian	26	Black	Some college			•				•
Mateo	29	Latino	GED	•		•	OTB			•
Alex	35	Latino	HS	•	•		OTB			•C
Hector	34	Latino-White	GED	•	•	•			•	•
Angel	33	Latino	Some college	•		•	•		•M	•C
Chase	27	White	Some college	•		•	•			•
Kurt	31	White-Black[w]	HS			•			•M	•
Declan	33	White	GED			•				
Jason	39*	White	GED			•				•
Frank	34	White	HS	•		•	•			•
Trevor	33	White	< HS	•		•				
Isaac	37	Black-White	GED	•		•	•		•M	•
Dennis	33	Latino	Some college		•		•		•M	•
Malcom	31	Black	HS				•			•C
Miles	33	Black	BA				•			
Tucker	35	Black	Some college				•		•	

* = Gen X (born 1979)

w = Presented as White, grouped with White men in analysis; •M = married; •C = custodial father

BA = bachelor of arts degree; GED = general equivalency diploma; HS = high school diploma; OTB = Off-the-books work

Notes

PREFACE

1. Fader, *Falling Back*.

2. All names of narrators mentioned from *Falling Back* (2013) and throughout the book are pseudonyms.

3. Fader, "'Game Ain't What It Used to Be.'"

4. Fader, "'Selling Smarter, Not Harder.'"

5. Crutchfield, *Get a Job*.

6. The 2020 annual report detailing juvenile arrests highlighted a flattening of the age-crime curve, at least for violent offenses, but I suspected these individuals were engaged in crime but largely going undetected. Puzzanchera, "Juvenile Arrests, 2018."

ACKNOWLEDGMENTS

1. Mazelis, *Surviving Poverty*; Jones, *Chosen Ones*; and Duck, *No Way Out*.

CHAPTER 1: INTRODUCTION

1. Van Dam, "Analysis."

2. Grusky et al., "Millennials in the United States."

3. Dilulio, "Coming of the Superpredators."

4. Feld, *Evolution of the Juvenile Court.*

5. Despite my inclination to keep "white" lowercase because of its association with White supremacist groups, I am convinced by an argument made by two writers of color at the Center for the Study of Social Policy, who point out: "To not name 'White' as a race is, in fact, an anti-Black act which frames Whiteness as both neutral and the standard. . . . We believe that it is important to call attention to White as a race as a way to understand and give voice to how Whiteness functions in our social and political institutions and our communities. Moreover, the detachment of 'White' as a proper noun allows White people to sit out of conversations about race and removes accountability from White people's and White institutions' involvement in racism." Nguyên and Pendleton, "Recognizing Race in Language."

6. Holzer, "Employment."

7. Fry, "Millennials Are the Largest Generation."

8. Upwork, "New 5th Annual 'Freelancing in America' Study."

9. Hanson, "Student Loan Debt by Generation."

10. Dynarski, "Student Debt."

11. Alexander, *New Jim Crow.*

12. Rios, *Punished.*

13. Clear, "Impacts of Incarceration on Public Safety."

14. Haggerty and Ericson, *New Politics of Surveillance and Visibility*; and Brayne, "Surveillance and System Avoidance."

15. Lageson and Maruna, "Digital Degradation."

16. Brayne, "Big Data Surveillance."

17. Hawley and Flint, "'It Looks Like a Demon'"; and Oeur, "Recognizing Dignity."

18. Jones, *Chosen Ones.*

19. Rosin, *End of Men.*

20. Binder and Bound, "Declining Labor Market Prospects."

21. Himes, "Men's Declining Labor Force Participation."

22. Case and Deaton, *Deaths of Despair and the Future of Capitalism.*

23. Thompson, "Many Young Men Giving Up?"

24. Reeves and Smith, "Male College Crisis."

25. Parker and Stepler, "Americans See Men as the Financial Providers."

26. Fry and Parker, "U.S. Adults without Spouse or Partner."

27. Haldipur, *No Place on the Corner.*

28. Brame et al., "Demographic Patterns of Cumulative Arrest."

29. Weaver, Papachristos, and Zanger-Tishler, "Great Decoupling."

30. Pettit and Western, "Mass Imprisonment and the Life Course," 151.

31. Pattillo et al., "Monetary Sanctions and Housing Instability"; and Wakefield and Uggen, "Incarceration and Stratification."

32. Significant economic advantages are associated with graduating from high school, even when compared to an equivalency certificate. Heckman, Humphries, and Mader, "GED.".

33. Of the twenty-four men identifying primarily as Black, four also identified as Latino, and two identified as also Asian or White; of the five who identified as Latino, one also identified as White; and of the seventeen who identified as White, two also identified as Black and Asian. One participant identified as biracial but looked White. He is coded as White because this was how he was most likely perceived by law enforcement agents.

34. Fader, VanZant, and Henson, "Crime and Justice Framing."

35. Edin and Lein, *Making Ends Meet*; and Venkatesh, *Gang Leader for a Day*.

36. Expenses included housing/utilities, food, entertainment, and debt; income sources included legal or OTB work, public assistance, or assistance from family. It should be noted that this budget represented a snapshot of finances that were likely to involve substantial fluctuation.

37. Schwartz and Wilson, "Who Can Afford a Home?"

38. It is likely that expenses that are counted previously as "rent" and "food" also fall into this category. These men's personal expenses were unlikely to be cleanly delineated from their contributions to others' support, especially since they receive help from them as well as give support to them.

39. Harris, Evans, and Beckett, "Drawing Blood from Stones."

40. Link and Roman, "Longitudinal Associations."

41. Thomas and Thomas, *Child in America*.

42. Becker, introduction to *Jack-Roller*.

43. Mead, *Mind, Self [and] Society*; and Cooley, *Human Nature and the Social Order*.

44. Goffman, *Presentation of Self in Everyday Life*.

45. Goffman, *Stigma*, 44.

46. Elder and Johnson, "Life Course and Aging"; and Elder, "Time, Human Agency."

47. Elder, *Children of the Great Depression*.

48. Erikson, *Childhood and Society*.

49. Bersani and Doherty, "Desistance from Offending."

50. Delgado and Stefancic, *Critical Race Theory*.

51. Alexander, *New Jim Crow*; and Bonilla-Silva, *Racism without Racists*.

52. Crenshaw, "Demarginalizing the Intersection of Race and Sex."

53. Schrock and Schwalbe, "Men, Masculinity, and Manhood Acts."

54. Bridges and Pascoe, "Hybrid Masculinities."

55. Connell, *Gender and Power*; Connell, *Masculinities*; Connell and Messerschmidt, "Hegemonic Masculinity"; and Messerschmidt and Messner, "Hegemonic, Nonhegemonic, and 'New' Masculinities."

56. Oeur and Grundy, "Allyship in the Time of Aggrievement," 255.

57. hooks, *We Real Cool.*

58. Whiton, "Mass Incarceration a Jobs Program."

59. Beck, *Risk Society*; and Giddens, "Risk and Responsibility."

60. Ericson and Haggerty, *Policing the Risk Society.*

61. Silva, *Coming Up Short.*

62. Bersani and Doherty, "Desistance from Offending"; and Sampson and Laub, *Crime in the Making.*

63. Carlsson, "Masculinities, Persistence, and Desistance."

64. Twine, "White Side of Black Britain"; and Jones, *Chosen Ones.*

65. Fader, *Falling Back.*

66. Rocque, "Lost Concept"; and Rocque, *Desistance from Crime.*

67. A version of chapter 4 was published as Jamie J. Fader, "'I Don't Have Time for Drama': Managing Risk and Uncertainty through Network Avoidance," *Criminology* 59, no. 2 (2021): 291–317.

68. A version of chapter 5 appeared in Jamie J. Fader, Abigail Henson, and Jesse Brey, "'I Don't Want to Be a Statistic': Racial-Criminal Stigma and Redemptive Generativity," *Crime & Delinquency* (forthcoming).

69. Goffman, *Stigma*, 44.

70. Ray, *Making of a Teenage Service Class.*

71. Jones, *Chosen Ones*; and Maruna, *Making Good.*

72. McAdams, *Redemptive Self.*

73. Mazelis, *Surviving Poverty.*

74. West and Zimmerman, "Doing Gender."

75. Silva, *Coming Up Short.*

76. Duck, *No Way Out.*

77. Kalleberg, *Precarious Lives.*

78. Simon, *Poor Discipline.*

79. Clear, "Impacts of Incarceration on Public Safety"; Klinenberg, *Palaces for the People*; and Sharkey, Torrats-Espinosa, and Takyar, "Community and the Crime Decline."

CHAPTER 2: PHILADELPHIA AS A SITE
OF SHIFTING GROUND

1. Fader, *Falling Back.*

2. US Census Bureau, "American Community Survey, One-Year Estimates, 2019."

3. Pew Charitable Trusts, "Philadelphians Living in Poverty, 2019."

4. Romero, "Data Reveals Huge Life Expectancy Gap"; for full data see Centers for Disease Control and Prevention, "U.S. Small-Area Life Expectancy Estimates Project."

5. US Census Bureau, "QuickFacts."

6. Bureau of Labor Statistics, "Philadelphia Area Employment—February 2022"; and Pew Charitable Trusts, "Philadelphia's Poor."

7. US Census Bureau, "American Community Survey, 5-Year Estimates."

8. Massey and Tannen, "Trends in Black Hypersegregation"; and Shukla and Bond, "Philly One of Most Racially Segregated Cities."

9. Pew Charitable Trusts, "Philadelphia's Changing Neighborhoods."

10. Otterbein, "Larry Krasner Wins DA's Race."

11. Philadelphia City Council, "Leaders Named to Special Committee."

12. MacArthur Foundation, "MacArthur Safety + Justice Challenge."

13. City of Philadelphia, "Philadelphia Prison Population Report."

14. Fleck and Stagoff-Belfort, "Reducing Policing's Footprint?"

15. Mancini, "Philadelphia Voters Approve Ballot Question."

16. City of Philadelphia, *2020 Annual Report Division of Substance Use.*

17. Whelan, "Here's How Safehouse Will Operate."

18. Feldman, "Judges Rule against 'Supervised' Site."

19. Schiraldi, "Pennsylvania Community Corrections Story."

20. Melamed and Purcell, "Probation Trap."

21. Schiraldi, "Pennsylvania Community Corrections Story."

22. Pennsylvania Community Legal Services, "Clean Slate."

23. Philadelphia Police Department, "Crime Maps & Stats."

24. Hutchinson, "'It's Just Crazy.'"

25. Palmer and Orso, "Philly's Homicide Crisis in 2021."

26. Wight et al., "What's in a Name?"

27. City of Philadelphia, "Philadelphia Roadmap to Safer Communities."

28. Philadelphia District Attorney's Office, "Report on Overturning Wrongful Convictions."

29. Melamed, "City May Face Civil Liability."

30. City of Philadelphia, "Police Department's Response to Plain View Project," 3.

31. "Plain View Project."

32. Jones, "Police in Spotlight for Bad Behavior."

33. Palmer, "Police 'Escalated Tensions' by Using Force."

34. Orso, McCrystal, and Newall, "Commissioner Sought to Use Tear Gas against Protesters."

35. Gross, "Death of Walter Wallace Jr."

36. Yu, "Philadelphia Settles with Mother."

37. Sances, "Police Budgets on the Ballot."

38. McCrystal, "Philly Budget Deal Cancels Increase."

39. Owens, "City Hall Will Never Defund Police."

40. Philadelphia City Council, "City Council Approves Equality Bills."

41. Zussman, "People in Places," 362.

42. US Census Bureau, "American Community Survey, 5-Year Estimates." Note that these numbers do not add up to 100 percent because many Hispanic residents also identified as Black or White.

43. Vella, "Walking Beat with Rookie Cop."

44. Roman et al., "Lasting Reforms for Prisoner Reentry."

45. Philadelphia Reentry Coalition, "People Released from Prison & Jail in 2015"; see also "Justice Mapping" online resource.

46. Leverentz, *Intersecting Lives*.

47. Hall and Ferrick, "Mapping Progress in 55 Neighborhoods."

48. Anderson, *Streetwise*.

49. Fairbanks, *How It Works*.

50. Smiley and Smiley, *Frankford Stories*, 6.

CHAPTER 3: LEAVING CRIME BEHIND
IN THE PROCESS OF MATURATION

1. Piquero, Farrington, and Blumstein, "Criminal Career Paradigm."

2. Bersani and Doherty, "Desistance from Offending"; Sampson and Laub, *Crime in the Making*.

3. Hays, Hayford, and Furstenberg, "Delayed Adulthood, Delayed Desistance?"

4. Giordano, Cernkovich, and Rudolph, "Gender, Crime, and Desistance."

5. Fader, *Falling Back*.

6. Crutchfield, *Get a Job*.

7. Anderson, *Code of the Street*; Contreras, *Stickup Kids*; and Fader, "'Game Ain't What It Used to Be.'"

8. Giordano, Cernkovich, and Rudolph, "Gender, Crime, and Desistance."

9. Edin, Nelson, and Paranal, "Fatherhood and Incarceration."

10. Boonstoppel, "'It's Not about Me No More.'"

11. Fader, *Falling Back*.

12. Paternoster and Bushway, "Desistance and the 'Feared Self.'"

13. Giordano, Cernkovich, and Rudolph, "Gender, Crime, and Desistance."

14. Shover, *Aging Criminals*.

15. Carlsson, "Masculinities, Persistence, and Desistance"; and Umamaheswar, "'When the Hell Are You Going to Grow Up?'"

16. The index ran from 0 to 5 and included a stable neighborhood, housing, families of origin, romantic relationships, and employment. "Stability" on each of these dimensions involved at least one year with no change.

17. Giordano, Cernkovich, and Rudolph, "Gender, Crime, and Desistance," 1026.

18. The small size of these subgroups makes it impossible to test the statistical significance of these differences.

19. Wakefield and Uggen, "Incarceration and Stratification."

20. Fader, *Falling Back.*

21. Soyer, "Imagination of Desistance."

22. Giordano, Cernkovich, and Rudolph, "Gender, Crime, and Desistance."

23. Massoglia and Uggen, "Settling Down and Aging Out."

24. Jones, *Chosen Ones.*

25. Matsueda and Heimer, "Role-Transitions, Role-Commitments, and Delinquency."

26. Rocque, "Lost Concept"; and Rocque, *Desistance from Crime.*

27. Soyer, *Dream Denied.*

28. Lemay et al., "Fatherhood among Young Urban Fathers."

29. Guy Johnson, *Standing at the Scratch Line* (New York: Villard, 2001). It is interesting to see how Vincent interpreted this novel, since according to *Library Journal*, "this novel presents a brief history of twentieth-century black America in the guise of a testosterone-fueled adventure yarn."

30. Robert Greene studied classics at UC-Berkeley and University of Michigan. The blurb for this book, which was published in 2000, says: "Amoral, cunning, ruthless, and instructive, this multi-million-copy *New York Times* bestseller is the definitive manual for anyone interested in gaining, observing, or defending against ultimate control in addition to having a strong following within the business world and a deep following in Washington, DC, Greene's books are hailed by everyone from war historians to the biggest musicians in the industry (including Jay-Z and 50 Cent)."

31. Dweck, "Mindsets."

32. Rocque, "Lost Concept"; and Rocque, *Desistance from Crime.*

33. Massoglia and Uggen, "Settling Down and Aging Out."

34. Shanahan, "Adulthood in Changing Societies."

35. Massoglia and Uggen, "Settling Down and Aging Out."

CHAPTER 4: ISOLATION AS A WAY OF AVOIDING TROUBLE AND MANAGING RISK

1. Anderson, *Code of the Street.*

2. Brunson and Miller, "Gender, Race, and Urban Policing"; and Haldipur, *No Place on the Corner.*

3. Duck, "Complex Dynamics of Trust and Legitimacy"; Jones, "'Regular Routine'"; and Rawls, Duck, and Turowetz, "Problems Establishing Identity/Residency."

4. See Urban Dictionary, s.v. "Drama."

5. In *Falling Back,* the much younger men I studied were very concerned with what they called "BMD," or "Baby's Momma Drama." It was indeed dramatic, as

these relationships seemed to be on-again and off-again on a near daily basis and involved mutual verbal and sometimes physical abuse. See Fader, *Falling Back*.

6. Panfil, "'I Was a Homo Thug.'"

7. This term was inspired by Brayne's work on "system avoidance," whereby those who have had contact with the CLS systematically "avoid institutions that keep formal records (i.e., 'put them in the system') and therefore heighten the risk of surveillance and apprehension by authorities." See Brayne, "Surveillance and System Avoidance, 368. Respondents who had even low-level contact such as arrest were less likely than their counterparts to engage with "surveilling" institutions such as hospitals and doctor's offices, banks, and schools, and most critically, with work.

8. Several scholars have noted that trouble is a "focal concern" for "lower-class youth," Black males, and men in inner-city communities. Miller, who advanced a subcultural theory of delinquency in urban neighborhoods, argues that lower-class youth are distinct from their middle-class counterparts in their concerns with trouble, autonomy, fate, excitement, toughness, and smartness. A concern with trouble, he argues, may be manifested either in a desire to stir up trouble by engaging in acts of delinquency or, in contrast, by avoiding trouble. This, he explains, is why we see offenders and police officers coming from the same communities. See Miller, "Lower Class Culture as Generating Milieu." Oliver, writing in a similar vein by focusing on cultural adaptations to the structural conditions of exclusion, argues that lower-class Black males engage in a compensatory form of masculinity that emphasizes toughness, which then exacerbates social problems such as violence, fear of "Blacks" by "Blacks," and emotional detachment. See Oliver, "Black Males and Tough Guy Image." See also Goffman, *On the Run*.

9. Safecam is a public-private partnership sponsored by the Philadelphia Police Department. Residents and business owners are encouraged to place cameras outdoors to monitor activities and to register them with the police so that the recordings are easily available for use in criminal investigations.

10. Bell, "Situational Trust."

11. Mitchell, "Philadelphia's Civil Payments."

12. Melamed and Purcell, "Probation Trap."

13. Reynolds et al., "Justice Reinvestment in Pennsylvania"; and Schiraldi, "Pennsylvania Community Corrections Story."

14. Corbett, "Burdens of Leniency."

15. Humes, *No Matter How Loud I Shout*; and Wacquant, "From Slavery to Mass Incarceration."

16. Fader, "Successful Status Graduation Ceremony"; and Ray, *Making of Teenage Service Class*.

17. Soyer, *Dream Denied*.

18. Anderson, *Streetwise*; and Anderson, *Code of the Street*.

19. West and Zimmerman, "Doing Gender."

20. Melamed and Purcell, "Probation Trap."

21. Mazelis, *Surviving Poverty*; and Furstenberg et al., *Managing to Make It*.

22. See also Haldipur, *No Place on the Corner*; and Jones, "'Regular Routine.'"

23. Silva, *Coming Up Short*.

24. Goffman, *On the Run*.

25. Bryan was incorrectly identified as Stallworth in Fader, "'I Don't Have Time for Drama.'"

26. Stevenson, *Just Mercy*.

27. Duck, "Complex Dynamics of Trust and Legitimacy," 135. See also Stuart and Benezra, "Criminalized Masculinities."

28. Anderson, *Black in White Space*.

29. See Roy, "Three-Block Fathers."

30. Glaser and Strauss, *Discovery of Grounded Theory*.

31. Wacquant points out the blurred boundaries between prisons and "the ghetto" in their shared function as "institutions of forced confinement entrusted with enclosing a stigmatized category so as to neutralize the material and/or symbolic threat it poses for the surrounding society." See Wacquant, "New 'Peculiar Institution,'" 377.

32. Klinenberg, "Social Isolation, Loneliness, and Living Alone"; and Putnam, *Bowling Alone*.

33. McFarland, Geller, and McFarland, "Police Contact and Urban Adolescents."

34. Mazelis, *Surviving Poverty*; and Stack, *All Our Kin*.

35. Granovetter, "Strength of Weak Ties."

36. Brayne, "Surveillance and System Avoidance."

37. Anderson, *Black in White Space*; and Fader, *Falling Back*.

38. Roy, "Three-Block Fathers."

39. Roberts, "Cost of Mass Incarceration."

40. Morenoff, Sampson, and Raudenbush, "Neighborhood Inequality Urban Violence"; and Rose and Clear, "Incarceration, Social Capital, and Crime."

41. Fader, VanZant, and Henson, "Crime and Justice Framing."

42. Miller and Stuart, "Carceral Citizenship"; and Sered, "Diminished Citizenship in Mass Incarceration."

43. Haldipur, *No Place on the Corner*; Jones, *Chosen Ones*; and Rios, *Punished*.

44. Ray, *Making of Teenage Service Class*; and Silva, *Coming Up Short*.

45. Foucault, *Foucault Effect*; and Garland, *Culture of Control*.

CHAPTER 5: STIGMA, GENERATIVITY, AND REDEMPTION

1. Twine, "White Side of Black Britain."

2. Maruna, *Making Good*.

3. See Doleac and Hansen's research on the racialized effects of Ban the Box legislation, which finds that employers use statistical discrimination in the absence of information on felony history, assuming that Black applicants have one and White applicants do not. See Doleac and Hansen, "Unintended Consequences of 'Ban the Box.'"

4. Goffman, *Stigma*.

5. Cooley, *Human Nature and Social Order*; and Mead, *Mind, Self [and] Society*.

6. Maruna, *Making Good*; and Stone, "Desistance and Identity Repair."

7. McAdams, *Redemptive Self*.

8. Pager, "Mark of a Criminal Record."

9. Muhammad, *Condemnation of Blackness*; Rios, *Punished*; and Russell-Brown, *Color of Crime*.

10. Fader, *Falling Back*.

11. hooks, *We Real Cool*, x (emphasis added).

12. Jones, *Chosen Ones*.

13. Jones, *Chosen Ones*; Lofland, *Deviance and Identity*; and Maruna, "'Virtue's Door Unsealed.'"

14. Brooms, "'I Didn't Want to Be a Statistic.'"

15. Anderson, *Code of the Street*, 73; see also Brezina et al., "Code of the Street."

16. Rios, *Punished*.

17. Ispa-Landa, "Believing in a Positive Future"; and McAdams, *Redemptive Self*.

18. I borrow and modify the notion of "identity projects," or a "consuming, defining passion," developed in DeLuca, Clampet-Lundquist, and Edin, *Coming of Age in the Other America*, 8.

19. McAdams, *Redemptive Self*, xi.

20. Erikson, *Childhood and Society*.

21. Shachar et al., "Criminal Justice or Public Health."

22. Anderson, *Black in White Space*.

23. Messerschmidt and Messner, "Hegemonic, Nonhegemonic."

24. Drake and Cayton, *Black Metropolis*; and Young, "Black Men and Black Masculinity."

25. See also Edin et al., "Tenuous Attachments of Working-Class Men."

26. Carlsson, "Masculinities, Persistence, and Desistance"; and Umamaheswar, "'When the Hell Are You Going to Grow Up?'"

27. Rios, *Punished*.

28. Jones, *Chosen Ones*.

29. Anderson, *Streetwise*.

30. Lofland, *Deviance and Identity*.

31. Anderson, *Cosmopolitan Canopy*.

32. Jones, *Chosen Ones*.

33. McAdams, *Redemptive Self*, xvii.

34. Edin et al., "Tenuous Attachments of Working-Class Men."

35. Pittman, "Managing Methadone Mile."

36. Oeur, *Black Boys Apart*.

37. Hawley and Flint, "'It Looks Like a Demon'."

38. Jones, "'Regular Routine'"; and Haldipur, *No Place on the Corner*.

CHAPTER 6: DURABLE SOCIAL TIES, LINKED LIVES, AND ADULT MASCULINITIES

1. Mazelis, *Surviving Poverty*; and Stack, *All Our Kin*.

2. Elder, "Time, Human Agency, and Social Change."

3. Comfort, *Doing Time Together*.

4. Elliott, "Caring Masculinities," 241.

5. See Comfort, *Doing Time Together*; and Goffman, *On the Run*.

6. Wilson, *Truly Disadvantaged*.

7. Giordano, Cernkovich, and Rudolph, "Gender, Crime, and Desistance."

8. The most recent *Diagnostic and Statistical Manual of Mental Health Disorders* (DSM-5) no longer recognizes Asperger's as a diagnosis, preferring to categorize it under the broader umbrella of autism spectrum disorder. See American Psychiatric Association, *DSM-5* However, Kurt still uses the term because it was still in use at the time of his diagnosis.

9. According to journalist Dan Nosowitz, the word *jawn* is both unique to Philadelphia and "unlike any other English word. In fact, according to the experts that I spoke to, it's unlike any other word in any other language. It is an all-purpose noun, a stand-in for inanimate objects, abstract concepts, events, places, individual people, and groups of people. It is a completely acceptable statement in Philadelphia to ask someone to 'remember to bring that jawn to the jawn.'" See Nosowitz, "Enduring Mystery of 'Jawn.'"

10. Fonzworth Bentley (played by Derek Watkins) is best known for being Sean (P-Diddy) Combs's personal valet and assistant and host of *From Gs to Gents* on MTV.

11. Silva, *Coming Up Short*.

12. This difference in our findings is also likely related to the fact that Jennifer Silva's sample included women, who were especially likely to assess men's economic contributions as lacking, thus representing greater risk.

13. Silva, *Coming Up Short*; and Edin and Kefalas, *Promises I Can Keep*.

14. According to the Urban Dictionary, "looking hit" means looking "like shit" or "below a 5 on a scale of 1–10. See Urban Dictionary, s.v. "Looking Hit."

15. Elliott, "Caring Masculinities," 241.

16. DeVault, *Feeding the Family*; and Hochschild and Machung, *Second Shift*.

17. Demantas and Myers, "'Step Up and Be a Man'"; and Melzer, *Manhood Impossible.*

18. Melzer, *Manhood Impossible.*

19. Men self-reported fatherhood, so this measure is based on the children that men know about.

20. Fader, *Falling Back.*

21. Boonstoppel, "'It's Not About Me No More'"; and Giordano, Cernkovich, and Rudolph, "Gender, Crime, and Desistance."

22. Henson, "Navigating Paternal Hurdles."

23. Paternoster and Bushway, "Desistance and the 'Feared Self.'"

24. Elliott, "Caring Masculinities."

25. Rawls and Duck, *Tacit Racism.*

26. Klinenberg, *Heat Wave*; and Putnam, *Bowling Alone.*

27. Murthy, *Together*; see also Case and Deaton, *Deaths of Despair.*

28. Resnick, "Millennial Loneliness Poll."

29. Silva, *Coming Up Short.*

30. See also Haldipur, *No Place on the Corner.*

31. Lopoo and Western, "Incarceration and Marital Unions."

32. Comfort, *Doing Time Together.*

33. Klinenberg, *Palaces for the People.*

CHAPTER 7: MEANINGS OF MANHOOD AND ADULTHOOD

1. These are four of the five markers of the transition to adulthood. The fifth, fatherhood, is perhaps the easiest to accomplish for men who have not achieved the others, although many respondents made careful distinctions between being a biological parent (a "daddy") and a father, which implies a more active role. See Arnett, "Emerging Adulthood"; and Shanahan, "Adulthood in Changing Societies."

2. West and Zimmerman, "Doing Gender."

3. Jones, *Chosen Ones.*

4. See Panfil, "'I Was a Homo Thug,'" for a nuanced treatment of "realness" in performing and constructing masculine identities among gay-identified gang members.

5. Shanahan, "Adulthood in Changing Societies"; and Silva, *Coming Up Short.*

6. Edin and Kefalas, *Promises I Can Keep.*

7. Connell and Messerschmidt, "Hegemonic Masculinity."

8. Schrock and Schwalbe, "Men, Masculinity, and Manhood Acts," 281.

9. Bridges and Pascoe, "Hybrid Masculinities."

10. One exception is Messerschmidt, "Becoming 'Real Men'." Another is Schrock and Schwalbe, "Men, Masculinity, and Manhood Acts."

11. Carlsson, "Masculinities, Persistence, and Desistance"; and Umama-heswar, "'When Are You Going to Grow Up?'"

12. Grundy, *Respectable*; and Kimmel, *Guyland*.

13. We also employed a masculinity checklist developed by Sand and colleagues to assess how they chose priorities for determining who was a "real man," what items were not important to their conceptions of manhood, and whether any of their own definitions were missing from the list. Most men thought the list lacked face validity, and it was difficult for me to parse what concepts like "being in control" meant to each man and how they were meaningfully distinct from others like "financial security." See Sand et al., "Erectile Dysfunction and Constructs of Masculinity."

14. West and Zimmerman, "Doing Gender."

15. See also Elliott, "Caring Masculinities"; and Rawls and Duck, *Tacit Racism*.

16. Melzer, *Manhood Impossible*.

17. Sand et al., "Erectile Dysfunction and Constructs of Masculinity."

18. DeVault, *Feeding the Family*; Goldscheider, *Ethnicity and New Family Economy*; and Randles, "Responsible Fatherhood Programming."

19. Connell, *Masculinities*.

20. Panfil, "'I Was a Homo Thug.'"

21. The Urban Dictionary defines *machisma* as a "male chauvinist" or "sexist guy" and is the female counterpart to *machismo*. See Urban Dictionary, s.v. "Machista."

22. Messerschmidt, "Becoming 'Real Men.'"

23. Anderson, *Code of the Street*.

24. Here, he appears to be referencing the phenomenon of selective fathering, noted in Edin and Nelson, *Doing the Best I Can*.

25. Granovetter, *Getting a Job*.

26. Jones, *Chosen Ones*.

27. Anderson, *Code of the Street*; and Bourgois, "In Search of Masculinity."

28. Grundy, *Respectable*.

29. Williams, Wilson, and Bergeson, "'It's Hard If You're a Black Felon.'"

CONCLUSION: NEW FRAMES FOR CREATING SOLIDARITY AND JUSTICE

1. Jones, *Chosen Ones*; Oeur, "Recognizing Dignity"; and Hawley and Flint, "'It Looks Like a Demon.'"

2. Silva, *Coming Up Short*.

3. Granovetter, "Strength of Weak Ties."

4. Brey and Fader, "Interactionist Theory of Human Agency."

5. Emirbayer and Mische, "What Is Agency?"

6. Carlsson, "Masculinities, Persistence, and Desistance"; Massoglia and Uggen, "Settling Down and Aging Out"; Rocque, "Lost Concept"; and Rocque, *Desistance from Crime.*

7. Erikson, *Childhood and Society.*

8. Erikson, *Childhood and Society.*

9. Brooms, "'I Didn't Want to Be a Statistic.'"

10. Stone, "Desistance and Identity Repair"; and Jones, *Chosen Ones.*

11. Calarco et al., "By Default."

12. Rosin, *End of Men.*

13. Cobbina-Dungy and Jones-Brown, "Too Much Policing," 10.

14. Forliti and Karnowski, "Chauvin Gets 22 1/2 Years."

15. Alexander, *New Jim Crow.*

16. Smith, *How the Word Is Passed.*

17. Simon, *Poor Discipline.*

18. Sered and Norton-Hawk, *Can't Catch a Break.*

19. Roman, "Evaluator's Reflections and Lessons Learned."

20. Ratcliffe, *Intelligence-Led Policing*; and Neusteter and O'Toole, "Every Three Seconds."

21. Natapoff, *Punishment without Crime.*

22. Pickett, Graham, and Cullen, "Racial Divide in Fear of the Police."

23. Coates, *Between the World and Me.*

24. Li and Lartey, "As Murders Spiked, Police Solved about Half."

25. Editorial Board, "More Likely to Win a Coin Toss."

26. Rhynhart, "Data Release."

27. Carr, Napolitano, and Keating, "We Never Call the Cops."

28. Soyer, *Dream Denied.*

29. Sabol and Baumann, "Justice Reinvestment."

30. Corburn et al., "Preventing Urban Firearm Homicides."

31. See Bell, "Next-Generation Policing Research." As Monica Bell notes, both efforts need rigorous evaluation, although READI has evaluation built into the model.

32. Heartland Alliance, "Evaluating and Understanding Our Impact"; and Cobbina-Dungy and Jones-Brown, "Too Much Policing."

33. Shaw and McKay, *Juvenile Delinquency and Urban Areas.*

34. Sampson, Raudenbush, and Earls, "Neighborhoods and Violent Crime."

35. Putnam, *Bowling Alone.*

36. Harvell et al., "Promoting Positive Youth Development."

37. Sharkey, Torrats-Espinosa, and Takyar, "Community and the Crime Decline."

38. Klinenberg, *Palaces for the People.*

39. Pearsall and Dickinson, "Impacts of COVID-19 on Outdoor Public Spaces."

40. Wellington, "City Pools That Will Be Open."

41. John Jay Center Research and Evaluation Center, "Reducing Violence without Police."

42. Klinenberg, *Palaces for the People*.

43. Clear, Hamilton, and Cadora, *Community Justice*.

44. Clear, Hamilton, and Cadora, *Community Justice*, 1.

45. Urban Institute, "Criminal Justice Expenditures."

46. Cobbina-Dungy and Jones-Brown, "Too Much Policing."

47. Clear, Hamilton, and Cadora, *Community Justice*, 3.

48. Ray, *Making of a Teenage Service Class*.

49. Maton et al., *Investing in Communities*; and Wright, Maylor, and Becker, "Young Black Males."

50. Sered and Norton-Hawk, *Can't Catch a Break*, 164.

51. American Civil Liberties Union, "U.S. and Human Rights."

52. Kendall, *Hood Feminism*; see also Collins, *Black Feminist Thought*; Crenshaw, *On Intersectionality*; and Levenstein, *They Didn't See Us Coming*.

53. Kendall, *Hood Feminism*, xiii.

54. "Health Justice Commons."

55. Krieger, "Enough."

56. Sered and Norton-Hawk, *Can't Catch a Break*; Potter, *Intersectionality and Criminology*; and León, "Critical Criminology and Race."

57. Williams, "Black Lives Matter in Research."

58. Williams, "Black Lives Matter in Research"; and Zuberi and Bonilla-Silva, *White Logic, White Methods*.

59. Becker, "Whose Side Are We On."

60. Collins, *Black Feminist Thought*; and Harding, "Rethinking Standpoint Epistemology."

61. Tutu, .

62. Bernard, "Criminal Justice."

63. León, "Critical Criminology and Race."

64. Murakawa and Beckett, "Penology of Racial Innocence."

65. Hinton and Cook, "Mass Criminalization of Black Americans"; Alexander, *New Jim Crow*; and Smith, *How the Word Is Passed*.

66. Reiman and Leighton, *Rich Get Richer*.

67. Muhammad, *Condemnation of Blackness*.

68. Muhammad, *Condemnation of Blackness*, xvii.

69. See MacDonald, "Myth of Systemic Police Racism," as cited in Pickett, Graham, and Cullen, "Racial Divide in Fear of the Police."

70. Edwards, Lee, and Esposito, "Risk of Being Killed by Police."

71. Brunson and Miller, "Gender, Race, and Urban Policing"; Jones, "'Regular Routine'"; and Rios, *Punished*.

72. Wrigley-Field, "Life Years Lost to Police Encounters."

73. Butts and Roman, "Good Questions."

74. Roman, "Evaluator's Reflections and Lessons Learned."

75. John Jay Center Research and Evaluation Center, "Reducing Violence without Police."

76. Roman, "Anticipating Mistakes"; see also Sharkey, *Uneasy Peace.*

77. Davis, *Are Prisons Obsolete?*; and Kaba, *We Do This 'Til We Free Us.*

78. Square One Project.

79. McNeill, *Pervasive Punishment.*

80. Weisburd and Piquero, "Do Criminologists Explain Crime?"

81. Solomon, "What Words We Use."

82. Williams, Wilson, and Bergeson, "'It's Hard If You're a Black Felon,'" 453.

83. Zuberi and Bonilla-Silva, *White Logic, White Methods.*

84. Becker, "Whose Side Are We On."

85. Pritchett et al., "Social Justice Is the Aim."

86. Guishard, "Nepantla and Ubuntu Ethics."

87. Alexander, *New Jim Crow.*

METHODOLOGICAL APPENDIX

1. Anderson, "Ideologically Driven Critique"; and Emerson, Fretz, and Shaw, *Writing Ethnographic Fieldnotes.*

2. Charmaz, *Constructing Grounded Theory.*

3. Bushway and Tahamont, "Modeling Long-Term Criminal Careers."

4. Weaver, Papachristos, and Zanger-Tishler, "Great Decoupling."

5. Uggen and Kruttschnitt, "Crime in the Breaking."

6. Maruna, *Making Good*; and Bushway et al., "Framework for Studying Desistance as a Process."

Bibliography

Alexander, Michelle. *The New Jim Crow: Mass Incarceration in the Age of Colorblindness*. New Press, 2010.

American Civil Liberties Union. "What You Should Know about the U.S. and Human Rights." 2013. www.aclu.org/sites/default/files/assets/121013 -humanrightsfacts.pdf.

American Psychiatric Association. *Diagnostic and Statistical Manual of Mental Disorders: DSM-5*. Vol. 5. American Psychiatric Association, 2013.

Anderson, Elijah. *Black in White Space: The Enduring Impact of Color in Everyday Life*. University of Chicago Press, 2022. https://doi.org/10.7208 /chicago/9780226815176.

———. *Code of the Street: Decency, Violence, and the Moral Life of the Inner City*. W. W. Norton, 1999.

———. *The Cosmopolitan Canopy: Race and Civility in Everyday Life*. W. W. Norton, 2011.

———. "The Ideologically Driven Critique." *American Journal of Sociology* 107, no. 6 (May 2002): 1533–50. https://doi.org/10.1086/342772.

———. *Streetwise: Race, Class, and Change in an Urban Community*. University of Chicago Press, 2013.

Arnett, Jeffrey Jensen. "Emerging Adulthood: A Theory of Development from the Late Teens through the Twenties." *American Psychologist* 55, no. 5 (2000): 469. https://doi.org/10.1037/0003-066X.55.5.469.

Beck, Ulrich. *Risk Society: Towards a New Modernity*. Sage, 1992.

Becker, Howard S. Introduction to *The Jack-Roller: A Delinquent Boy's Own Story*, by C. R. Shaw. University of Chicago Press, 1966.

———. "Whose Side Are We On." *Social Problems* 14, no. 3 (1967): 239–47.

Bell, Monica C. "Next-Generation Policing Research: Three Propositions." *Journal of Economic Perspectives* 35, no. 4 (2021): 29–48.

———. "Situational Trust: How Disadvantaged Mothers Reconceive Legal Cynicism." *Law & Society Review* 50, no. 2 (2016): 314–47. https://doi.org/10.1111/lasr.12200.

Bernard, Thomas J. "Criminal Justice." *Britannica*, 2019. www.britannica.com/topic/criminal-justice.

Bersani, Bianca E., and Elaine Eggleston Doherty. "Desistance from Offending in the Twenty-First Century." *Annual Review of Criminology* 1, no. 1 (2018): 311–34. https://doi.org/10.1146/annurev-criminol-032317-092112.

Binder, Ariel J., and John Bound. "The Declining Labor Market Prospects of Less-Educated Men." *Journal of Economic Perspectives* 33, no. 2 (May 2019): 163–90. https://doi.org/10.1257/jep.33.2.163.

Bonilla-Silva, Eduardo. *Racism without Racists: Color-Blind Racism and the Persistence of Racial Inequality in the United States*. Rowman & Littlefield, 2006.

Boonstoppel, Sarah. "'It's Not about Me No More': Fatherhood and Mechanisms of Desistance Among At-Risk Men." *Journal of Developmental and Life-Course Criminology* 5, no. 3 (2019): 335–65. https://doi.org/10.1007/s40865-019-00120-9.

Bourgois, Philippe. "In Search of Masculinity: Violence, Respect and Sexuality among Puerto Rican Crack Dealers in East Harlem." *British Journal of Criminology* 36, no. 3 (1996): 412–27.

Brame, Robert, Shawn D. Bushway, Ray Paternoster, and Michael G. Turner. "Demographic Patterns of Cumulative Arrest Prevalence by Ages 18 and 23." *Crime & Delinquency* 60, no. 3 (2014): 471–86. https://doi.org/10.1177/0011128713514801.

Brayne, Sarah. "Big Data Surveillance: The Case of Policing." *American Sociological Review* 82, no. 5 (October 1, 2017): 977–1008. https://doi.org/10.1177/0003122417725865.

———. "Surveillance and System Avoidance: Criminal Justice Contact and Institutional Attachment." *American Sociological Review* 79, no. 3 (2014): 367–91. https://doi.org/10.1177/0003122414530398.

Brey, Jesse, and Jamie J Fader. "Developing an Interactionist Theory of Human Agency for Men of Color." Unpublished manuscript, n.d.

Brezina, Timothy, Robert Agnew, Francis T. Cullen, and John Paul Wright. "The Code of the Street: A Quantitative Assessment of Elijah Anderson's Subculture of Violence Thesis and Its Contribution to Youth Violence Research." *Youth Violence and Juvenile Justice* 2, no. 4 (2004): 303–28. https://doi.org/10.1177/1541204004267780.

Bridges, Tristan, and C. J. Pascoe. "Hybrid Masculinities: New Directions in the Sociology of Men and Masculinities." *Sociology Compass* 8, no. 3 (2014): 246–58. https://doi.org/10.1111/soc4.12134.

Brooms, Derrick R. "'I Didn't Want to Be a Statistic': Black Males, Urban Schooling, and Educational Urgency." *Race Ethnicity and Education* 25, no. 3 (2020): 351–69. https://doi.org/10.1080/13613324.2020.1803821.

Brunson, Rod K., and Jody Miller. "Gender, Race, and Urban Policing: The Experience of African American Youths." *Gender & Society* 20, no. 4 (2006): 531–52. https://doi.org/10.1177/0891243206287727.

Bureau of Labor Statistics. "Philadelphia Area Employment—February 2022." www.bls.gov/regions/mid-atlantic/news-release/2022/areaemployment_philadelphia_20220408.htm.

———. "Table 1: Employees on Nonfarm Payrolls by Industry Supersector, Philadelphia Metropolitan Area and Its Components, Not Seasonally Adjusted (Numbers in Thousands)." Bureau of Labor Statistics, 2022. www.bls.gov/regions/mid-atlantic/news-release/areaemployment_philadelphia.htm.

Bushway, Shawn D., Alex R. Piquero, Lisa M. Broidy, Elizabeth Cauffman, and Paul Mazerolle. "An Empirical Framework for Studying Desistance as a Process." *Criminology* 39, no. 2 (2001): 491–516. https://doi.org/10.1111/j.1745-9125.2001.tb00931.x.

Bushway, Shawn D., and Sarah Tahamont. "Modeling Long-Term Criminal Careers: What Happened to the Variability?" *Journal of Research in Crime and Delinquency* 53, no. 3 (2016): 372–91. https://doi.org/10.1177/0022427815618706.

Butts, Jeffrey A., and John K. Roman. "Good Questions: Building Evaluation Evidence in a Competitive Policy Environment." *Justice Evaluation Journal* 1, no. 1 (2018): 15–31. https://doi.org/10.1080/24751979.2018.1478237.

Calarco, Jessica McCrory, Emily Meanwell, Elizabeth M. Anderson, and Amelia S. Knopf. "By Default: How Mothers in Different-Sex Dual-Earner Couples Account for Inequalities in Pandemic Parenting." *Socius* 7 (2021). https://doi.org/23780231211038783.

Carlsson, Christoffer. "Masculinities, Persistence, and Desistance." *Criminology* 51, no. 3 (2013): 661–93. https://doi.org/10.1111/1745-9125.12016.

Carr, Patrick J., Laura Napolitano, and Jessica Keating. "We Never Call the Cops and Here Is Why: A Qualitative Examination of Legal Cynicism in Three Philadelphia Neighborhoods." *Criminology* 45, no. 2 (2007): 445–80. https://doi.org/10.1111/j.1745-9125.2007.00084.x.

Case, Anne, and Angus Deaton. *Deaths of Despair and the Future of Capitalism. Deaths of Despair and the Future of Capitalism.* Princeton University Press, 2020. https://doi.org/10.1515/9780691199955.

Centers for Disease Control and Prevention. "U.S. Small-Area Life Expectancy Estimates Project (USALEEP): Life Expectancy Estimates File for Philadelphia, 2010–2015." 2018. www.cdc.gov/nchs/nvss/usaleep/usaleep.html.

Charmaz, Kathy. *Constructing Grounded Theory: A Practical Guide through Qualitative Analysis*. Sage, 2006.

City of Philadelphia. "Philadelphia Prison Population Report—July 2015–September 2021." First Judicial District of Pennsylvania Department of Research and Development. 2021. www.phila.gov/media/20211013141356/Full-Public-Prison-Report-September-2021.pdf.

———. "Philadelphia Roadmap to Safer Communities." Office of Policy and Strategic Initiatives for Criminal Justice and Public Safety, April 14, 2021. www.phila.gov/documents/the-philadelphia-roadmap-to-safer-communities/.

———. "A Review of the Philadelphia Police Department's Response to the Plain View Project." 2020. /www.phila.gov/media/20201015091951/PAC-Report-A-review-of-the-PPDs-Response-to-the-Plain-View-Project.pdf.

———. *2020 Annual Report of the Division of Substance Use Prevention and Harm Reduction*. Department of Public Health, Philadelphia, 2022.

Clear, Todd R. "The Impacts of Incarceration on Public Safety." *Social Research: An International Quarterly* 74, no. 2 (2007): 613–30.

Clear, Todd R., John R. Hamilton, and Eric Cadora. *Community Justice*. Routledge, 2011.

Coates, Ta-Nehisi. *Between the World and Me*. Text Publishing Company, 2015.

Cobbina-Dungy, Jennifer E., and Delores Jones-Brown. "Too Much Policing: Why Calls Are Made to Defund the Police." *Punishment & Society* 25, no. 1 (2021): 3–20. https://doi.org/10.1177/14624745211045652.

Collins, Patricia Hill. *Black Feminist Thought: Knowledge, Consciousness, and the Politics of Empowerment*. Routledge, 1990. https://doi.org/10.4324/9780203900055.

Comfort, Megan. *Doing Time Together: Love and Family in the Shadow of the Prison*. University of Chicago Press, 2009. https://doi.org/10.7208/9780226114682.

Connell, R. W. *Gender and Power: Society, the Person and Sexual Politics*. Allen & Unwin, 1987.

———. *Masculinities*. Polity, 1995.

Connell, Robert W., and James W. Messerschmidt. "Hegemonic Masculinity: Rethinking the Concept." *Gender & Society* 19, no. 6 (2005): 829–59.

Contreras, Randol. *The Stickup Kids: Race, Drugs, Violence, and the American Dream*. University of California Press, 2013.

Cooley, Charles Horton. *Human Nature and the Social Order*. Scribner, 1902.

Corbett, Ronald P., Jr. "Burdens of Leniency: The Changing Face of Probation." *Minnesota Law Review* 99, no. 5 (2014): 1697–1734.

Corburn, Jason, DeVone Boggan, Khaalid Muttaqi, and Sam Vaughn. "Preventing Urban Firearm Homicides during COVID-19: Preliminary Results from Three Cities with the Advance Peace Program." *Journal of Urban Health* 99, no. 4 (August 1, 2022): 626–34. https://doi.org/10.1007/s11524-022-00660-4.

Crenshaw, Kimberlé. "Demarginalizing the Intersection of Race and Sex: A Black Feminist Critique of Antidiscrimination Doctrine, Feminist Theory and Antiracist Politics." *University of Chicago Legal Forum* 1989, 139–68.

———. *On Intersectionality: Essential Writings*. New Press, 2017.

Crutchfield, Robert D. *Get a Job: Labor Markets, Economic Opportunity, and Crime*. NYU Press, 2014.

Davis, Angela Y. *Are Prisons Obsolete?* Seven Stories Press, 2011.

Delgado, Richard, and Jean Stefancic. *Critical Race Theory: An Introduction*. 3rd ed. New York University Press, 2017. https://doi.org/10.18574/97814798 51393.

DeLuca, Stefanie, Susan Clampet-Lundquist, and Kathryn Edin. *Coming of Age in the Other America*. Russell Sage Foundation, 2016.

Demantas, Ilana, and Kristen Myers. "'Step Up and Be a Man in a Different Manner': Unemployed Men Reframing Masculinity." *Sociological Quarterly* 56, no. 4 (2015): 640–64. https://doi.org/10.1111/tsq.12099.

DeVault, Marjorie L. *Feeding the Family: The Social Organization of Caring as Gendered Work*. University of Chicago Press, 1991.

Dilulio, John J. "The Coming of the Superpredators." *Weekly Standard*, November 27, 1995.

Doleac, Jennifer L., and Benjamin Hansen. "The Unintended Consequences of 'Ban the Box': Statistical Discrimination and Employment Outcomes When Criminal Histories Are Hidden." *Journal of Labor Economics* 38, no. 2 (2020): 321–74. https://doi.org/10.1086/705880.

Drake, St. Clair, and Horace R. Cayton. *Black Metropolis: A Study of Negro Life in a Northern City*. 1st ed. University of Chicago Press, 1945.

Duck, Waverly. "The Complex Dynamics of Trust and Legitimacy: Understanding Interactions between the Police and Poor Black Neighborhood Residents." *ANNALS of the American Academy of Political and Social Science* 673, no. 1 (2017): 132–49. https://doi.org/10.1177/0002716217726065.

———. *No Way Out: Precarious Living in the Shadow of Poverty and Drug Dealing*. University of Chicago Press, 2015.

Dweck, Carol S. "Carol Dweck Revisits the Growth Mindset." *Education Week* 35, no. 5 (2015): 20–24.

Dynarski, Susan. "Student Debt." In *The State of the Union on Poverty and Inequality Report*. Stanford Center on Poverty & Inequality, 2019. https://inequality.stanford.edu/sites/default/files/Pathways_SOTU_2019_Student Debt.pdf.

Edin, Kathryn, and Maria Kefalas. *Promises I Can Keep: Why Poor Women Put Motherhood before Marriage*. University of California Press, 2011.

Edin, Kathryn, and Laura Lein. *Making Ends Meet: How Single Mothers Survive Welfare and Low-Wage Work*. Russell Sage Foundation, 1997.

Edin, Kathryn, and Timothy J. Nelson. *Doing the Best I Can: Fatherhood in the Inner City*. University of California Press, 2013.

Edin, Kathryn, Timothy Nelson, Andrew Cherlin, and Robert Francis. "The Tenuous Attachments of Working-Class Men." *Journal of Economic Perspectives* 33, no. 2 (2019): 211–28. https://doi.org/10.1257/jep.33.2.211.

Edin, Kathryn, Timothy J. Nelson, and Rechelle Paranal. "Fatherhood and Incarceration as Potential Turning Points in the Criminal Careers of Unskilled Men." In *Imprisoning America: The Social Effects of Mass Incarceration*, edited by Bruce Western, Mary Pattillo, and David Weiman, 46–75. Russell Sage Foundation, 2004.

Editorial Board. "You Are More Likely to Win a Coin Toss than Be Caught for Murder in Philadelphia: Editorial." *Philadelphia Inquirer*, August 29, 2019. www.inquirer.com/opinion/editorials/philadelphia-police-unsolved-murders-homicide-clearance-rate-20190829.html.

Edwards, Frank, Hedwig Lee, and Michael Esposito. "Risk of Being Killed by Police Use of Force in the United States by Age, Race–Ethnicity, and Sex." *Proceedings of the National Academy of Sciences* 116, no. 34 (2019): 16793–98. https://doi.org/10.1073/pnas.1821204116.

Elder, Glen H. *Children of the Great Depression: Social Change in Life Experience.* 25th ed. Routledge, 1974. https://doi.org/10.4324/9780429501739.

———. "Time, Human Agency, and Social Change: Perspectives on the Life Course." *Social Psychology Quarterly* 57, no. 1 (1994): 4–15. https://doi.org/10.2307/2786971.

Elder, Glen H., and Monica Kirkpatrick Johnson. "The Life Course and Aging: Challenges, Lessons, and New Directions." In *Invitation to the Life Course: Toward New Understandings of Later Life*, 49–81. Routledge, 2018.

Elliott, Karla. "Caring Masculinities: Theorizing an Emerging Concept." *Men and Masculinities* 19, no. 3 (2016): 240–59. https://doi.org/10.1177/1097184X15576203.

Emerson, Robert M., Rachel I. Fretz, and Linda L. Shaw. *Writing Ethnographic Fieldnotes, Second Edition.* University of Chicago Press, 2011.

Emirbayer, Mustafa, and Ann Mische. "What Is Agency?" *American Journal of Sociology* 103, no. 4 (1998): 962–1023. https://doi.org/10.1086/231294.

Ericson, Richard Victor, and Kevin D. Haggerty. *Policing the Risk Society.* Clarendon Press, 1997.

Erikson, Erik H. *Childhood and Society.* W. W. Norton, 1950.

Fader, Jamie J. "Conditions of a Successful Status Graduation Ceremony: Formerly Incarcerated Urban Youth and Their Tenuous Grip on Success." *Punishment & Society* 13, no. 1 (2011): 29–46. https://doi.org/10.1177/1462474510385636.

———. *Falling Back: Incarceration and Transitions to Adulthood among Urban Youth.* Rutgers University Press, 2013.

———. "'The Game Ain't What It Used to Be': Drug Sellers' Perceptions of the Modern Day Underground and Legal Markets." *Journal of Drug Issues* 49, no. 1 (2019): 57–73. https://doi.org/10.1177/0022042618803057.

———. "'I Don't Have Time for Drama': Managing Risk and Uncertainty through Network Avoidance." *Criminology* 59, no. 2 (2021): 291–317. https://doi.org/10.1111/1745-9125.12271.

———. "'Selling Smarter, Not Harder': Life Course Effects on Drug Sellers' Risk Perceptions and Management." *International Journal of Drug Policy* 36 (October 1, 2016): 120–29. https://doi.org/10.1016/j.drugpo.2016.04.011.

Fader, Jamie J., Scott W. VanZant, and Abigail R. Henson. "Crime and Justice Framing in an Era of Reform: How the Local Matters." *Justice Quarterly* 37, no. 6 (2019): 1119–39. https://doi.org/10.1080/07418825.2019.1589555.

Fairbanks, Robert P. *How It Works: Recovering Citizens in Post-Welfare Philadelphia*. University of Chicago Press, 2009.

Federal Bureau of Investigation. *Uniform Crime Report*. 2017. https://cde.ucr.cjis.gov/LATEST/webapp/#/pages/explorer/crime/crime-trend.

Feld, Barry C. *The Evolution of the Juvenile Court: Race, Politics, and the Criminalizing of Juvenile Justice*. New York University Press, 2017. https://doi.org/10.18574/9781479856664.

Feldman, Nina. "In Philadelphia, Judges Rule against Opening 'Supervised' Site to Inject Opioids." *NPR News*, January 14, 2021. www.npr.org/sections/health-shots/2021/01/14/956428659/in-philadelphia-judges-rule-against-opening-a-medical-site-to-safely-inject-hero.

Fleck, Mary, and Aaron Stagoff-Belfort. "Reducing Policing's Footprint? Racial Disparities and Arrest Trends after Decriminalization and Legalization in Denver and Philadelphia." Vera Institute of Justice, May 2021. www.vera.org/downloads/publications/reducing-policings-footprint.pdf.

Forliti, Amy, and Steve Karnowski. "Chauvin Gets 22 1/2 Years in Prison for George Floyd's Death." Associated Press, June 25, 2021. https://apnews.com/article/derek-chauvin-sentencing-23c52021812168c579b3886f8139c73d.

Foucault, Michel. *The Foucault Effect: Studies in Governmentality*. University of Chicago Press, 1991.

Fry, Richard. "Millennials Are the Largest Generation in the U.S. Labor Force." April 11, 2018. https://policycommons.net/artifacts/617408/millennials-are-the-largest-generation-in-the-us/1598209/.

Fry, Richard, and Kim Parker. "Rising Share of U.S. Adults Are Living without a Spouse or Partner." PEW Research Center, October 5, 2021. www.pewresearch.org/social-trends/wp-content/uploads/sites/3/2021/10/PSDT_10.05.21_unpartnered_adults_report-1.pdf.

Furstenberg, Frank F., Thomas D. Cook, Jacquelynne Eccles, and Glen H. Elder Jr. *Managing to Make It: Urban Families and Adolescent Success*. University of Chicago Press, 2000.

Garland, David. *The Culture of Control: Crime and Social Order in Contemporary Society*. University of Chicago Press, 2001.

Giddens, Anthony. "Risk and Responsibility." *Modern Law Review* 62, no. 1 (1999): 1–10.

Giordano, Peggy C., Stephen A. Cernkovich, and Jennifer L. Rudolph. "Gender, Crime, and Desistance: Toward a Theory of Cognitive Transformation." *American Journal of Sociology* 107, no. 4 (2002): 990–1064. https://doi.org/10.1086/343191.

Glaser, Barney G., and Anselm Strauss. *The Discovery of Grounded Theory: Strategies for Qualitative Research*. Aldine Publishing, 1967.

Goffman, Alice. *On the Run: Fugitive Life in an American City*. Picador, 2014.

Goffman, Erving. *The Presentation of Self in Everyday Life*. Knopf Doubleday Publishing Group, 1959.

———. *Stigma: Notes on the Management of Spoiled Identity*. Simon and Schuster, 1963.

Goldscheider, Frances K. *Ethnicity and the New Family Economy: Living Arrangements and Intergenerational Financial Flows*. Routledge, 2019.

Granovetter, Mark S. *Getting a Job: A Study of Contacts and Careers*. University of Chicago Press, 1974.

———. "The Strength of Weak Ties." *American Journal of Sociology* 78, no. 6 (1973): 1360–80. https://doi.org/10.1086/225469.

Gross, Jenny. "What We Know about the Death of Walter Wallace Jr. in Philadelphia." *New York Times*, October 29, 2021, sec. U.S. www.nytimes.com/article/walter-wallace-jr-philadelphia.html.

Grundy, Saida. *Respectable: Politics and Paradox in Making the Morehouse Man*. University of California Press, 2022.

Grusky, David B., Marybeth Mattingly, Charles Varner, and Stephanie Garlow. "Millennials in the United States." In *The State of the Union on Poverty and Inequality Report*. Stanford Center on Poverty & Inequality, 2019.

Guishard, Monique A. "Nepantla and Ubuntu Ethics Para Nosotros: Beyond Scrupulous Adherence toward Threshold Perspectives of Participatory/Collaborative Research Ethics." PhD diss., City University of New York, 2015. www.proquest.com/docview/1689440096/abstract/E552004CE9614AE3PQ/1.

Haggerty, Kevin, and Ericson, Richard. *The New Politics of Surveillance and Visibility*. University of Toronto Press, 2019. https://doi.org/10.3138/9781442681880.

Haldipur, Jan. *No Place on the Corner: The Costs of Aggressive Policing*. New York University Press, 2018. https://doi.org/10.18574/9781479871407.

Hall, Olivia, and Tom Ferrick. "Mapping Progress in 55 Philadelphia Neighborhoods." Next City, 2017. https://nextcity.org/features/philadelphia-neighborhoods-gentrification-mapping-growth.

Hanson, Melanie. "Student Loan Debt by Generation." Education Data Initiative, 2021. https://educationdata.org/student-loan-debt-by-generation.

Harding, Sandra. "Rethinking Standpoint Epistemology: What Is 'Strong Objectivity'?" *Centennial Review* 36, no. 3 (1992): 437–70.

Harris, Alexes, Heather Evans, and Katherine Beckett. "Drawing Blood from Stones: Legal Debt and Social Inequality in the Contemporary United States." *American Journal of Sociology* 115, no. 6 (2010): 1753–99. https://doi.org/10.1086/651940.

Harvell, Samantha, Hanna Love, Elizabeth Pelletier, Chloe Warnberg, and Constance Hull. "Matching Services and Promoting Positive Youth Development." Fact Sheet. The Urban Institute, 2018. www.urban.org/sites/default/files/2018/10/31/chapter_4_two-pager_bridging_research.pdf.

Hawley, Jamie D., and Staycie L. Flint. "'It Looks Like a Demon': Black Masculinity and Spirituality in the Age of Ferguson." *Journal of Men's Studies* 24, no. 2 (2016): 208–12.

Hays, Jake J., Sarah R. Hayford, and Frank F. Furstenberg. "Delayed Adulthood, Delayed Desistance? A Brief Report on Changing Age Schedules of Risky Behaviors." *Emerging Adulthood* 9, no. 3 (2020): 252–58. https://doi.org/10.1177/2167696820956477.

"Health Justice Commons." Accessed June 21, 2022. www.healthjusticecommons.org.

Heartland Alliance. "Evaluating and Understanding Our Impact." Accessed February 23, 2023. https://support.heartlandalliance.org/page/32956/data/1?locale=en-US.

Heckman, James J., John E. Humphries, and Nick S. Mader. "The GED." *Handbook of the Economics of Education* 3 (2011): 423–83.

Henson, Abigail. "Navigating Paternal Hurdles: A Strengths-Based Exploration of the Ways Young Black Men Construct and Enact Fatherhood in Southwest Philadelphia." PhD diss., Temple University, 2020. www.proquest.com/docview/2411058560/abstract/66BB87326E09439DPQ/1.

Himes, Douglas. "Men's Declining Labor Force Participation." *Monthly Labor Review*, May 2018. www.bls.gov/opub/mlr/2018/beyond-bls/mers-declining-labor-force-participation.htm.

Hinton, Elizabeth, and DeAnza Cook. "The Mass Criminalization of Black Americans: A Historical Overview." *Annual Review of Criminology* 4, no. 1 (2021): 261–86. https://doi.org/10.1146/annurev-criminol-060520-033306.

Hochschild, Arlie, and Anne Machung. *The Second Shift: Working Families and the Revolution at Home*. Penguin, 1989.

Holzer, Harry J. "Employment." In *The State of the Union on Poverty and Inequality Report*. Stanford Center on Poverty & Inequality, 2019. https://inequality.stanford.edu/sites/default/files/Pathways_SOTU_2019_Employment.pdf.

hooks, bell. *All about Love: New Visions*. Women's Press, 1999.

———. *We Real Cool: Black Men and Masculinity*. Psychology Press, 2004.

Humes, Edward. *No Matter How Loud I Shout: A Year in the Life of Juvenile Court*. Simon and Schuster, 1996.

Hutchinson, Bill. "'It's Just Crazy': 12 Major Cities Hit All-Time Homicide Records." *ABC News*, 2021. https://abcnews.go.com/US/12-major-us-cities -top-annual-homicide-records/story?id=81466453.

Ispa-Landa, Simone. "Believing in a Positive Future as a Form of Stigma Resistance: Narratives of Denied Expungement-Seekers." *Deviant Behavior* 40, no. 11 (2019): 1428–44. https://doi.org/10.1080/01639625.2019.1596550.

John Jay Center Research and Evaluation Center. "Reducing Violence without Police: A Review of Research Evidence." John Jay Center Research and Evaluation Center, November 9, 2020. https://johnjayrec.nyc/2020/11/09/av2020/.

Jones, Layla, A. "10 Times Philly Police Were in the National Spotlight for Bad Behavior." Billy Penn, June 6, 2020. https://billypenn.com/2020/06/06/10 -times-philly-police-were-in-the-national-spotlight-for-bad-behavior/.

Jones, Nikki. *The Chosen Ones: Black Men and the Politics of Redemption.* University of California Press, 2018.

———. "'The Regular Routine': Proactive Policing and Adolescent Development among Young, Poor Black Men." *New Directions for Child and Adolescent Development*, no. 143 (2014): 33–54. https://doi.org/10.1002/cad.20053.

"Justice Mapping," 2017. www.justicemapping.org.

Kaba, Mariame. *We Do This 'Til We Free Us: Abolitionist Organizing and Transforming Justice.* Haymarket Books, 2021.

Kalleberg, Arne L. *Precarious Lives: Job Insecurity and Well-Being in Rich Democracies.* John Wiley & Sons, 2018.

Kendall, Mikki. *Hood Feminism: Notes from the Women That a Movement Forgot.* Penguin, 2020.

Kimmel, Michael. *Guyland: The Perilous World Where Boys Become Men.* HarperCollins, 2008.

Klinenberg, Eric. *Heat Wave: A Social Autopsy of Disaster in Chicago.* University of Chicago Press, 2003.

———. *Palaces for the People: How Social Infrastructure Can Help Fight Inequality, Polarization, and the Decline of Civic Life.* Crown, 2018.

———. "Social Isolation, Loneliness, and Living Alone: Identifying the Risks for Public Health." *American Journal of Public Health* 106, no. 5 (2016): 786–87. https://doi.org/10.2105/AJPH.2016.303166.

Krieger, Nancy. "Enough: COVID-19, Structural Racism, Police Brutality, Plutocracy, Climate Change—and Time for Health Justice, Democratic Governance, and an Equitable, Sustainable Future." *American Journal of Public Health* 110, no. 11 (2020): 1620–23. https://doi.org/10.2105/AJPH.2020 .305886.

Lageson, Sarah E., and Shadd Maruna. "Digital Degradation: Stigma Management in the Internet Age." *Punishment & Society* 20, no. 1 (January 1, 2018): 113–33. https://doi.org/10.1177/1462474517737050.

Lemay, Celeste A., Suzanne B. Cashman, Dianne S. Elfenbein, and Marianne E. Felice. "A Qualitative Study of the Meaning of Fatherhood among Young Urban Fathers." *Public Health Nursing* 27, no. 3 (2010): 221–31. https://doi .org/10.1111/j.1525-1446.2010.00847.x.

León, Kenneth Sebastián. "Critical Criminology and Race: Re-Examining the Whiteness of US Criminological Thought." *Howard Journal of Crime and Justice* 60, no. 3 (2021): 388–408. https://doi.org/10.1111/hojo.12441.

Levenstein, Lisa. *They Didn't See Us Coming: The Hidden History of Feminism in the Nineties.* Basic Books, 2020.

Leverentz, Andrea. *Intersecting Lives: How Place Shapes Reentry.* University of California Press, 2022.

Li, Weihua, and Jamiles Lartey. "As Murders Spiked, Police Solved about Half in 2020." The Marshall Project, January 12, 2022. www.themarshallproject .org/2022/01/12/as-murders-spiked-police-solved-about-half-in-2020.

Link, Nathan W., and Caterina G. Roman. "Longitudinal Associations among Child Support Debt, Employment, and Recidivism after Prison." *Sociological Quarterly* 58, no. 1 (2017): 140–60. https://doi.org/10.1080/00380253.2016 .1246892.

Lofland, John. *Deviance and Identity.* Prentice-Hall, 1969.

Lopoo, Leonard M., and Bruce Western. "Incarceration and the Formation and Stability of Marital Unions." *Journal of Marriage and Family* 67, no. 3 (2005): 721–34. https://doi.org/10.1111/j.1741-3737.2005.00165.x.

MacArthur Foundation. "MacArthur Foundation Safety + Justice Challenge: One-Year Implementation Update." June 8, 2017. www.phila.gov/media /20181023151853/MacArthur-Powerpoint-One-Year-Presentation-to-City -Council-6.8.17.pdf.

MacDonald, Heather. "The Myth of Systemic Police Racism." *Wall Street Journal*, June 2, 2020. www.wsj.com/articles/the-myth-of-systemic-police -racism-11591119883.

Mancini, Maggie. "Philadelphia Voters Approve Ballot Question Calling for Marijuana Decriminalization in Pennsylvania." PhillyVoice, November 3, 2021. www.phillyvoice.com/philadelphia-municipal-ballot-questions-2021 -election-marijuana-legalization-civil-service-hiring-afforable-housing/.

Maruna, Shadd. *Making Good: How Ex-Convicts Reform and Rebuild Their Lives.* American Psychological Association, 2001.

———. "Virtue's Door Unsealed Is Never Sealed Again': Redeeming Redemption and the Seven-Year Itch." In *Contemporary Issues in Criminal Justice Policy: Policy Proposals From the American Society of Criminology Conference*, 52–60. Cengage/Wadsworth Belmont, CA, 2009.

Massey, Douglas S., and Jonathan Tannen. "A Research Note on Trends in Black Hypersegregation." *Demography* 52, no. 3 (2015): 1025–34. https://doi.org/10 .1007/s13524-015-0381-6.

Massoglia, Michael, and Christopher Uggen. "Settling Down and Aging Out: Toward an Interactionist Theory of Desistance and the Transition to Adulthood." *American Journal of Sociology* 116, no. 2 (2010): 543–82. https://doi.org/10.1086/653835.

Maton, Kenneth I., Cynthia J. Schellenbach, Bonnie J. Leadbetter, and Andrea L. Solarz. *Investing in Children, Youth, Families, and Communities: Strengths-Based and Policy.* American Psychological Association, 2004.

Matsueda, Ross L., and Karen Heimer. "A Symbolic Interactionist Theory of Role-Transitions, Role-Commitments, and Delinquency." In *Developmental Theories of Crime And Delinquency*, edited by Terence P. Thornberry, 163–214. Transaction Publishers, 1997.

Mazelis, Joan Maya. *Surviving Poverty: Creating Sustainable Ties among the Poor.* NYU Press, 2017.

McAdams, Dan P. *The Redemptive Self: Stories Americans Live By.* Rev. and exp. ed. Oxford University Press, 2013.

McCrystal, Laura. "Philly Budget Deal Cancels $19 Million Increase in Police Funding, Moves Another $14 Million Elsewhere." *Philadelphia Inquirer*, June 18, 2020. www.inquirer.com/news/budget-police-philadelphia-kenney-covid-20200618.html.

McFarland, Michael J., Amanda Geller, and Cheryl McFarland. "Police Contact and Health among Urban Adolescents: The Role of Perceived Injustice." *Social Science & Medicine* 238 (2019): 112487. https://doi.org/10.1016/j.socscimed.2019.112487.

McNeill, Fergus. *Pervasive Punishment: Making Sense of Mass Supervision.* Emerald Group, 2018.

Mead, George Herbert. *Mind, Self [and] Society: From the Standpoint of a Social Behaviorist.* University of Chicago Press, 1934.

Melamed, Samantha. "As Philly Tops Two Dozen Exonerations, City May Face Tens of Millions in Civil Liability." *Philadelphia Inquirer*, June 13, 2021. www.inquirer.com/news/wrongful-convictions-philadelphia-civil-settlements-lawsuits-20210613.html.

Melamed, Samantha, and Dylan Purcell. "The Probation Trap: The Marijuana Paradox." *Philadelphia Inquirer*, November 26, 2019. www.inquirer.com/news/inq/probation-parole-pennsylvania-philadelphia-marijuana-criminal-justice-system-20191126.html.

Melzer, Scott. *Manhood Impossible: Men's Struggles to Control and Transform Their Bodies and Work.* Rutgers University Press, 2018.

Messerschmidt, James W. "Becoming 'Real Men': Adolescent Masculinity Challenges and Sexual Violence." *Men and Masculinities* 2, no. 3 (2000): 286–307.

Messerschmidt, James W., and Michael A. Messner. "Hegemonic, Nonhegemonic, and 'New' Masculinities." In *Gender Reckonings: New Social Theory and Research*, 35–56. New York University Press, 2018.

Miller, Reuben Jonathan, and Forrest Stuart. "Carceral Citizenship: Race, Rights and Responsibility in the Age of Mass Supervision." *Theoretical Criminology* 21, no. 4 (2017): 532–48. https://doi.org/10.1177/1362480617731203.

Miller, Walter. B. "Lower Class Culture as a Generating Milieu of Gang Delinquency." *Journal of Social Issues* 14, no. 3 (1958): 5–19. https://doi.org/10.1111/j.1540-4560.1958.tb01413.x.

Mitchell, Max. "Philadelphia's Civil Payments from Police Abuse Have Been on the Rise." *Legal Intelligencer*, June 22, 2020. www.law.com/thelegalintelligencer/2020/06/22/phila-s-civil-payments-from-police-abuse-have-been-on-the-rise-thats-likely-to-accelerate/.

Morenoff, Jeffrey D., Robert J. Sampson, and Stephen W. Raudenbush. "Neighborhood Inequality, Collective Efficacy, and the Spatial Dynamics of Urban Violence." *Criminology* 39, no. 3 (2001): 517–58. https://doi.org/10.1111/j.1745-9125.2001.tb00932.x.

Muhammad, Khalil Gibran. *The Condemnation of Blackness*. Harvard University Press, 2010.

Murakawa, Naomi, and Katherine Beckett. "The Penology of Racial Innocence: The Erasure of Racism in the Study and Practice of Punishment." *Law & Society Review* 44, nos. 3–4 (2010): 695–730. https://doi.org/10.1111/j.1540-5893.2010.00420.x.

Murthy, Vivek. *Together: Why Social Connection Holds the Key to Better Health, Higher Performance, and Greater Happiness*. HarperCollins, 2020.

Natapoff, Alexandra. *Punishment without Crime: How Our Massive Misdemeanor System Traps the Innocent and Makes America More Unequal*. Basic Books, 2018.

Neusteter, Rebecca, and Megan O'Toole. "Every Three Seconds: Unlocking Police Data on Arrests." Vera Institute of Justice, 2019. www.vera.org/publications/arrest-trends-every-three-seconds-landing/arrest-trends-every-three-seconds/overview.

Nguyên, Ann Thûy, and Maya Pendleton. "Recognizing Race in Language: Why We Capitalize 'Black' and 'White.'" Center for the Study of Social Policy, *Ideas into Action* (blog), March 23, 2020. https://cssp.org/2020/03/recognizing-race-in-language-why-we-capitalize-black-and-white/.

Nosowitz, Dan. "The Enduring Mystery of 'Jawn,' Philadelphia's All-Purpose Noun." *Atlas Obscura*, March 24, 2016.

Oeur, Freeden Blume. *Black Boys Apart: Racial Uplift and Respectability in All-Male Public Schools*. University of Minnesota Press, 2018.

———. "Recognizing Dignity: Young Black Men Growing Up in an Era of Surveillance." *Socius* 2 (2016). https://doi.org/2378023116633712.

Oeur, Freeden Blume, and Saida Grundy. "Allyship in the Time of Aggrievement: The Case of Black Feminism and the New Black Masculinities." In *Black Feminist Sociology: Perspectives and Praxis*, 1st ed., edited by Zakiya Luna and Whitney N. Laster Pirtle, 253–66. Routledge, 2021.

Oliver, William. "Black Males and the Tough Guy Image: A Dysfunctional Compensatory Adaptation." *Western Journal of Black Studies* 8, no. 4 (1984): 199–203.

Orso, Anna, Laura McCrystal, and Mike Newall. "Philly Police Commissioner Sought to Use Tear Gas against Protesters as Kenney Hesitated, Investigation Says." *Philadelphia Inquirer*, January 27, 2021. www.inquirer.com/news /philadelphia/philadelphia-police-danielle-outlaw-tear-gas-protests-kenney -20210127.html.

Otterbein, Heather. "'Completely Unelectable' Progressive Larry Krasner Wins DA's Race." *Philadelphia Magazine*, November 7, 2017. www.phillymag.com /news/2017/11/07/larry-krasner-wins-district-attorney-general-election/.

Owens, Ernest. "Philly's New Budget Makes It Clear City Hall Will Never Defund the Police." *Philadelphia Magazine*, July 8, 2021. www.phillymag .com/news/2021/07/08/philadelphia-defund-police/.

Pager, Devah. "The Mark of a Criminal Record." *American Journal of Sociology* 108, no. 5 (2003): 937–75. https://doi.org/10.1086/374403.

Palmer, Chris. "When Danielle Outlaw Was Chief in Portland, Ore., Police 'Escalated Tensions' by Using Force against Protesters, Report Finds." *Philadelphia Inquirer*, February 10, 2021. www.inquirer.com/news/danielle -outlaw-police-philadelphia-protests-portland-unrest-tear-gas-20210210 .html.

Palmer, Chris, and Anna Orso. "Philly's Homicide Crisis in 2021 Featured More Guns, More Retaliatory Shootings, and a Decline in Arrests and Convictions." *Philadelphia Inquirer*, December 31, 2021, sec. News, news, news. www.inquirer.com/news/philadelphia-murders-shootings-gun-violence -2021-20211231.html.

Panfil, Vanessa R. "'I Was a Homo Thug, Now I'm Just Homo': Gay Gang Members' Desistance and Persistence." *Criminology* 58, no. 2 (2020): 255–79. https://doi.org/10.1111/1745-9125.12240.

Parker, Kim, and Renee Stepler. "Americans See Men as the Financial Providers, Even as Women's Contributions Grow." *Pew Research Center* (blog), September 20, 2017. www.pewresearch.org/fact-tank/2017/09/20/americans-see -men-as-the-financial-providers-even-as-womens-contributions-grow/.

Paternoster, Ray, and Shawn Bushway. "Desistance and the 'Feared Self': Toward an Identity Theory of Criminal Desistance." *Journal of Criminal Law and Criminology* 99, no. 4 (2009): 1103–56.

Pattillo, Mary, Erica Banks, Brian Sargent, and Daniel J. Boches. "Monetary Sanctions and Housing Instability." *RSF: The Russell Sage Foundation Journal of the Social Sciences* 8, no. 2 (January 1, 2022): 57–75. https://doi.org /10.7758/RSF.2022.8.2.03.

Pearsall, Hamil, and Stephen T Dickinson. "Short- and Long-Term Impacts of COVID-19 on Outdoor Public Spaces." Policy Brief. Temple University, Public

Policy Lab, July 20, 2021. https://scholarshare.temple.edu/handle/20.500
   .12613/7062.

Pennsylvania Community Legal Services. "Clean Slate." My Clean Slate PA,
   2019. https://mycleanslatepa.com/.

Pettit, Becky, and Bruce Western. "Mass Imprisonment and the Life Course:
   Race and Class Inequality in U.S. Incarceration." *American Sociological
   Review* 69 (2004): 151–69.

Pew Charitable Trusts. "Philadelphia's Changing Neighborhoods." May 2016.
   www.pewtrusts.org/~/media/assets/2016/05/philadelphias_changing
   _neighborhoods.pdf.

———. "Philadelphia's Poor: Experiences from Below the Poverty Line," September 26, 2018. https://pew.org/2NyZSJG.

———. "The State of Philadelphians Living in Poverty, 2019." April 2019.

Philadelphia City Council. "City Council Approves Member Thomas's Driving
   Equality Bills." October 14, 2021. https://phlcouncil.com/city-council
   -approves-councilmember-thomas-driving-equality-bills/.

———. "Community & Law Enforcement Leaders Named to Special Committee
   on Criminal Justice Reforms." February 4, 2016. https://phlcouncil.com
   /community-law-enforcement-leaders-named-to-special-committee-on
   -criminal-justice-reforms/.

Philadelphia District Attorney's Office. "DA Krasner, Conviction Integrity Unit
   Release Report on Overturning Era of Wrongful Convictions in Philly." *The
   Justice Wire* (blog), June 15, 2021. https://medium.com/philadephia-justice
   /da-krasner-conviction-integrity-unit-release-report-on-overturning-era-of
   -wrongful-convictions-in-5270431f8412.

The Philadelphia Inquirer. DataHub. Accessed June 13, 2023. https://data
   .philly.com/.

Philadelphia Police Department. "Crime Maps & Stats." 2022. www.phillypolice
   .com/crime-maps-stats/index.html.

Philadelphia Reentry Coalition. "People Released to Philadelphia from Prison &
   Jail in 2015." 2018. https://data.phila.gov/visualizations/prison-releases/.

Pickett, Justin T., Amanda Graham, and Francis T. Cullen. "The American
   Racial Divide in Fear of the Police." *Criminology* 60, no. 2 (2022): 291–320.
   https://doi.org/10.1111/1745-9125.12298.

Piquero, Alex R., David P. Farrington, and Alfred Blumstein. "Criminal Career
   Paradigm: Background, Recent Developments, and the Way Forward
   Research." *International Annals of Criminology* 41, nos. 1–2 (2003): 243–70.

Pittman, Adam W. "Managing Methadone Mile: Dynamics of Neighborhood
   Change and Social Control in Boston's South End." PhD diss., University of
   Massachusetts Boston, 2020. www.proquest.com/docview/2418753147
   /abstract/9785CAE99A0F47F1PQ/1.

"Plain View Project." June 20, 2019. www.plainviewproject.org/.

Potter, Hillary. *Intersectionality and Criminology: Disrupting and Revolutionizing Studies of Crime*. Routledge, 2015. https://doi.org/10.4324/978020 3094495.

Pritchett, Malika, Shahla Ala'i-Rosales, Alicia Re Cruz, and Traci M. Cihon. "Social Justice Is the Spirit and Aim of an Applied Science of Human Behavior: Moving from Colonial to Participatory Research Practices." *Behavior Analysis in Practice* 15 (2022): 1074–92. https://doi.org/10.1007 /s40617-021-00591-7.

Putnam, Robert D. *Bowling Alone: The Collapse and Revival of American Community*. Simon and Schuster, 2000.

Puzzanchera, Charles. "Juvenile Arrests, 2018." *Juvenile Justice Statistics: National Report Series Bulletin*, June 2020. https://ojjdp.ojp.gov/sites/g/files /xyckuh176/files/media/document/254499.pdf.

Randles, Jennifer. "The Means to and Meaning of 'Being There' in Responsible Fatherhood Programming with Low-Income Fathers." *Family Relations* 69, no. 1 (2020): 7–20. https://doi.org/10.1111/fare.12376.

Ratcliffe, Jerry H. *Intelligence-Led Policing*. Routledge, 2016.

Rawls, Anne Warfield, and Waverly Duck. *Tacit Racism*. University of Chicago Press, 2020. https://doi.org/10.7208/9780226703725.

Rawls, Anne W., Waverly Duck, and Jason Turowetz. "Problems Establishing Identity/Residency in a City Neighborhood during a Black/White Police–Citizen Encounter: Reprising Du Bois' Conception of Submission as 'Submissive Civility.'" *City & Community* 17, no. 4 (2018): 1015–50. https://doi.org/10 .1111/cico.12345.

Ray, Ranita. *The Making of a Teenage Service Class: Poverty and Mobility in an American City*. University of California Press, 2017.

Reeves, Richard V., and Ember Smith. "The Male College Crisis Is Not Just in Enrollment, but Completion." Brookings, October 8, 2021. www.brookings .edu/blog/up-front/2021/10/08/the-male-college-crisis-is-not-just-in -enrollment-but-completion/.

Reiman, Jeffrey, and Paul Leighton. *The Rich Get Richer and the Poor Get Prison: Thinking Critically about Class and Criminal Justice*. Routledge, 2020.

Resnick, Brian. "Millennial Loneliness Poll: 22 Percent Say They Have 'No Friends.'" Vox, August 1, 2019. www.vox.com/science-and-health/2019/8/1 /20750047/millennials-poll-loneliness.

Reynolds, Carl, Marc Pelka, Ed Weckerly, Patrick Armstrong, and Dan Altman. "Justice Reinvestment in Pennsylvania: Second Presentation to the Working Group." Council of State Governments Justice Center, 2016. https://csgjustice center.org/wp-content/uploads/2020/10/PA-Second-Presentation.pdf.

Rhynhart, Rebecca. "Data Release: Gun Violence Clearance Rates and Case Outcomes." City of Philadelphia, Office of the Controller, 2022. https:// controller.phila.gov/philadelphia-audits/data-release-gun-violence-trends/.

Rios, Victor M. *Punished: Policing the Lives of Black and Latino Boys*. NYU Press, 2011.

Roberts, Dorothy E. "The Social and Moral Cost of Mass Incarceration in African American Communities." *Stanford Law Review* 56, no. 5 (2004): 1271–1306.

Rocque, Michael. *Desistance from Crime: New Advances in Theory and Research*. Springer, 2017.

———. "The Lost Concept: The (Re)Emerging Link between Maturation and Desistance from Crime." *Criminology & Criminal Justice* 15, no. 3 (2014): 340–60. https://doi.org/10.1177/1748895814547710.

Roman, Caterina G. "An Evaluator's Reflections and Lessons Learned about Gang Intervention Strategies: An Agenda for Research." *Journal of Aggression, Conflict and Peace Research* 13, nos. 2/3 (2021): 148–67. https://doi.org/10.1108/JACPR-02-2021-0576.

Roman, John. "Anticipating Mistakes." *External Processing* (blog), November 30, 2020. https://johnkroman.substack.com/p/anticipating-mistakes.

Roman, John, Michael Kane, Emily Turner, and Beverly Frazier. "Instituting Lasting Reforms for Prisoner Reentry in Philadelphia." The Urban Institute, 2006. https://doi.org/10.1037/e719922011-001.

Romero, Melissa. "Data Reveals Huge Life Expectancy Gap among Philly Neighborhoods." Curbed Philly, April 7, 2016. https://philly.curbed.com/2016/4/7/11380408/life-expectancy-in-philly-neighborhoods.

Rose, Dina R., and Todd R. Clear. "Incarceration, Social Capital, and Crime: Implications for Social Disorganization Theory." *Criminology* 36, no. 3 (1998): 441–80. https://doi.org/10.1111/j.1745-9125.1998.tb01255.x.

Rosin, Hanna. *The End of Men: And the Rise of Women*. Penguin, 2012.

Roy, Kevin. "Three-Block Fathers: Spatial Perceptions and Kin-Work in Low-Income African American Neighborhoods." *Social Problems* 51, no. 4 (2004): 528–48. https://doi.org/10.1525/sp.2004.51.4.528.

Russell-Brown, Katheryn. *The Color of Crime*. NYU Press, 2009.

Sabol, William J., and Miranda L. Baumann. "Justice Reinvestment: Vision and Practice." *Annual Review of Criminology* 3, no. 1 (2020): 317–39. https://doi.org/10.1146/annurev-criminol-011419-041407.

Sampson, Robert J., and John H. Laub. *Crime in the Making: Pathways and Turning Points Through Life*. Harvard University Press, 1993.

Sampson, Robert J., Stephen W. Raudenbush, and Felton Earls. "Neighborhoods and Violent Crime: A Multilevel Study of Collective Efficacy." *Science* 277, no. 5328 (1997): 918–24.

Sances, Michael. "Police Budgets on the Ballot before and after George Floyd's Murder." Temple University Public Policy Lab Brief Series, January 6, 2022. https://drive.google.com/file/d/1H-Fdlj74Htr_CJCbokt9oTg1F95LjkEX/view?usp=embed_facebook.

Sand, Michael S., William Fisher, Raymond Rosen, Julia Heiman, and Ian Eardley. "Erectile Dysfunction and Constructs of Masculinity and Quality of Life in the Multinational Men's Attitudes to Life Events and Sexuality (MALES) Study." *Journal of Sexual Medicine* 5, no. 3 (2008): 583–94. https://doi.org/10.1111/j.1743-6109.2007.00720.x.

Schiraldi, Vincent. "The Pennsylvania Community Corrections Story." Columbia University Justice Lab, April 25, 2018. justicelab.columbia.edu/sites/default/files/content/PACommunityCorrections4.19.18finalv3.pdf.

Schrock, Douglas, and Michael Schwalbe. "Men, Masculinity, and Manhood Acts." *Annual Review of Sociology* 35 (2009): 277–95.

Schwartz, Mary, and Ellen Wilson. "Who Can Afford to Live in a Home? A Look at Data from the 2006 American Community Survey." US Census Bureau, 2008. www.basicknowledge101.com/pdf/housing/who-can-afford.pdf.

Sered, Susan Starr. "Diminished Citizenship in the Era of Mass Incarceration." *Punishment & Society* 23, no. 2 (2021): 218–40. https://doi.org/10.1177/14624 74520952146.

Sered, Susan Starr, and Maureen Norton-Hawk. *Can't Catch a Break: Gender, Jail, Drugs, and the Limits of Personal Responsibility.* University of California Press, 2014.

Shachar, Carmel, Tess Wise, Gali Katznelson, and Andrea Louise Campbell. "Criminal Justice or Public Health: A Comparison of the Representation of the Crack Cocaine and Opioid Epidemics in the Media." *Journal of Health Politics, Policy and Law* 45, no. 2 (2020): 211–39. https://doi.org/10.1215 /03616878-8004862.

Shanahan, Michael J. "Pathways to Adulthood in Changing Societies: Variability and Mechanisms in Life Course Perspective." *Annual Review of Sociology* 26 (2000): 667–92.

Sharkey, Patrick. *Uneasy Peace: The Great Crime Decline, the Renewal of City Life, and the Next War on Violence.* W. W. Norton, 2018.

Sharkey, Patrick, Gerard Torrats-Espinosa, and Delaram Takyar. "Community and the Crime Decline: The Causal Effect of Local Nonprofits on Violent Crime." *American Sociological Review* 82, no. 6 (December 1, 2017): 1214–40. https://doi.org/10.1177/0003122417736289.

Shaw, C. R., and H. D. McKay. *Juvenile Delinquency and Urban Areas.* University of Chicago Press, 1942.

Shover, Neal. *Aging Criminals.* Sage, 1985.

Shukla, Aseem, and Michaelle Bond. "Philly Remains One of the Most Racially Segregated Cities in America." *Philadelphia Inquirer*, October 19, 2021, sec. Philadelphia News. www.inquirer.com/news/philadelphia/inq2/philadelphia -racial-segregation-remains-high-census-analysis-20211019.html.

Silva, Jennifer M. *Coming Up Short: Working-Class Adulthood in an Age of Uncertainty.* Oxford University Press, 2013.

Simon, Jonathan. *Poor Discipline*. University of Chicago Press, 1993.

Smiley, Robert F., and Patricia M. Smiley. *Frankford Stories: Reflections on Life in a Philadelphia Neighborhood*. Smiley Publishing, 2022.

Smith, Clint. *How the Word Is Passed: A Reckoning with the History of Slavery across America*. Little, Brown, 2021.

Solomon, Akiba. "What Words We Use—and Avoid—When Covering People and Incarceration." The Marshall Project, April 12, 2021. www.themarshallproject.org/2021/04/12/what-words-we-use-and-avoid-when-covering-people-and-incarceration.

Soyer, Michaela. *A Dream Denied: Incarceration, Recidivism, and Young Minority Men in America*. University of California Press, 2016.

———. "The Imagination of Desistance: A Juxtaposition of the Construction of Incarceration as a Turning Point and the Reality of Recidivism." *British Journal of Criminology* 54, no. 1 (2013): 91–108. https://doi.org/10.1093/bjc/azt059.

Square One Project. Accessed June 13, 2023. https://squareonejustice.org/.

Stack, Carol B. *All Our Kin: Strategies for Survival in a Black Community*. Basic Books, 1974.

Stevenson, Bryan. *Just Mercy: A Story of Justice and Redemption*. Random House, 2014.

Stone, Rebecca. "Desistance and Identity Repair: Redemption Narratives as Resistance to Stigma." *British Journal of Criminology* 56, no. 5 (2016): 956–75. https://doi.org/10.1093/bjc/azv081.

Stuart, Forrest, and Ava Benezra. "Criminalized Masculinities: How Policing Shapes the Construction of Gender and Sexuality in Poor Black Communities." *Social Problems* 65, no. 2 (2018): 174–90. https://doi.org/10.1093/socpro/spx017.

Thomas, William I., and Dorothy Swaine Thomas. *The Child in America*. Knopf, 1928.

Thompson, Derek. "Why Are So Many Young Men Giving Up on College?" *The Atlantic*, September 14, 2021. www.theatlantic.com/ideas/archive/2021/09/young-men-college-decline-gender-gap-higher-education/620066/.

Tutu, Desmond. *Desmond Tutu at Stanford University*. Stanford University Video Collection, January 21, 1986.

Twine, France Winddance. "A White Side of Black Britain: The Concept of Racial Literacy." *Ethnic and Racial Studies* 27, no. 6 (2004): 878–907. https://doi.org/10.1080/0141987042000268512.

Uggen, Christopher, and Candance Kruttschnitt. "Crime in the Breaking: Gender Differences in Desistance." *Law & Society Review* 32, no. 2 (1998): 339–66.

Umamaheswar, Janani. "'When the Hell Are You Going to Grow Up?': A Life-Course Account of Hybrid Masculinities among Incarcerated Men."

Journal of Developmental and Life-Course Criminology 6, no. 1 (2020): 127–51. https://doi.org/10.1007/s40865-020-00137-5.

Upwork. "New 5th Annual 'Freelancing in America' Study Finds That the U.S. Freelance Workforce, Now 56.7 Million People, Grew 3.7 Million since 2014." Upwork Global, 2018. www.upwork.com/press/releases/freelancing-in -america-2018.

Urban Dictionary. S.v. "Drama." Accessed June 13, 2023. www.urbandictionary .com/define.php?term=Drama.

———. S.v. "Looking Hit." Accessed June 13, 2023. www.urbandictionary.com /define.php?term=Looking%20Hit.

———. S.v. "Machista." Accessed June 13, 2023. www.urbandictionary.com /define.php?term=Machista.

Urban Institute. "Criminal Justice Expenditures: Police, Corrections, and Courts." Urban Institute. Accessed February 21, 2023. www.urban.org/policy -centers/cross-center-initiatives/state-and-local-finance-initiative/state-and -local-backgrounders/criminal-justice-police-corrections-courts -expenditures.

US Census Bureau. "American Community Survey, 5-Year Estimates, Table DP05 (ACS Demographic and Housing Estimate)." 2016. https://data .census.gov/cedsci/table?g=860XX00US19124&tid=ACSDP5Y2020.DP05.

———. "American Community Survey, One-Year Estimates, 2019, Table S1701 (Poverty Status in the Past 12 Months)." 2021. https://data.census.gov /cedsci/table?q=United%20States&t=Poverty&g=1600000US4260000&y =2019.

———. "QuickFacts: Philadelphia County, Pennsylvania, 2021 Estimates." 2022. www.census.gov/quickfacts/philadelphiacountypennsylvania.

Van Dam, Andrew. "Analysis: The Unluckiest Generation in U.S. History." *Washington Post*, May 27, 2020. www.washingtonpost.com/business/2020 /05/27/millennial-recession-covid/.

Vella, Vinny. "In City's Busiest Police District, Walking the Beat with a Rookie Cop." *Philadelphia Inquirer*, October 4, 2014, sec. News, news, news. www .inquirer.com/philly/news/20141005_In_city_s_busiest_police_district_ _walking_the_beat_with_a_rookie_cop.html.

Venkatesh, Sudhir. *Gang Leader for a Day: A Rogue Sociologist Takes to the Streets.* Penguin, 2008.

Wacquant, Loïc. "From Slavery to Mass Incarceration." *New Left Review* 13 (January 1, 2002): 41–60.

———. "The New 'Peculiar Institution': On the Prison as Surrogate Ghetto." *Theoretical Criminology* 4, no. 3 (2000): 377.

Wakefield, Sara, and Christopher Uggen. "Incarceration and Stratification." *Annual Review of Sociology* 36, no. 1 (2010): 387–406. https://doi.org/10.1146 /annurev.soc.012809.102551.

Weaver, Vesla M., Andrew Papachristos, and Michael Zanger-Tishler. "The Great Decoupling: The Disconnection between Criminal Offending and Experience of Arrest across Two Cohorts." *RSF: The Russell Sage Foundation Journal of the Social Sciences* 5, no. 1 (February 1, 2019): 89–123. https://doi.org/10.7758/RSF.2019.5.1.05.

Weisburd, David, and Alex R. Piquero. "How Well Do Criminologists Explain Crime? Statistical Modeling in Published Studies." *Crime and Justice* 37 (2008): 453–502. https://doi.org/10.1086/524284.

Wellington, Elizabeth. "Here Are the City Pools That Will Be Opening in Philadelphia This Summer." *Philadelphia Inquirer*, June 28, 2021. www.inquirer.com/philly-tips/philadelphia-city-pools-20210628.html.

West, Candace, and Don H. Zimmerman. "Doing Gender." *Gender & Society* 1, no. 2 (1987): 125–51. https://doi.org/10.1177/0891243287001002002.

Whelan, Aubrey. "Here's How Safehouse, Philly's Proposed Safe-Injection Site, Will Operate." *Philadelphia Inquirer*, October 8, 2018. www.inquirer.com/philly/health/addiction/safe-injection-site-philadelphia-safehouse-faq-20181008.html.

Whiton, Jacob. "In Too Many American Communities, Mass Incarceration Has Become a Jobs Program." Brookings, June 18, 2020. www.brookings.edu/blog/the-avenue/2020/06/18/in-too-many-american-communities-mass-incarceration-has-become-a-jobs-program/.

Wight, Hayley, Brook Kearley, Jesse Brey, Jamie J. Fader, and Natalie Flath. "What's in a Name? The Contested Framing of 'Gangs' in a City Plagued by Group-Based Violence." *Justice Quarterly*, in press.

Williams, Jason M. "Black Lives Matter in Research." Virtual Workshop, Montclair University, November 12, 2020.

Williams, Jason M., Sean K. Wilson, and Carrie Bergeson. "'It's Hard Out Here If You're a Black Felon': A Critical Examination of Black Male Reentry." *Prison Journal* 99, no. 4 (2019): 437–58. https://doi.org/10.1177/0032885519852088.

Wilson, William Julius. *The Truly Disadvantaged: The Inner City, the Underclass, and Public Policy.* University of Chicago Press, 1987.

Wright, Cecile, Uvanney Maylor, and Sophie Becker. "Young Black Males: Resilience and the Use of Capital to Transform School 'Failure.'" *Critical Studies in Education* 57, no. 1 (2016): 21–34. https://doi.org/10.1080/17508487.2016.1117005.

Wrigley-Field, Elizabeth. "Life Years Lost to Police Encounters in the United States." *Socius* 6 (2020): 2378023120948718. https://doi.org/2378023120948718.

Young, Alford A., Jr. "Black Men and Black Masculinity." *Annual Review of Sociology* 47 (2021): 437–57.

Yu, Alan. "Philadelphia Settles with Mother Police Dragged from Car and Assaulted in Front of Toddler." WHYY News, September 14, 2021. https://

whyy.org/articles/philadelphia-settles-with-mother-police-dragged-from
-car-and-beat-in-front-of-toddler/.

Zuberi, Tukufu, and Eduardo Bonilla-Silva, eds. *White Logic, White Methods: Racism and Methodology.* Rowman and Littlefield, 2008.

Zussman, Robert. "People in Places." *Qualitative Sociology* 27, no. 4 (2004): 351–63. https://doi.org/10.1023/B:QUAS.0000049237.24163.e5.

Index

Founded in 1893,
UNIVERSITY OF CALIFORNIA PRESS
publishes bold, progressive books and journals
on topics in the arts, humanities, social sciences,
and natural sciences—with a focus on social
justice issues—that inspire thought and action
among readers worldwide.

The UC PRESS FOUNDATION
raises funds to uphold the press's vital role
as an independent, nonprofit publisher, and
receives philanthropic support from a wide
range of individuals and institutions—and from
committed readers like you. To learn more, visit
ucpress.edu/supportus.

www.ingramcontent.com/pod-product-compliance
Lightning Source LLC
Chambersburg PA
CBHW030818270326
41928CB00007B/797